REFLECTIONS ON SOCIOLOGY OF SPORT: TEN QUESTIONS, TEN SCHOLARS, TEN PERSPECTIVES

RESEARCH IN THE SOCIOLOGY OF SPORT

Series Editor: Kevin Young

Recent Volumes:

RESEARCH IN THE SOCIOLOGY OF SPORT   VOLUME 10

REFLECTIONS ON SOCIOLOGY OF SPORT: TEN QUESTIONS, TEN SCHOLARS, TEN PERSPECTIVES

EDITED BY

KEVIN YOUNG
University of Calgary, Canada

United Kingdom – North America – Japan
India – Malaysia – China

Emerald Publishing Limited
Howard House, Wagon Lane, Bingley BD16 1WA, UK

First edition 2018

Reprints and permissions service
Contact: permissions@emeraldinsight.com

British Library Cataloguing in Publication Data
A catalogue record for this book is available from the British Library

ISBN: 978-1-78714-643-3 (Print)
ISBN: 978-1-78714-642-6 (Online)
ISBN: 978-1-78743-001-3 (Epub)

ISSN: 1476-2854 (Series)

Printed and bound by CPI Group (UK) Ltd, Croydon, CR0 4YY

ISOQAR certified
Management System,
awarded to Emerald
for adherence to
Environmental
standard
ISO 14001:2004.

Certificate Number 1985
ISO 14001

INVESTOR IN PEOPLE

CONTENTS

LIST OF CONTRIBUTORS

Toni Bruce	Faculty of Education and Social Work, University of Auckland, New Zealand
Cora Burnett	Department of Sport and Movement Studies, University of Johannesburg, South Africa
Jay Coakley	Department of Sociology, University of Colorado at Colorado Springs, USA
Agnes Elling	Mulier Institute, Utrecht, The Netherlands
Steven J. Jackson	School of Physical Education, Sport & Exercise Sciences, University of Otago, New Zealand
Mary Jo Kane	Tucker Center for Research on Girls & Women in Sport, College of Education and Human Development, University of Minnesota, USA
Joseph Maguire	School of Sport, Exercise and Health Sciences, Loughborough University, UK
Roy McCree	Sir Arthur Lewis Institute of Social and Economic Studies, University of the West Indies, Trinidad and Tobago
Fabien Ohl	Faculty of Social and Political Sciences, ISSUL University of Lausanne, Switzerland
Gertrud Pfister	Department of Nutrition, Exercise and Sports, University of Copenhagen, Denmark
Kevin Young	Department of Sociology, University of Calgary, Canada

INTRODUCTION

Kevin Young

Following quickly on the heels of, and conceptually tied to, Volume 9 of *Research in the Sociology of Sport* (*Sociology of Sport: A Global Subdiscipline in Review*), this volume now completes the 'double celebration' of this book series as the sociology of sport subfield turns 50.

Ten recognized and influential scholars from around the world (five women and five men) have been invited to reflect on their respective academic journeys. Specifically, they have been asked to couch their experiences and to frame their papers around the following ten questions, grouped into four main themes: *About the Author* (Who are your Mentors and Influential Figures? What is your Research Trajectory?); *About Sport* (Why does Sport Matter? How Should Sport be Studied? Is Sport a Panacea for Social Problems?); *About Practising Sociology of Sport* (Is Teaching Sociology of Sport Easy? Do Sociologists of Sport Like Sport? Is the Sociologist of Sport a 'Public Intellectual'?); and *About Sociology of Sport in the Academy* (Does Sociology of Sport Face Institutional/ Industry Barriers? What is the Future of the Sociology of Sport?).

To my knowledge, this sort of approach has never been taken before. While the ten questions are salient for everyone in the academy irrespective of field of study, they seem particularly trenchant for sociologists of sport as the subfield reaches a chronological milestone and continues to undergo its own 'growing pains' and maturation (as discussed at more length in the Introduction to Volume 9). The underpinning objective is thus plainly serious but, in style, the volume (often written in a conversational first-person tone) is definitely 'lighter' than a conventionally scholarly empirical or theoretical research approach. It is nevertheless suitably celebratory of, and introspective towards, the subfield. Once again, it represents a fitting complement to RSS9 where 23 chapters written by recognized scholars summarized the subdisciplinary 'state of play' across the globe in the most substantial and inclusive set of subfield summaries ever collated in one source. To avoid any perception of priority or proportional ordering, the ten chapters in the current volume simply follow an author surname alphabetical protocol.

When I acknowledged (with then co-editor Joe Maguire) in 2002 that '*Theory, Sport & Society* is the opening volume in a new series entitled *Research in the Sociology of Sport*', I could never have imagined that 15 years later I'd be writing similar prefatory comments for the 10th volume of the series. Clearly, the series has progressed at a respectable pace and, cumulatively, has offered up a valuable catalogue of information about the sports process. Over the past 15 years, the previous nine volumes have dealt with a wide diversity of sociological matters: theory; sports injury; the Olympic Games; sport subcultures; cultural diversity; qualitative methods; indigineity; sport, social development and peace; as well as the status of the subfield across the globe. Including this volume, well over 200 authors have contributed their ideas culminating in, at this point, an impressive corpus of research papers and knowledge. The future looks equally rosy, with Volumes 11 (on sport and forms of mental illness) and 12 (on sport and risk, pain and injury) already 'in the works'.

It is an absolute pleasure to introduce Volume 10 of *Research in the Sociology of Sport*, and it is my hope that you enjoy these careful, contemplative and sometimes cautious 'reflections' as much as I have in earlier preparatory stages. My guess is that wherever and however you approach 'sport', these ten chapters will resonate with you and, in them, you will find many of your own experiences mirrored.

Once again, Happy Anniversary!

CHAPTER 1

STORIES FROM AN ACADEMIC LIFE: REFLECTIONS ON BEING/ DOING/THINKING/TEACHING IN SOCIOLOGY OF SPORT

Toni Bruce

INTRODUCTION

My first real exposure to organized sport did not happen until high school, partly because I grew up on a sheep farm with no near neighbors. This isolation left my sister and me to create our own recreational activities grounded in the natural environment: exploring and swimming in streams, sliding down clay banks on flattened cardboard boxes, or swinging on supplejack vines. Even holidays at my grandparents' beach house focused more on water-based play than anything resembling organized sport. Arriving at boarding school, aged 13, knowing no-one, I was drawn to team sports by the sense of instant community. I discovered that I was physically competent, and tried all the available sports, finally settling on basketball, through which I have had opportunities to travel, coach and referee, and to connect with people whenever I arrived in a new place. Many of my strongest memories, both good and bad, are tied to sport. For me, sport was a powerful space of learning about myself and others, about leadership, friendship, and resilience in the face of failure or (perceived) unfairness, about gender, racial difference, sexuality, and many other social issues. What eventually led me to the sociology of sport was working on summer camps in the United States with underprivileged inner city children, which ignited a desire to gain an undergraduate degree in sport or physical education.

Reflections on Sociology of Sport: Ten Questions, Ten Scholars, Ten Perspectives
Research in the Sociology of Sport, Volume 10, 1–15
Copyright © 2018 by Emerald Publishing Limited
All rights of reproduction in any form reserved
ISSN: 1476-2854/doi:10.1108/S1476-285420170000010001

At university I discovered a love of learning that eventually led to a scholarship for postgraduate study in the United States, where my interest in the social aspects of sport and previous experience in news and sports journalism set me on the path to study the sociology of sport and issues of sport media representation.

ABOUT THE AUTHOR

Mentors and Influential Figures

Mentors have come in different forms throughout my career. Some appeared in formal roles, such as my MSc and PhD main supervisor, Susan Greendorfer, who ensured I was well-grounded in the history and recent developments in sociology of sport, and taught me fundamental research skills, including the importance of systematicity, detail, and the non-negotiability of accurate referencing. Sue also weathered and supported my unsettling and emotional shift from a positivist desire to learn *the one right way* to do research and then return home and apply it, to embracing fundamentally different ontologies and epistemologies in cultural studies and feminisms.

Other mentors came in the form of teachers, such as Syndy Sydnor and Norman Denzin, who fostered and validated different ways of representing research (e.g., Denzin, 1996; Kohn & Slowikowski, 1998; Sydnor, 1998) and introduced me to the work of C. Wright Mills and Laurel Richardson. Larry Grossberg provided a strong grounding in cultural studies (e.g., Grossberg, 1992, 1996) and introduced me to Stuart Hall's writings, which have become the bedrock of my theoretical approach to, and interpretation of, sports media representations. All of them challenged me to think differently than I had before, and introduced me to concepts and ideas that I hold close, that act like points of light, orienting my research. For example, through Hall's work (e.g., 1984, 1985, 1997a, 1997b; Hall, Evans, & Nixon, 2013) I came to understand that media stories teach us *how* to think about aspects of identity, such as gender, sexuality, race or ethnicity, nationalism, and dis/ability, by establishing the boundaries within which we *can* think. I continue to find the cultural studies concept of articulation a particularly valuable way to make sense of some of the intractable discourses of difference that permeate sports media. My work attempting to challenge dominant discourses that marginalize, de-legitimate, and reduce groups to stereotypes is also firmly grounded in the belief that such articulations, discourses, and stories have real effects and affects on people's lives and possibilities. I have long drawn inspiration from Richardson's belief that "stories that deviate from standard cultural plots provide new narratives" and that hearing such narratives "legitimates replotting one's own life" (1990,

p. 26). For her, "The story of the transformed life, then, becomes a part of the cultural heritage affecting future stories, future lives" (Richardson, 1990, p. 26).

Other mentors came in the form of peers at the University of Illinois, Pirkko Markula, David Andrews, Nancy Spencer, Bob Rinehart, Jim Denison, Steve Jackson, Jeremy Howell, Lesley Fishwick, and others, with whom I spent many hours drinking beer or coffee as we debated the finer points of the theories and methods of sport sociology, cultural studies, postmodernism, and feminisms. In the North American Society for the Sociology of Sport (NASSS) I found an academic home, which exposed me to multiple perspectives, fierce debates, and senior academics who encouraged and supported graduate students. After moving back to New Zealand from the United States, the International Sociology of Sport Association (ISSA) conferences became a second home and started me down the path of international collaborations, seeking patterns and differences in multiple cultural contexts (e.g., Bruce, 2016a; Bruce, Hovden, & Markula, 2010; see also Markula, 2009).

Beyond research, Norm Denzin embodied a form of teaching practise that I embrace, one that values the knowledge and experiences students bring to learning, recognizes and makes visible the tentative and limited nature of academic knowledge, and values debate and discussion, alongside immersion in personally relevant topics. Similarly, Vicky Paraschak and I have shared many 5:30 am morning walks at NASSS, discussing our shared philosophy of strengths-based, student-centered, teaching practise (e.g., Paraschak & Thompson, 2014).

Rather than unintentionally ignoring some of the many colleagues, supervisors, teachers, and peers whose words and ideas have helped me navigate my way into and through an academic career, I finish instead with a story. At a recent writing retreat, we were asked to imagine ourselves in a room facing a writing problem, then to imagine a knock at the door. Our task was to explain our problem to the writing mentor we found standing outside, who would give us the answer. Opening the door, I "saw" Laurel Richardson and Norm Denzin holding hands, and together they said, "Write from the heart." I treasure these four powerful and inspirational words as a foundation upon which to build the rest of my research, writing, and teaching career.

Research Trajectory

Throughout my career, I have been engaged in what another mentor, journalist and writer Don Murray, called exploring "the questions that itch" our lives (Murray, 1991, p. 73). As with many researchers, my early questions emerged from my own biography (Richardson, 2001) as a female basketball player and sports journalist. I began with small-scale feminist and cultural studies-informed studies of various aspects of sports media, including women basketball fans' experiences of watching televised coverage of women's games and women sportswriters' experiences covering men's college and professional sport. Since then my work has expanded into issues of mediated nationalism, masculinity, and dis/ability. The diversity of topics – gender/sexuality, race/ethnicity, nationalism, and disability – is held together through my focus on the power of dominant cultural discourses to include or exclude, to reify or marginalize, and a desire to create spaces where silenced or marginalized voices and experiences can be heard.

Right now, I am trying to understand two key issues. The first is the remarkable historical and global continuity in sports media narratives. I am asking questions such as: under what conditions and in what ways do different forms of difference matter (or are *made* to matter), and what effects does that "mattering" have on the possibilities for making sense of sport, sports media, and various forms of identity? The question that has been "itching" me asks what kinds of articulations would need to emerge for sportswomen and other marginalized groups in sport to become part of the mediasport furniture, so to speak? Cultural studies allows me to imagine even potent articulations as unstable and (potentially) able to be articulated in different ways. This leads to a focus on instabilities within the default settings of mediasport.

The second key issue involves investigating the spaces in which "normal" media discourses are (usually temporarily) disrupted: the moments when those who are usually marginalized, such as sportswomen, cross the boundary into respectful public visibility. My search for positive disruptions, resulting from frustration at the persistent mainstream media marginalization of sportswomen, led to analyses of the possibilities of the Web 2.0 environment for sportswomen and supporters of women's sport to create and circulate new narratives. This new focus led me to Margaret Wetherell's work around emotion as a social practise (Wetherell, 2012), and Leslie Heywood and Shari Dworkin's work around third-wave feminism (Heywood & Dworkin, 2003), which influence the way I am looking at the changing nature of female sporting embodiment and (self-) representation (e.g., Bruce, 2016a). I am increasingly interested in the diversity of representation and its ambivalent nature; the way that, in Hall's (1997b) terms, difference "can be both positive and negative" (p. 238) – along with the conditions under which it falls into either category (or both at once).

I am simultaneously saddened by the failure of women's sport advocates to make any significant impact on the amount of coverage of sportswomen, and troubled by why this is the case. Given the cultural studies insistence on strategic intervention, I question why advocates for women's sport (and I would include those fighting for "better" representation of disabled, racial or ethnic minority and LGBTI athletes) have failed so miserably to dis-articulate sport (and sports media in particular) from cultural ideals of heterosexual, able-bodied, white masculinity. It appears that part of the failure is to find the right layers or levels at which to intervene in mediasport's role in reifying and constantly re-articulating the relationship between sport and masculinity. In an interview, Grossberg proposed that

> if you keep fighting battles and you keep losing (on all sorts of sites and fronts, including institutional and popular struggles), it must be that there is something wrong with the story you are telling, the story from which you are deriving political strategies. Somehow, you don't understand the rules of the game, you are not playing the right game, you are not playing on the right field ...You don't understand what's happening well enough. (Liang, Wong, Wong, & Chan, 2005, para. 13)

He suggests that if we gain "a better sense of the state of play on the field of forces in popular culture and daily life," this opens up the chance to "see more clearly where struggles are possible and, in some cases, even actual. Then we can try to find ways to oppose them, or help articulate them, to nurture and support them and perhaps, to bring them into visible relations with other struggles" (Grossberg, 1992, p. 66). It was these words that created the space in my thinking to write a novel exploring these issues in women's sport (Bruce, 2016b), "to take risks and go places that would not be possible" in other forms of writing (Richardson, 1994, p. 521). If we need to find ways to create new narratives or tell new stories, as Richardson (2001) and Grossberg (see Liang et al., 2005) advocate, then a novel seemed one way to liberate possibilities that research had not yet brought into visible relations.

Yet, the still-unanswered question remains: How can we tell new stories and create new connections to help journalists and media workers articulate femininity, disability, and homosexuality to sport, and present all athletes, no matter their race, ethnicity, or nationality, in nuanced and non-stereotypical ways? Certainly, this is no simple task of informing sports media outlets and journalists that they are inequitable and/or discriminatory (as so many disability and gay rights activists, and women's sport researchers, foundations and organizations, and even government departments have tried and failed to achieve). Instead, we need to understand how and where to make strategic alliances that make a difference. What seems to be missing is the ability of advocates for women, disabled, and LGBTI athletes, and those fighting against the echoes of racial stereotyping, to find ways to build new coalitions and create alternative articulations.

ABOUT SPORT

Why Does Sport Matter?

Sport matters because it has physical, social, psychological, community, economic, political, and national effects and affects. In Arnold's (1992) words, sport is "a culturally valued human practise" organized by its own rules that, like other forms of cultural activity, constitutes the "source of our possibilities" and understandings of "what it is to be a person" (p. 237). For Arnold, sport helps create "a meaningful pattern of life in which individuals can both find and extend themselves" through initiation "into the ways, customs and prac-tises of a given culture," which include the need for co-operation to achieve shared goals, an ethical framework within which to play, and value of passing on sporting knowledge to future generations (1992, p. 253). Similarly, in sociol-ogy of sport's most-used text book, the authors explain that

> we study sports because they are given special meaning by particular people in societies, they are tied to important ideas and beliefs in many cultures, and they are connected with major spheres of social life such as the family, religion, education, the economy, politics and the media. (Coakley, Hallinan, Jackson, & Mewett, 2009, pp. 15−16)

Whether individuals love or hate sport, the cultural visibility and impact of elite and professional sport is undeniable. So, too, is the impact of sport in the lives of families and communities, whose weekends are often organized around their children's sporting activities, including driving, coaching, managing, refereeing, planning half-time sustenance and awards, and washing and repair-ing uniforms. Participating in sport can contribute to the maintenance of cul-tural and ethnic connections (Hokowhitu, 2007). It can profoundly impact individual, community, and national identities, bringing people together and/or dividing them. It also matters because, in the right contexts, it can achieve some of the many things it is believed to do: integrate, provide purpose, and teach culturally valued skills such as teamwork, perseverance, the value of hard work and resilience. The economic impact of sport, which includes sales of sport and sports team merchandise and equipment, building of stadia, hosting international sports events, television rights, ticket sales to sports events, and player and coach salaries, is also undeniable.

How Should Sport be Studied?

A short answer would be that sport should be studied systematically, in depth, with a sense of curiosity, and from multiple perspectives. Like every important element of society, sport is far too complex, layered, and multifaceted to be studied in only one way: there is no one-size-fits-all way to understand sport. I support Lather's (2006) exhortation to embrace multiplicity and proliferation in methods and theories, as we seek ways "into a less comfortable social science full of stuck places and difficult philosophical issues of truth, interpretation and responsibility" (p. 52). As a field, sociology of sport has periodically been through major debates about appropriate and valid ways to study sport. Although one of the advantages in sociology of sport research is the diversity of theories and methods, some intractable issues may require us to work in a more cross-, inter-, or trans-disciplinary manner (e.g., Lather, 2006; Thorpe, 2006), much as we see in the burgeoning field of pleasure, emotion, and affect (e.g., Pringle, Rinehart, & Caudwell, 2015). The priority is that sociologists of sport conduct high-quality research, no matter which paradigmatic, theoretical, or methodological approaches they embrace, driven by a concern with how our research can be useful, how it can "ask what might be thought and done otherwise" (Lather, 2006, p. 45). Thus, the field would do well to reflect and foster openness toward different approaches, even ones that fundamentally challenge our individual ontological and epistemological commitments.

Is Sport a Panacea for Social Problems?

As with so many questions about sport's connection to broader society, my answer is yes *and* no. Sport, in its many forms and dimensions, has the *potential* to contribute positively to society, as structural functionalists have always maintained, often based on an unshakable belief that sport builds character (Coakley, 2015; Crabbe, 2000; Sugden, 2015). Increasingly, global organizations like the United Nations have shown interest in mobilizing sport's potential to address "social ills" to meet Millennium Development Goals (Burnett, 2015). One example is UNESCO's learning values through sport campaign, which identifies "Equality, inclusion, respect, and fairness" as "core values triggered by sport" and supports "using sport in order to empower learners to be self-determined, responsible, and contribute to society" (United Nations, 2016, para. 2). It further argues that "Not only is sport a bridge between individuals and nations, it can also be an active tool for overcoming stereotypes, rising above exclusion, and fostering citizenship" (United Nations, 2016, para. 5). Although such aims are laudable, the "problem" occurs when this belief is accepted in an unquestioning, taken-for-granted way. Such beliefs negate the need for critical analysis and engagement with what sport *actually* does, rather than focusing on what it is *believed* to do (see also Coakley, 2015; Sugden, 2015). Perhaps because of the "uncritical stance of practitioners and funding agencies about assumed impact," there appears to be only limited evidence of the effectiveness of programs using sport to increase physical and psychological well-being, teach life skills, improve educational outcomes, increase safety and reduce crime or drug use, regenerate communities, and create positive economic impacts (Burnett, 2015; Crabbe, 2000). This is not to argue that such programs have no effect but, rather, that there is little systematic or holistic evaluation that captures the complexity of outcomes, power relations, relationships, and local struggles (Burnett, 2015). Despite the need to challenge the widespread and taken-for-granted beliefs about sport as a panacea, I agree with Sugden (2015) that we need to think seriously about how, as sociologists of sport, we can use our knowledge in hands-on ways, including working toward "practical interventions that may help sport play a role in saving the world" (p. 611).

ABOUT PRACTISING SOCIOLOGY OF SPORT

Is Teaching Sociology of Sport Easy?

Teaching of any kind is never "easy" but teaching sociology of sport is one of the great joys of my academic life. It literally changes some students' lives, as they come to understand how the stories we tell ourselves as a society – often circulated through media – intersect with their own experiences and understandings. Turning a sociological lens on sport provides students with some distance to think about why they think and act the way they do. A focus on cultural discourses and their impacts on people's lives enables students to locate their own experiences into a bigger picture. Because I teach in sport and physical education programs where most students are sport fans, there is never a shortage of current and relevant examples of all kinds of issues that provide sources for fruitful discussion and student-selected content for assignments. Teaching similar kinds of students 33 years ago, McKay and Pearson (1984) argued that teaching a sociologically critical view of sport "is usually a difficult task" because students "often react in an incredulous or hostile fashion" when their taken-for-granted assumptions are debunked (p. 134). More recently, Dart (2015) also reported initial reluctance from "students who enjoyed sport at school" (p. 9) to engaging with critical viewpoints. In contrast, my experience has been very different. Perhaps because I have taught for the past 15 years in programs underpinned by critical perspectives, I find students are usually willing to consider alternative perspectives. As a result, I have not faced the challenges of sociologists of sport interviewed by Dart (2015) who reported that their work sat "uneasily alongside" other disciplines "that taught 'sport' in an uncritical fashion" and faced the "constant risk of exclusion" because their courses acted "as a dissenting voice" in more positivist programs (p. 10). It appears that I have been in "a rare, but advantageous position" in programs that value interdisciplinary and critical perspectives (Dart, 2015, p. 5). Over time, I have developed a pedagogical approach that explicitly structures the course as a discussion between students' lived experiences and the results of systematic sociological research. This approach validates students' experiential knowledge and simultaneously provides them with additional resources to make sense of what they see and experience. Like Blinde (1995), my focus is on applying rather than memorizing information, and embraces a reciprocal approach in which "the teacher and the students learn from each other" (p. 267). An early example that both reflects, and reinforces, this commitment resulted from the objections of undergraduate students to the conclusions of a published analysis of racism in basketball commentary. In response, I initiated a summer research project in which I interviewed basketball commentators and analyzed racial ideologies in a televised commentary of 43 men's college and professional basketball games. The results supported the students' rather than the researchers' explanations.

My overall aim is to facilitate a psychologically safe and supportive learning community where the students are comfortable with me, the content of the course, and with each other and, most importantly, "feel that their ideas are respected and encouraged" (Bonk & Khoo, 2014, p. 45). Authentic learning requires a classroom climate and assignments that are "open and active, involve genuine tasks, respect students' ideas, and embed student-driven activities" (Bonk & Khoo, 2014, pp. 45–46; Cochrane, 2014). I measure the success of this approach through course evaluations and students' responses, including their reported use of course content and assignments in their own teaching practise. In recent years, students in my sociocultural foundations course have described it as "the life course" because they see the learning as directly relevant to their everyday lives.

Do Sociologists of Sport Like Sport?

Bairner (2009) identifies two kinds of sociologists of sport: the "many" critical scholars who have an antipathy for sport, and others "who truly enjoy the aesthetic pleasure and the emotional engagement that sport can offer" (p. 118). From my experience, most sociologists of sport do like sport, or even loved it before they encountered critical theory, but somehow our published research seldom makes this clear. Most likely reflecting the theoretical turn toward critical questions about power, inequality, and difference, much sociological research on sport leans strongly toward critiquing existing structures and discourses. It is only recently that we are beginning to see a broader shift back toward investigating why so many people invest so much time, money, and emotion playing and/or consuming it via media or merchandise. This shift encourages us to remember that joy, pleasure, challenge, and self-, or group-actualization are among the many reasons sport can be a positive influence in people's lives, and to consider exploring these possibilities in more depth. At the same time, as someone who takes great pleasure in playing and consuming sport but has also been described by a sports journalist as at risk of being seen as one of the great killjoys of our time, I agree with Bairner (2009) that sports fandom and being a critical sociologist creates an "inevitable tension" between loving and consuming mediated sport while recognizing its problematic aspects (p. 118). I also believe he is correct that balancing these two competing intellectual and experiential positions places us in "a more advantageous position than those who are anti-sport to critique and potentially to combat those aspects of the sporting world that are morally and ideologically unacceptable to us" (Bairner, 2009, pp. 118–119), even if it takes greater than normal efforts to establish our pro-sport credentials. In my case, after widespread coverage of my research critiquing the dominant discourse that all New Zealanders loved rugby, a newspaper journalist decided to start a profile piece like this: "Let's clear one matter up. Toni Bruce likes footy. 'I was raised to be a rugby fan,' says the sport sociologist" (Stone, 2015, paras. 1–2).

Is the Sociologist of Sport a "Public Intellectual"?

Not all sociologists of sport are public intellectuals but I believe at least some of us should be. We have valuable knowledge and research to share, and if we do not enter public debates then our knowledge is often excluded from the most powerful forums in which members of society gain their understandings, and decisions affecting how sport is practised and administered are made. Donnelly (2015) argues that not only does engaged and relevant sociological research have the power to change lives but that our work "*should* make a difference" (p. 422), in part through being shared beyond the academy. Pike, Jackson, and Wenner (2015) believe that sociologists of sport are already active as public sociologists, and argue that the field "has had considerable influence, playing diverse roles in policy development" and directing the attention of the public and media "to a myriad of pressing issues facing sport in society today" (p. 359). In contrast, Bairner (2009) argues that institutional constraints and the antipathy some critical sociologists of sport show toward their subject matter has made it challenging for sociologists of sport to "assume the mantle of public intellectuals" (p. 115).

Most higher education institutions espouse a belief in the role of academics as public intellectuals. Indeed, this role is embedded in New Zealand law, where the Education Act (1989) states that one of five characteristics of universities is that "they accept a role as critic and conscience of society" (p. 282). Until recently, that role involved active engagement with the most powerful story-tellers of our time — the mainstream mass media — even though the level of support and training for us to enact that role varies widely. So why do so few of us actively engage in the rough-and-tumble world of public debate? Agreeing with Bairner (2009) that public intellectualism can negatively affect individuals' academic careers, colleagues have reported fear of backlash from their own colleagues, including snide remarks about seeking public visibility, or raising questions about research methodology or quality, as journalists or commentators simplify complex ideas into simple, catchy, click-bait-enticing headlines. In addition, taking the role seriously almost inevitably reduces the quantum of researchers' publications, which can pose a threat to tenure and promotion (Bairner, 2009; Dudding, 2016). Additionally, unlike our preparation in theory, methodology, and even teaching, few of us are taught media skills. Learning them requires training in how best to gain attention, how best to frame your research for a public rather than academic audience, as well as an understanding of the increasingly cut-throat nature of media, a sense of humor, and thick skin (Bruce, 2014). Research that challenges deeply held cultural beliefs can attract negative and scathing public attacks. I have been variously described as an ugly bone-carving wearing woman of questionable sexuality, a tiny mind, a wet blanket, and as conducting sloppy research. At the same time, publicizing such research-informed challenges can be empowering for people whose voices were previously invisible. For example, responses such as those of the 80-year-old retired farmer who emailed me privately to share that hearing about my results *"made my day, as I feel almost main stream"* or the 45-year-old woman who wrote, *"Thanks for the opportunity for this survey, its fantastic for non rugby fans to have a voice"* validate the importance of publicly sharing research results.

As the mixed reactions above suggest, public intellectualism is not necessarily easy. Despite attempts to control your message, once you enter the mass media fray, the results are unpredictable. More often than not, mainstream media coverage highlights simplicity rather than nuance, and represents results in black and white terms rather than the shades of gray in which academics usually deal. However, in the Web 2.0 environment we now have more opportunities to share and control our messages (through blogs, tweets, Instagram, etc.), and many academics are taking up this opportunity, suggesting that being a public intellectual in the 21st century looks somewhat different from the past. Perhaps, like professional sportspeople, sport sociologists too are now in the position to bypass media gatekeepers and circulate our messages in our own nuanced ways − if we can build an audience, and our institutional policies value and allow this form of interaction.

ABOUT SOCIOLOGY OF SPORT IN THE ACADEMY

Does Sociology of Sport Face Institutional/Industry Barriers?

I suspect the answer to this question varies significantly by national context. In New Zealand, the research field seems in reasonable health, although sport-related Faculties and Departments around the country are undergoing significant restructuring and there is increasing pressure to do more with less. Pike et al. (2015) recently summarized the state of the field by arguing that

> the subject does appear to be thriving in some institutions and countries, offering a legitimate research and career pathway, and attracting the critical scholarly gaze of academics from a wide range of disciplinary fields, including anthropology, communication, economics, gender, international relations and politics and even mainstream sociology. (pp. 358−359)

In many countries, sociologists of sport are valued as expert commentators on sport and regularly approached by media to comment on current issues. However, just as institutional rewards do not always advantage the public intellectual (Bairner, 2009; Dudding, 2016), they may also function as barriers to building connections with those working in professional contexts (e.g., coaches, marketers, media workers, policy-makers, or national and international sport federations and organizations). Building such connections takes time and does not always lead to fast academic publications, especially if the findings are designed to be directly useful to the organizations concerned.

Another barrier is that sport sociology research is often critical of current practises in sport, which seldom endears us to those working in those contexts. For example, in my main area of sports media research, researchers have faced significant challenges in trying to convince mainstream media workers to accept or act upon the results of our research (Fountaine & McGregor, 1999; McKee, 2003). McKee (2003) – who describes many cultural studies researchers as wanting "to change the kinds of texts that are published, particularly by journalists in newspapers and in television news, wishing for texts which are less racist, less sexist, less homophobic, less capitalist" (p. 53) – has suggested that journalists resist our findings because they interpret them as suggesting they are sexist or racist, for example. New Zealand researchers attempting such work have had similar experiences, finding that sports journalists did not react well when researchers tried to bring inequities in sports media coverage to their attention. Such research was "persistently rejected as irrelevant" and the findings "often ignored or trivialized by news management and journalists" (Fountaine & McGregor, 1999, p. 113). McKee (2003) suggests we might focus less on brow-beating media producers and, instead, apply our energies to providing widely accessible resources to enable the public to change how they interpret what the media produce. This is one form of intervention that is often embraced by those who would benefit from change (Bruce, Rankine, & Nairn, 2017). However, it still seems worthwhile to persevere with attempts to build bridges and collaborate with those working in sport, even if our institutions do not necessarily value it.

What is the Future of the Sociology of Sport?

In New Zealand we have a well-known saying: *He aha te mea nui o te ao. He tangata, he tangata, he tangata* (What is the most important thing in the world? It is the people, it is the people, it is the people). I begin with this saying because I fear that unless we can better connect ourselves to the actual field of play of sport and, in the case of sports media, build connections and conversations with mass media producers, we will end up speaking only to ourselves and our students. In the introduction to the *International Review for the Sociology of Sport* journal's fiftieth anniversary issue, the editors made a similar point, arguing that because sociologists of sport work primarily in sport-focused departments and publish in sport-related journals, this "may serve to limit their engagement with, and influence on, the wider community within and outside academia" (Pike et al., 2015, p. 358).

Many, if not most, sociologists of sport are drawn to research that identifies issues and strives to make sport a better place, whether that is more financially stable, better managed, more supportive of personal or community development, or more fair and equitable. However, unless we can find ways to enter into the conversations that matter, with the people who can enact the differences we believe are needed, our field runs the risk of being seen as obsolete or irrelevant "to the real world."

Although some sociologists of sport are already actively engaging in this way, it might be valuable to consistently host conference sessions on these issues in order to reveal the pleasures and pains, and provide signposts for success, of trying to build relationships, and make change outside the academy and beyond our classrooms. We may also need to develop a strategy for circulating our work more widely into other disciplines (Bruce, 2015; Pike et al., 2015). As sport has become increasingly culturally important, other disciplines have entered the fray, and many of these "newcomers" appear completely unaware that sport sociology exists. Nor do they cite the excellent research and theorizing that has already been produced by sociologists of sport, which suggests that our work still has to find its place in the broader sociological field. As Pike et al. (2015) conclude: "In order to effectively challenge the marginalization of the field and to transact more integrally with the worlds of sport and sociology, sociologists of sport will need to facilitate meaningful dialogue and collaborations with scholars working in other social sciences, sport sciences and mainstream sociology" (p. 361). Are we up for the challenge?

REFERENCES

Arnold, P. J. (1992). Sport as a valued human practice: A basis for the consideration of some moral issues in sport. *Journal of Philosophy of Education, 26*(2), 237–255.

Bairner, A. (2009). Sport, intellectuals and public sociology: Obstacles and opportunities. *International Review for the Sociology of Sport, 44*(2), 115–130.

Blinde, E. M. (1995). Teaching sociology of sport: An active learning approach. *Teaching Sociology, 23*(3), 264–268.

Bonk, C. J., & Khoo, E. (2014). *Adding some TEC-VARIETY: 100+ activities for motivating and retaining learners online.* Bloomington, IN: Open World Books.

Bruce, T. (2014). Battered in the media: The value of theorizing as a method for lessening the pain of lived experience. In R. E. Rinehart, K. N. Barbour, & C. Pope (Eds.), *Ethnographic worldviews: Transformations and social justice* (pp. 187–203). Netherlands: Springer Press.

Bruce, T. (2015). Assessing the sociology of sport: On media and representations of sportswomen. *International Review for the Sociology of Sport, 50*(4-5), 380–384.

Bruce, T. (2016a). New rules for new times: Sportswomen and media representation in the third wave. *Sex Roles, 74*, 361–376.

Bruce, T. (2016b). *Terra Ludus: A novel about media, gender and sport.* Rotterdam: Sense Publishers.

Bruce, T., Hovden, J., & Markula, P. (Eds.) (2010). *Sportswomen at the Olympics: A global comparison of newspaper coverage.* Rotterdam: Sense Publishers.

Bruce, T., Rankine, J., & Nairn, R. (2017). Critical discourse analysis. In M. L. Silk, D. L. Andrews, & H. Thorpe (Eds.), *Routledge handbook of physical cultural studies* (pp. 467–475). New York, NY: Routledge.

Burnett, C. (2015). Assessing the sociology of sport: On sport for development and peace (SfDP). *International Review for the Sociology of Sport, 50*(4-5), 385–390.

Coakley, J. (2015). Assessing the sociology of sport: On cultural sensibilities and the great sport myth. *International Review for the Sociology of Sport, 50*(4-5), 402–406.

Coakley, J. J., Hallinan, C., Jackson, S., & Mewett, P. (2009). *Sports in Society: Issues and controversies in Australia and New Zealand.* North Ryde: McGraw-Hill.

Cochrane, T. (2014). Critical success factors for transforming pedagogy with mobile Web 2.0. *British Journal of Educational Technology, 45*(1), 65–82.

Crabbe, T. (2000). A sporting chance? Using sport to tackle drug use and crime. *Drugs: Education, Prevention and Policy, 7*(4), 381–391.

Dart, J. (2015). Sports tribes and academic identity: Teaching the sociology of sport in a changing disciplinary landscape. *Sport, Education and Society,* doi:10.1080/13573322.2015.1102724

Denzin, N. K. (1996). *Interpretive ethnography: Ethnographic practices for the 21st century.* London: Sage.

Donnelly, P. (2015). Assessing the sociology of sport: On public sociology of sport and research that makes a difference. *International Review for the Sociology of Sport, 50*(4-5), 419–423.

Dudding, A. (2016, May 7). National portrait: Michelle Dickinson, aka Nanogirl. *Stuff.co.nz.* Retrieved from http://i.stuff.co.nz/national/79686257/National-Portrait-Michelle-Dickinson-aka-Nanogirl

Education Act, No. 80. (1989). Retrieved from http://www.legislation.govt.nz/act/public/1989/0080/latest/DLM175959.html

Fountaine, S., & McGregor, J. (1999). The loneliness of the long distance gender researcher: Are journalists right about the coverage of women's sport? *Australian Journalism Review, 21*(3), 113–126.

Grossberg, L. (1992). *We gotta get out of this place: Popular conservatism and postmodern culture.* New York, NY: Routledge.

Grossberg, L. (1996). On postmodernism and articulation: An interview with Stuart Hall. In D. Morley & K-H. Chen (Eds.), *Stuart Hall: Critical dialogues in cultural studies* (pp. 131–150). London: Routledge.

Hall, S. (1984). The narrative construction of reality. *Southern Review, 17*, 3–17.

Hall, S. (1985). Signification, representation, ideology: Athusser and the post-structuralist debates. *Critical Studies in Mass Communication, 2*(2), 91–114.

Hall, S. (1997a). Introduction. In S. Hall (Ed.), *Representation: Cultural representations and signifying practices* (pp. 1–12). London: Sage.

Hall, S. (1997b). The spectacle of the 'Other'. In S. Hall (Ed.), *Representation: Cultural representations and signifying practices* (pp. 223–290). London: Sage.

Hall, S., Evans, J., & Nixon, S. (2013). *Representation* (2nd ed.). London: Sage.

Heywood, L., & Dworkin, S. L. (2003). *Built to win: The female athlete as cultural icon.* Minneapolis, MN: University of Minnesota Press.

Hokowhitu, B. (2007). Maori sport: Pre-colonisation to today. In C. Collins & S. Jackson (Eds.), *Sport in Aotearoa/New Zealand society* (pp. 78–95). Palmerston North, NZ: Dunmore Press.

Kohn, N., & Slowikowski, S. S. (1998). 'How do you warm up for a stretch class?' Sub/in/di/verting hegemonic shoves toward sport. In G. Rail (Ed.), *Sport in postmodern times* (pp. 21–32). Albany, NY: State University of New York Press.

Lather, P. (2006). Paradigm proliferation as a good thing to think with: Teaching research in education as a wild profusion. *International Journal of Qualitative Studies in Education, 19*(1), 35–57.

Liang, X., Wong, P., Wong, H-w., & Chan, S-h. (2005, June). *Let's tell a different story: An interview with Lawrence Grossberg.* Hong Kong: Lingnan University. Retrieved from http://www.ln.edu.hk/mcsln/3rd_issue/interview_01.htm

Markula, P. (Ed.). (2009). *Olympic women and the media: International perspectives.* Hampshire: Palgrave Macmillan.

McKay, J., & Pearson, K. (1984). Objectives, strategies and ethics in teaching introductory courses in sociology of sport. *Quest, 36*, 134–146.

McKee, A. (2003). *Textual analysis: A beginner's guide.* Thousand Oaks, CA: Sage.

Murray, D. M. (1991). All writing is autobiography. *College Composition and Communication, 42*(1), 66–73.

Paraschak, V., & Thompson, K. (2014). Finding strength(s): Insights on Aboriginal physical cultural practices in Canada. *Sport in Society, 17*(8), 1046–1060.

Pike, E. C. J., Jackson, S. J., & Wenner, L. A. (2015). Assessing the sociology of sport: On the trajectory, challenges and future of the field. *International Review for the Sociology of Sport, 50*(4–5), 357–362.

Pringle, R. G., Rinehart, R., & Caudwell, J. (2015). *Sport and the social significance of pleasure.* New York, NY: Routledge.

Richardson, L. (1990). *Writing strategies: Reaching diverse audiences.* Newbury Park, CA: Sage.

Richardson, L. (1994). Writing: A method of inquiry. In N. K. Denzin & Y. S. Lincoln (Eds.), *Handbook of qualitative research* (pp. 516–529). Thousand Oaks, CA: Sage.

Richardson, L. (2001). Getting personal: Writing-stories. *International Journal of Qualitative Studies in Education, 14*(1) 33–38.

Stone, A. (2015, November 7). Standing out from the crowd. *New Zealand Herald.* Retrieved from http://m.nzherald.co.nz/sport/news/article.cfm?c_id=4&objectid=11541279

Sugden, J. (2015). Assessing the sociology of sport: On the capacities and limits of using sport to promote social change. *International Review for the Sociology of Sport, 50*(4–5), 606–611.

Sydnor, S. (1998). A history of synchronized swimming. *Journal of Sport History, 25*(2), 252–267.

Thorpe, H. (2006). Beyond "decorative sociology": Contextualizing female surf, skate, and snowboarding. *Sociology of Sport Journal, 23*, 205–228.

United Nations. (2016). *The power of sport values.* Retrieved from http://www.un.org/youthenvoy/2016/04/learning-values-sport/

Wetherell, M. (2012). *Affect and emotion: A new social science understanding.* London: Sage.

CHAPTER 2

THE SOCIOLOGY OF SPORT IN SERVICE OF HUMANITY

Cora Burnett

ABOUT THE AUTHOR

Mentors and Influential Figures

Writing about yourself and your life's work is both challenging and rewarding. The questions posed by the editor provided a guideline for introspection and critical reflection. Emerging as a young researcher at the peak of the Apartheid years shaped how I chose mentors who would serve the cause of humanity, often in open defiance of institutional discrimination. My career path developed as I found opportunities opening up through partnerships, being exposed to influential thinkers and paradigms that would aid my understanding of the world. I realized that the knowledge production process is flawed with biases and remains obscure unless it can translate into agency that often entails unchartered territory. Being relevant means that you have to be strategic in walking on a tightrope of criticizing and contributing to positive social transformation and institutional reform.

I, like many young people from rural towns of the Northern Cape Province, went to the University of Stellenbosch after completing high school. Coming from a highly patriarchal society during the Apartheid era, I opted for a teaching career and having excelled in sport, I entered a degree program in physical education. During the 1970s, Professor Danie Craven (a famous rugby personality) brought a philosophy of enlightenment and openly challenged the government's Apartheid policies. He was an influential figure in the sport movement who, on the one hand, opposed the nationalist policies of the white minority

Reflections on Sociology of Sport: Ten Questions, Ten Scholars, Ten Perspectives
Research in the Sociology of Sport, Volume 10, 17–31
Copyright © 2018 by Emerald Publishing Limited
All rights of reproduction in any form reserved
ISSN: 1476-2854/doi:10.1108/S1476-285420170000010002

ruling party yet, on the other hand, negotiated for bringing rugby tours to South Africa during the boycott era (1970s and 1980s). He was also a leading figure of the National Party government and the African National Congress in the early 1990s, prior to the release of Nelson Mandela from prison and his subsequent selection as the first black president of a new democratic South Africa in 1994. As Head of the Department of Physical Education at the University of Stellenbosch, Danie Craven's open-mindedness allowed for influential women to take leadership positions and run multicultural programs. Professor Edith Katzenellenbogen became my mentor and I completed a Master's degree in dance choreography, following with a PhD in Dance Ethnology (completed in 1984).

At that stage, I accepted a position as junior lecturer at the Rand Afrikaans University and met with anthropologists and experts in the field of dance ethnology. In a politically explosive environment, the leadership at many conservative universities was openly challenged by growing opposition from liberal anthropologists who broke away from the *Volkekunde* paradigm. This paradigm supported a separatist ideology and scholars in the field argued for the legitimacy of cultural and racial divides on the basis that they represent separate nations to be granted self-governance in a homeland system. Professor Kotzé (1993) was one such scholar who publicly opposed the political establishment and published a boundary-shifting text entitled *In their Shoes: Understanding black South Africans through their experiences of life*. He and Professor Kees van der Waal became my supervisors for a doctorate that focused on the understanding of poverty and violence as related phenomena in a gang-ridden township of Davidsonville, north-west of Johannesburg. Anthropology provided an intellectual home and opportunity for praxis, whereas physical education and sociology at the university level during the 1990s were relatively a-political.

At that stage, sociology of sport was not taught as an independent subject and it was only when Professor Eric Dunning and his team from Leicester University visited South Africa that students were recruited for a post-graduate qualification in sport management and the sociology of sport. The restructuring of physical education departments in the late 1980s and the popularization of sport management provided an opportunity for the sociology of sport to become a service subject.

On a visit to Ohio State University in 1994, I discovered Jay Coakley's textbook *Sport and Society: Issues and Controversies* which I prescribed for my students, and continued to do so despite the lack of local case studies for contextual relevance (Coakley, 1997).[1] The *Handbook of Sport Studies* by Jay Coakley and Eric Dunning (2000) became another prescribed textbook. The co-authored publication *Sport in Society in Southern Africa* with Jay Coakley in 2014[2] was a most rewarding experience as it became the preferred textbook for most South African universities offering the sociology of sport as a subject. Continued contact with him has been most inspiring and he remains an important influence in the production and updation of learning material in the sociology of sport at the university level.

In post-apartheid South Africa, several international agencies required impact assessments and Sophie Beauvais from the Australian Sport Commission (ASC) became a key influence in shaping the methodology for intercountry comparative research. Wim Hollander (a colleague in the field of sport management and co-designer of the Sport for Development Impact Assessment Tool (S·DIAT))[3] and I were nominated by the ASC to a workshop for experts at UNICEF New York in 2005. The research tool was well-received and would undergo significant changes to allow for focused impact assessments in the fields of health (H·DIAT, Health-development Impact Assessment Tool) and education (E·DIAT, Education-Impact Assessment Tool) (Burnett & Hollander, 2006).

The S·DIAT gained traction and when presented to representatives of the European Union and German Development Corporation in 2006, we were contracted for a 2010 FIFA World Cup sport for development program. Gerald Guskowski, as the Project Manager of the GIZ/YDF (German Development Corporation's Youth Development through Football) program, welcomed in-depth research in addition to indicator-guiding impact assessments. The collaboration allowed for a fruitful enduring relationship and contributed to multiple academic research outputs and innovative research approaches (Burnett, 2013, 2015a). Under his leadership, additional funding was made available for a 12-month extension of research in the Cape Flats relating to the study of gang-related violence and the publication of *Stories from the Field* (Burnett, 2012).

At the international level, the International Sociology of Sport Association became a significant influence, particularly under the leadership of Joe Maguire, Kari Fasting, Steve Jackson, and Elisabeth Pike. Focusing on the sport for development field was a natural transition from anthropology and the sociology of sport. To me, the most influential personalities and collaborators in the field are John Sugden and Fred Coalter. We often shared a forum at international conferences and consequently a close relationship developed with the University of Brighton through John Sugden and his colleagues around the common interest of the Football4Peace initiative. Other colleagues such as Frank van Eekeren (Utrecht University) and Simona Safarikova (Palacky University) are currently collaborators in exchange programs and continue to shape Global North–Global South relationships.

Research Trajectory

After having completed a Master's degree in choreography, the consequent publications had an educational focus as I was located in the Faculty of Education (at the then Rand Afrikaans University that later became the University of Johannesburg in 2005) and lecturing courses in physical education. Within this paradigm, doctoral studies were followed by focusing on the socioethnic dances of the Venda. The in-depth understanding and collecting of educational material across ethnic divides in South Africa served the broader vision. I realized that research in service of a greater cause is a much more meaningful road to travel than merely collecting indigenous material and packaging it for educational purposes. It was thus inevitable that my research interests changed from publishing in dance ethnology and physical education (play and indigenous games).[4] Having gained understanding of a traditional African society (Venda) and studying the manifestations of poverty in a colored township equipped me with knowledge of diverse cultural contexts. Yet, it was the sport focus that returned in my subsequent publications.

Eric Dunning invited me to publish on soccer violence from a figurative sociological perspective. He and a team of academics visited South African public universities to recruit post-graduate students and lecturers for research in the field of the sociology of sport and sport management in the early 1990s. A post-graduate student from Venda, who later became the President of the South African Football Association during the 2010 FIFA World Cup, accompanied me to soccer games.[5] Engaging with the wider soccer community paved the way for being elected as President of the Football Club at the Rand Afrikaans University (now the University of Johannesburg) where there were political issues to deal with.

My main consideration was to do meaningful research in the interest of improving human conditions and challenge institutionalized forms of discrimination and the rights of disenfranchised populations. The socialization of athletes who competed in the All Africa Games in 1999 (in Johannesburg) provided the opportunity for larger scale research and for post-graduate students to become part of a research team. A comprehensive report was produced, and this was the first time that the Supreme Council of Sport for Africa allowed psycho-social research. Various papers were published – first on socialization dynamics and influences, followed by a critical stance where third-world and lingering apartheid-related justices still perpetuated structural inequalities.[6]

During the 1999 and the following 2004 (All Africa Games) research, it was observed that the multiple social discriminatory layers that the intersecting modalities of gender and race, and the fact that I could drive research (as a woman), would serve as a next level of agency through research. The critical work of Hargreaves (1997) and Pelak (2005) who also published on South African women in sport, and radical feminist paradigms provided a theoretical framework for further research. The lack of agency by women to negotiate access to decision-making positions in different sport sectors remains a challenge in the new political dispensation in South Africa. Even producing a national-level research report contracted by the Ministry of Sport (Sport and Recreation South Africa) had no guarantee for action, regardless of the merit of strategic insights.

In post-apartheid South Africa, international sporting bodies such as UK Sport and the Australian Sport Commission offered such opportunities through various development programs. It was around this time (1999–2005) that the United Nations accepted various resolutions and actions that would enable a Sport for Development and Peace (SDP) movement to flourish. It is in this genre that I would direct most of my future research.

Being involved in national-scale projects and strategic research enabled the development of the now relatively widely used Sport for Development Impact Assessment Tool (S·DIAT) and ensured the refinement of the methodology and training of local fieldworkers to assist in data collection. About 30 research outputs (reports, articles, and conference proceedings) followed on the Australian Sport Commission's research alone, following various critical paradigms, neo-classical capital theory (Bourdieu), Coleman's rational choice theory, the network theory, and Putnam's framework of civil engagement, integrated by the Marshallian concept of citizenship, informed the conceptual framework for analysis of social capital (Burnett, 2006).

The ASC's research attracted other development agencies such as GIZ/YDF, which would direct the majority of research outputs and led to a fruitful research partnership. The German Development Agency, co-funded by the European Union ensured a reciprocally beneficial partnership and funding for supplementing impact assessments with academic inquiry. For instance, they provided additional funding for research on violence (gangs at the Cape Flats) and the publication of *Stories from the Field*.[7] In this way strategic research, praxis, and academic objectives merged as a "win-win" scenario for all stakeholders involved.

On invitation of Gideon Sam, President of the South African Sport Commission and Olympic Committee (SASCOC) and Chair of the Commonwealth Games Development Committee, I received an invitation to do research at the 2014 Glasgow Commonwealth Games. The research aimed to investigate the perceptions, experiences, and expectations relating to development work of Commonwealth Games Associations (of which most are also serving as National Olympic Committees), and provided insights on which the development of a Commonwealth Games Foundation was formed in 2016, with "SDP" as a fifth pillar.[8] This experience motivated the application for the IOC's Advanced Olympic Research Grant. In 2015, I was awarded this grant and conducted a study on *Olympic Movement Stakeholder Collaboration for Delivering on Sport Development in Eight African (SADC) Countries* (Burnett, 2015b). The research was underpinned by stakeholder theory and bridged into the sport management field.

The focus on broader scale strategic research also severed national-level stakeholders; namely, an impact assessment of SRSA's community mass sport program (2004–2006), the school sport mass participation program (2008), and *The Status of SA Women in Sport & Recreation: 1994–2004* (Burnett, 2004).[9] Funding was also available for mobilizing 11 South African Public Universities to engage in an indigenous games research project, and in 2010, University Sport South Africa (USSA) requested a national research on the *Delivery for the Sport Industry by South African Universities* (Burnett, 2010).[10] The drive for meaningful research has recently culminated in another national research project under the leadership of a newly established organization, the South African University Physical Education Association. I developed the methodology and in collaboration with UNICEF (funding and strategic partner), SRSA, and the Department of Basic Education (DBE), was commissioned to do a situation analysis of the current school-based physical education/life orientation and school sport practises in which nine public universities took part.

As a South African researcher, the meaningfulness lies in knowledge production for positive societal change and strategic praxis – to have a voice in discourse development from the Global South, to influence multiple stakeholders (from government, to NGOs, and international sport agencies) through critical inquiry.

ABOUT SPORT

Why Does Sport Matter?

As a physical educator and academic in the sociology of sport there is indeed a convincing case to build for the multiple benefits of sport participation. Being exposed to structured physical activities from a very young age provides the key building blocks for human growth and development. School sport provides a microcosm for learning life skills, and for the talented, it provides the foundation for specialization and a pathway to competitive sport participation.

At the global political level, sport featured as a major tool to rally support against the Apartheid regime since the 1960s when South Africa became increasingly isolated from international sport competitions. In the 1990s, it was sport that was used by the first democratically elected government to bridge the racial divides. Nelson Mandela became known for his strategic actions and philosophy that still inspire notions of nation-building. He gave an inspiring speech at the 2000 Laureus World Sports Awards Ceremony which reads:

> Sport has the power to change the world. It has the power to inspire. It has the power to unite people in a way that little else can. Sport can awaken hope where there was previously despair.[11]

Sport also matters in building international relationships and for showcasing a nation through the hosting of major international sport competitions such as the 1995 Rugby World Cup (which South Africa won) and the 2010 FIFA World Cup. Sport has become a major industry worldwide and globalization became a formative force. Such influences contributed to international interuniversity partnerships and curriculum developments at South African public universities.

Studying sport sociologically provides a valuable lens from which to consider race, gender, and class in South African society. There is a long academic tradition of studying South African sport-related phenomena with most sociological inquiries focused on critiquing apartheid sport. Political issues still provide rich material for critical research such as studying social transformation (e.g., sport quotas), the hosting of national events (e.g., 2010 FIFA World Cup and the, now canceled 2022 Commonwealth Games), and the "transgression" of breaking gender and (dis)ability boundaries encapsulated by public debates and academic discourses surrounding Caster Semenya and Oscar Pistorius.

How Should Sport be Studied?

Sociologists of sport in many first-world countries have the opportunity to specialize and focus on a specific thematic field or even work within specific theoretical frameworks. In the first instance, sport sociologists should have a critical lens and focus on controversial issues in sport and related phenomena. In a way, they construct the discourses that may shed new light on issues, which in turn bear influence for positive social change. Tapping into Marxian approaches, feminism, and the work of Foucault and Bourdieu, as well as concepts such as Gramsci's conceptualization of hegemonic power relations, provides researchers with the necessary analytical tools. Globally, the clustering of scholars around main thematic areas provides a variety of material from which critical and innovative insights may be drawn.

Radical thinking and agency, as encapsulated by Badiou's Kantian ideas (Watkin, 2011) and Césaire's advocacy (Grosfoguel, 2012) for an international left, challenge the status quo of powerful neocolonial networks built around mega events and multinational foundations. New World Black thinkers like C.L.R. James and W.E.B. Du Bois warn against neoliberal thinking and the structuring of development courses that perpetuate western-centric practises (Pithouse, 2013). Development is a contentious phenomenon as it is not always clear who are to benefit most, and where the real ownership lies. Focusing on sport only provides a limited understanding of how it articulates with other, and often more dominant, spheres within an individual's life. The danger in this is to lose sight of the complexity of phenomena under study. Deductive approaches and a choice of paradigm may in some ways obscure real power struggles – even within the academic realm. The challenge is to discover new ways of knowing, and multiple layers of sense-making reflection of sociocultural realities.

Contextual understandings and reflective interpretations from the research community in articulation with discourse development are often absent from knowledge production within the social sciences. In this sense, data is manipulated and mediated to serve, rather than inform new insights or understand the full complexity of an issue under academic scrutiny. For instance, in the African context, feminist debates are only partly accepted by those who regard themselves as "womanists" which is embedded in traditional culture, religious beliefs, and a historical context of prioritizing race to gender in a struggle against colonial oppression. At the same time, further interrogation of subtle ways of oppression and possible social change to improve the situation of all, necessitate the understandings of complex phenomena from multiple perspectives.

Possible strategies to bring about innovative, new understandings and praxis, would be to: (i) utilize theoretical insights as they may apply to the study at hand, while adding a layer of indigenous reflective understandings; (ii) put the complexity back in the research process; (iii) engage in grounded research approaches to generate new insights; (iv) act boldly in disseminating research to various institutions and those with the political power which will bring about meaningful societal change – if they know differently, they may act differently; and (v) never compromise your integrity in search of the truth.

Is Sport a Panacea for Social Problems?

In the field of the sport for development, contractual research, and working with practitioners who, often with evangelical seal, vouch for the magical power of sport, obscuring the reality of the potential role of sport in addressing social ills. Coalter (2013, p. 3) refers to Gramsci's advice to radicals to live without illusions, yet not to become disillusioned, stating "I'm a pessimist because of intelligence, but optimist because of the will" (Letter from Prison, December 19, 1929; Gramsci, 1994). He applies this paraphrase to the investigation of the benefits of sport for development programs delivering on "promises" of donors which echoed in the evangelical rhetoric of implementers.

The focus on sport only, without investigating the social problem in its complex manifestations, contributes to a biased or reductionist understanding and overstatement of how sport can serve as an antidote. For instance, the belief that sport keeps young boys off the street and as such prevents them from committing crime, encapsulated by the rhetoric of "a child in sport is a child out of court," rings hollow in conflicting evidence. Sport participation offers a site where many influences may play out such as mentorship from a coach, friendships with peers, and learning from experiences on the playing field. Even if a potentially positive outcome such as social cohesion is claimed, it can turn sour in cases where a tight-knit sport team engages in antisocial behavior such as excessive drinking, risk taking, or even criminal acts.

Not only do many claims of the positive effects of sport participation remain unsubstantiated, but addressing symptoms of deeper-rooted social problems through sport is doomed to fail. In *Stories from the Field*, all 45 case studies illustrate the potential role of sport in addressing social issues – from unemployment, exclusion, teenage pregnancies, and public violence (Burnett, 2012). Although significant in the manipulation of positive and transforming sport experiences, it remains wedged in with multiple other influences and life philosophies that would filter its effect. Longitudinal studies such as the one from Forde (2008) bring a sense of perspective to the claim of enduring positive effects of sport as a life changer.

ABOUT PRACTISING SOCIOLOGY OF SPORT

Is Teaching Sociology of Sport Easy?

The teaching of the sociology of sport to a diverse group of students, many of whom are sport science students, does not go without challenges. In sport departments, critical approaches and multiple perspectives inherent in the sociological argument do not sit well with students having been exposed to experimental work and "theories to proof" approaches. A narrow focus on high-performance sport, an uncritical stance relating to issues of overtraining (positive deviance) and emphasis on the bio-sciences, pose unique challenges to established common sense reality and dogma of the natural sciences.

The same rings true when exposing mainstream sociology students to the study of sport, who have a limited understanding of what sport participation or various sport-related phenomena entail. For many, sport remains an abstract concept with little relevance to how athletes or people structure their lives around sport, and construct sport to fit in with their identities and social worlds.

In post-apartheid South Africa, teaching the sociology of sport is most relevant in addressing broader societal issues and social policy development. Discussions on issues relating to politics (e.g., social transformation), the economy (including the hosting of major sport events), gender, race, and class often lead to heated debates, but bring an acute awareness that sport is a social construction which does not operate in a value and influence free vacuum. Racial stereotypes lead to high levels of sensitivity and political affiliations generate feelings of hostility in a society (and class) where "us" and "them" are barely covered under a veneer of tentative argumentation.

The current *fees must fall* campaign at public South African universities clearly demonstrates the existing social fault lines and disparate socioeconomic realities in an unequal society. Inequality remains a stark reality, even in providing sport facilities and opportunities to students after the national restructuring of the public higher education sector in 2005. During this restructuring process, existing public universities were merged and relatively better resourced (dominantly white) institutions had to merge with less resources (and inner-city or peri-urban) institutions. The South African society thus remains a politically volatile environment that provides real-life examples and a rich frame of reference for teaching the sociology of sport.

Do Sociologists of Sport Like Sport?

During a national project where research was conducted at all 23 public universities in 2010, it became clear that most academics in the field of sport studies participated in sport during their careers. In the transition from physical education to multidisciplinary departments, the sociology of sport is only offered at eight public universities and considered a relatively new subject by lecturers within existing departments who took on the teaching of the subject. There is a keen interest in engaging in sport practises where it contributes to a healthy lifestyle by pursuing earlier interests and becoming engaged in outdoor pursuits.

In addition to active participation, interests would inevitably shift to viewing sport as a field of study and as a career. Like other international scholars (e.g., Jay Coakley and Michael Messner), drawing insights from being involved and studying the sport participation of their children and grandchildren, I did the same. My son's involvement in competitive rugby and athletics within a racially loaded sport environment provided rich material and led to some publications on "race and sport," as perceived by elite school rugby players.

Attending sport events and watching televised programmes became a way of gathering information for lecturing purposes and reflecting on public debates. It continues to create a realistic frame of reference and at the same time provides material for academic engagement. Attending the 2014 Commonwealth Games as an on-site researcher rendered a completely different perspective on the event than merely observing it as a spectator. Themes of national pride, power relations, and intergroup tensions made participant-observation a highly worthwhile experience − getting an understanding of what it meant for CGA representatives to be "part of the Commonwealth family."

Is the Sociologist of Sport a "Public Intellectual"?

In the sociology of sport, and among others, Donnelly (2015) pitched the emergence of subdisciplines through the fragmentation of physical education's transformation into an academic discipline at the same time when Michael Burawoy's professional sociology drew widespread critique. Since the 1980s, leading sport sociologists increasingly engaged with Marxian and other critical approaches at a time when antipoverty and pro-women environmentalists and civil rights activists launched successful protest actions in different spheres of society. The positionality of the researcher (on whose side s/he might be on), is key in delivering research that may address the plight of various populations, guiding critical debates, and exposing unethical practises or corruption of sport powerhouses as evidenced in the work of Jennings (2011). Geoff Arbourne (now a producer of documentary films) left his post-graduate studies to make protest documentaries – first it was *Tin Town* to demonstrate the plight of local impoverished people who were forcefully removed in cleaning up Cape Town for the 2010 FIFA World Cup, followed by *Forever Pure* that exposed the ethic racism in Jewish football.[12]

In South Africa, social scientists span over a wide spectrum. Not only was the apartheid ideology informed by the then *Volkekunde* insights of separate cultural, and therefore a fragmented socio-political dispensation, but it was from the enlightened anthropologists and sociologists that severe opposition and activism emerged. Publications such as *Political Keywords* (Boonzaier & Sharp, 1988) interrogated the political vocabulary constructed within the Apartheid paradigm and provided critical insights for argumentation and activism.

In the field of sport discussions around match-fixing (in cricket and soccer), usage of performance-enhancing substances and athlete's rights necessitates the scrutiny of the discourse to provide insights to meaningful public debates. An example would be the case of the Caster Semenya saga which exploded from a gender debate to one of human justice and the questioning of political power and ethical conduct of sport powerhouses (e.g., the International Amateur Athletic Association and the International Olympic Committee). Caster Semenya is currently considered a very influential female athlete who won a gold medal in the 2016 Rio Olympic Games, yet at the international level of competition she remains a controversial figure in terms of being labeled as inter-gender with an assumed advantage over other female athletes.

Without sociologists and feminists arguments interrogating the social consequences of banning athletes with an "inter-sex condition," outlier female athletes may fall victim to what "Miranda Fricker has termed epistemic injustice – a condition that arises as a result of the absence of concepts and language that would enable us to articulate reality differently" (Dee, 2010, p. 311). It is thus up to sport and mainstream sociologists to reveal reality in its messy manifestations, rather than to abide by quick fix and neat (politically correct) solutions.

ABOUT SOCIOLOGY OF SPORT IN THE ACADEMY

Does Sociology of Sport Face Institutional/Industry Barriers?

The existing divisionary structures along the lines of disciplinary practises contribute to the marginalization of the sociology of sport within mainstream sociology and within sport science communities. Sport is not always taken seriously in mainstream sociological work, whereas applied sociology as evidenced in many sociology of sport practises often fails to demonstrate theoretical depth and scientific rigor. 2016 is the first time that a mainstream sociological text for South African students included a chapter on *The significance of sports to sociology* (Burnett, 2016). Disciplinary divisions at the level of the university produce similar fragmented bodies of knowledge, while many societal issues would benefit from interdisciplinary work.

Currently in many African countries, there is a call for decolonizing knowledge, which holds the danger of reversed political biases and limits the utilization of influential and meaningful theoretical frameworks in search of counter-ideologies emanating from indigenous knowledge systems. Scrutinizing sociological knowledge for Eurocentric or neocolonial biases is essential to empower African-based academics to produce, rather than consume knowledge – making it relevant and contextual. However, in a globalized world, shared meanings are crucial for a community of scholars dedicated to take the discipline forward.

In most public universities in South Africa, the sociology of sport is a service subject or comprises modules in support of sport science and sport management coursework. Only recently did the subject make inroads in the field of physical education by addressing issues of equality, empowerment, and citizenship (Stidder & Hayes, 2013). Career paths are limited for a sociology major or post-graduate qualification in the sociology of sport. It is for that reason that a strategy is to recruit post-graduate students from people already working in the field of sport such as governance, coaching, media, or management, who would then benefit from a sociological focus.

The fact that the sociology of sport has made limited impact on mainstream sociological and developmental studies remains a challenge for academics and practitioners. It seems that the issue of relevance plays a part in adding value to mainstream development and youth work in impoverished communities (Darnell & Black, 2011). In many such communities, sport is seen as a luxury and, for governments, investing in sport is seen as irresponsible when faced with high levels of unemployment, combating epidemics such as HIV/AIDS and where literacy levels are relatively low. Undue critical stances without strategic insights to improve human conditions create high levels of animosity rather than finding ways for collaboration or where critical sociological insights may be harnessed for policy development and just practises.

What is the Future of the Sociology of Sport?

Increased levels of specialization within the field would continue to create pockets of academic excellence and shape scholars into "super-specialization," which has a positive impact on theoretical and discourse development. Their work is, however, seldom questioned in academic publications. The danger is that emerging researchers tend to uncritically paraphrase the work of such scholars without engaging in a critical discourse and review contextual limitations or realities.

Putting complexity back into the sociological study of sport, may contribute to meaningful interdisciplinary research collaboration which, in turn, may ensure that the sociology of sport makes inroads into mainstream disciplinary fields and practises. Collaboration should honor the integrity of partnerships without dictation from a dominant entity. This would find expression in the development of joint degree courses where post-graduate students may be exposed to the different sources or experts, who in turn would reciprocally benefit from such engagement with students from different localities.

Practises emanating from global sporting bodies may require the (re)packaging of the sociology of sport such as in the case of Olympic Studies or Community Sport Studies. The selection of relevant content for such focused coursework may lead to undermine a more comprehensive understanding of, and exposure to the sociology of sport. The emergence of such applied bodies of knowledge would inevitably find maturity in the development of theoretical insights and scholarly activity to constitute a body of scientific knowledge.

Scholars in the field of the sociology of sport may find international collaboration around central research themes particularly fruitful. Tapping into global funding for intercontinental and intercountry research, may advance the understanding of a particular social discourse and create an understanding of the manifestations influenced by the society as context.

The African proverb which is also reflective of the spirit of "brotherhood," stating that "If you want to go quickly, go alone. If you want to go far, go together," rings true in my life where I was fortunate to have met so many people who have dedicated their lives and careers of serving humanity through professional and personal agency. As a researcher, you are often humbled by the wisdom of your research participants with whom you often find a relationship of reciprocal agency. You realize that everybody knows differently, and that induced discourses often obscure rather reveal the truth within its complex contextual manifestations. In diversity lies innovation and the richness of meaning to be harnessed for discovering multiple sociological truths in the complexity of real-life contexts. As I reflect on these issues, I realize that there is an obligation to inspire as others have inspired me, to serve the field with integrity, and find a collective voice to bring about meaningful and lasting change for the creation of a more just and equal society.

NOTES

1. Jay Coakley's textbook *Sport in Society: Issues and Controversies* had several editions between 1997 and 2015, as well as several regional adaptations (e.g., Canada, the United Kingdom, and southern Africa).

2. Jay Coakley and Cora Burnett collaborated in writing *Sport in Society: Issues and Controversies* (Southern African Edition).

3. Several papers were published on the Sport in Development Impact Assessment Tool (S·DIAT) with Burnett as the main author. The methodology was also recognized in *Mapping research on the impact of sport and development interventions. Comic Relief Review* — a Comic Relief publication.

4. Under the leadership of Cora Burnett and Wim Hollander, the South African Indigenous Games Research Project of 2001/2002 was conducted in all 9 provinces by 11 collaborating tertiary institutions.

5. Several papers by Cora Burnett were published on soccer violence between two Professional Soccer League teams, namely Orlando Pirates and Kaizer Chiefs as articles in research journals and a book chapter.

6. Cora Burnett produced several papers on the sociological perspectives and socialization of elite African athletes following her research at the 1999 and 2003 All Africa Games, respectively.

7. The publication, *Stories from the field: GIZ/YDF Footprint in Africa,* includes a more popular version and CD with 45 case studies for coursework in the teaching of the sociology of sport.

8. Cora Burnett and Wim Hollander conducted research at the 2014 Glasgow Commonwealth Games to come up with a development framework for the Commonwealth Games Federation for implementation at the global and national (Commonwealth Games Association) levels.

9. The various national-level impact assessments include two on mass participation sport programmes and tracing the status of South African girls and women in sport (1994–2004).

10. Cora Burnett conducted a national survey among all 23 public universities in South Africa (during 2010) to establish the delivery of these institutions to the sport industry. The study was commissioned by University Sport South Africa (USSA).

11. A copy of Mandela's speech can be found at: www.pennlive.com/sports/index.ssf/2013/12/nelson_mandela_believed_in_the.html.

12. Geoff Arbourne (a producer of documentary films) showed both films at different ISSA World conferences, *Tin Town* featured at the congress in Havana (2011) and *Forever Pure* featured in Paris (2015). See http//duckinandivinfilms.com.

REFERENCES

Boonzaier, E., & Sharp, J. S. (Eds.). (1988). *South African keywords: The uses & abuses of political concepts.* Cape Town: David Philip Publishers.

Burnett, C. (2004). *The status of SA Women in Sport & Recreation 1994 to 2004.* Pretoria: South African Sports Commission.

Burnett, C. (2006). Building Social Capital through an 'Active Community Club'. *International Review for the Sociology of Sport, 41*(3-4), 283–294.

Burnett, C. (2010). *Delivery for the sport industry by South African Universities.* Johannesburg: University of Johannesburg.

Burnett, C. (2012). *Stories from the field: GIZ/YDF footprint in Africa*. Pretoria: GIZ GmbH Youth Development Project.

Burnett, C. (2013). GIZ/YDF and youth as drivers for sport for development in the African context. *Journal of Sport for Development*, *1*(1), 1–10. (Online, www.jsfd.org/publications).

Burnett, C. (2015a). Assessing the sociology of sport: On Sport for Development and Peace. *International Review for the Sociology of Sport*, *50*(4-5): 385–390.

Burnett, C. (2015b). *Olympic Movement Stakeholder Collaboration for Delivering on Sport Development in Eight African (SADC) Countries. Advanced Olympic Research Grant Programme*. Lausanne: IOC.

Burnett, C. (2016). The significance of sports to sociology. In J. Ferante, M. Seedat-Khan, Z. Jansen, & R. Smith (Eds.), *Sociology. A South African perspective* (pp. 294–307). Andover: Cengage Learning EMEA.

Burnett, C., & Hollander, W. J. (2006). *The impact of the Mass Participation Project of Sport and Recreation South Africa (Siyadlala) 2004/5*. Pretoria: Sport and Recreation South Africa.

Coakley, J. (1997). *Sport in society: Issues & controversies* (6th ed.). New York, NY: McGraw-Hill.

Coakley, J., & Dunning, E. (Eds.). (2000). *Handbook of sports studies*. New York, NY: Sage.

Coalter, F. (2013). *Sport for development. What game are we playing?* London: Routledge.

Darnell, S. C., & Black, D. R. (2011). Mainstreaming sport into international development studies. *Third World Quarterly*, *32*(3), 367–378.

Dee, A-C. (2010). Doing epistemic (in)justice to Semenya. *International Journal of Media and Cultural Politics*, *6*(3): 311–326.

Donnelly, P. (2015). Assessing the sociology of sport: On public sociology of sport and research that makes a difference. *International Review for the Sociology of Sport*, *50*(4-5), 419–423.

Forde, S. (2008). *Playing by their rules: Coastal teenage girls in Kenya on life, love and football*. Kalifi: Moving the Goalposts.

Gramsci, A. (1994). *Letters from prison, Volumes 1 and 2*. In: F. Rosengarten (Ed. & Trans.). New York, NY: Columbia University Press.

Grosfoguel, R. (2012). Decolonizing Western universalisms: Decolonial pluriversalism from Aimé Césaire to the zapatistas. *Transmodernity*, *1*(3), 88–104.

Hargreaves, J. (1997). Women's sport, development, and cultural diversity: The South African experience. *Women's Studies International Forum*, *20*(2), 191–209.

Jennings, A. (2011). Investigating corruption in corporate sport: The IOC and FIFA. *International Review for the Sociology of Sport*, *46*(4), 367–387.

Kotzé, J. C. (1993). *In their shoes: Understanding black South Africans through their experiences of life*. Johannesburg: Juta Publishers.

Pelak, C. F. (2005). Negotiating gender/race/class constraints in the New South Africa A Case Study of Women's Soccer. *International Review for the Sociology of Sport*, *40*(1), 53–70.

Pithouse, R. (2013). 'The open door of every consciousness'. *The South Atlantic Quarterly*, *112*(1), 91–98.

Stidder, G., & Hayes, S. (2013). *Equity and inclusion in physical education and sport*. London: Routledge.

Watkin, C. (2011). *Difficult atheism: Post-theological thinking in Alain Badiou, Jean-Luc Nancy and Quentin Meillassoux*. Edinburgh: Edinburgh University Press.

CHAPTER 3

THE SOCIOLOGY OF SPORT AS A CAREER AND ACADEMIC DISCIPLINE

Jay Coakley

ABOUT THE AUTHOR

Introduction

As I grew up on the North side of Chicago, my early experiences revolved around sports. Most of those experiences consisted of playing informal games in parks and other spaces. I immersed myself into sandlot baseball and softball, swimming, ice hockey and speed skating, all forms of basketball competition, horseshoes, darts, tennis, table tennis, bike racing, street and garage hockey, and just about anything that involved physical challenges. I did play golf on "caddy day" at the country club where I carried clubs for wealthy members who I learned to dislike as a caddy and as a paid member of the grounds crew between the ages of 14 and 17 years.

The sports I played were clearly gendered, segregated by race and ethnicity and social class, and sponsored by schools, churches, local businesses, and civic organizations. They gave rise to no grand illusions about "the power of sport" to transform people or social and economic circumstances. They were physical challenges that offered fun, occasional flow, and reaffirmation of what it meant to be a male during the 1950s and 1960s in the United States. I saw "athletes" engage in various forms of deviant behavior and face serious trouble with law enforcement. I also witnessed the planning of crimes by some of the young

Reflections on Sociology of Sport: Ten Questions, Ten Scholars, Ten Perspectives
Research in the Sociology of Sport, Volume 10, 33–48
Copyright © 2018 by Emerald Publishing Limited
All rights of reproduction in any form reserved
ISSN: 1476-2854/doi:10.1108/S1476-285420170000010003

"athletes" with whom I played basketball at the DePaul Settlement House in Chicago.

I loved to play sports of all kinds, and I was drawn to them because of the joy associated with participation. I saw sports as an enjoyable life experience and never saw it as a magical elixir that produced social integration or character development, although I did develop bonds with certain teammates during my sport experiences, and I did learn things about myself as I faced challenges in connection with organizing and playing sports through and beyond my college years. These experiences combined with my interest in sociology attracted me to the sociology of sport.

Mentors and Influential Figures

While completing my PhD coursework at the University of Notre Dame in 1969, I had not heard of the sociology of sport. My degrees, including a BA and MA, were in sociology with a consistent emphasis on theory, methods, social psychology, urban sociology, and race and ethnicity. Eager to begin what I perceived as a teaching career in higher education, Nancy (my wife), our two children, and I departed from South Bend, Indiana in 1970 so I could assume a position as assistant professor in sociology at Northern Arizona University in Flagstaff, Arizona.

During my first year in Arizona, I read *Athletics for Athletes* (1969) and *The Athletic Revolution* (1971) by Jack Scott and *The Revolt of the Black Athlete* (1969) by Harry Edwards. Having played basketball in college with a majority of black teammates in a nearly all-white institution, I had followed the media coverage of the boycott of the 1968 Olympic Games by black athletes and saw Edwards as an influential sociologist-activist in the civil rights movement. Experiences with my teammates primed me to agree with Edwards that sports at all levels were riddled with personal and systemic racism.

When I also read *Sport, Culture, and Society* edited by Loy and Kenyon (1969), *Aspects of Contemporary Sport Sociology* edited by Kenyon (1969), and *The Cross-Cultural Analysis of Sport and Games* edited by Lüschen (1970), I decided in 1971 to propose a one-off special studies seminar titled "Sport in Society" for advanced undergraduates. Over 50 students applied for the seminar and my department chair suggested that I choose the 15 who would make up the class. Without a system to prioritize the registrants, I chose students so that women comprised half the class; half were athletes (male and female), including four African American men; and five were students that I identified as "socially curious, open-minded thinkers."

We met at my house which was close to the campus and spent the first two weeks reading selected sections from all the above sources. At the end of the second session the students identified 10 questions that they wanted to explore through readings and discussions.[1] The seminar was a hit and this led me to propose, with the support of the sociology chair who was a strong faculty advocate, a sociology of sport course to the college curriculum committee. The proposal was promptly rejected, with the committee members concluding that the topic was frivolous.

During the same semester I was identified as a problem faculty member by the Board of Regents and the president of the university. This came about because I used material from Robin Morgan's anthology, *Sisterhood is Powerful: An Anthology of Writings From The Women's Liberation Movement* (1970) in a race and ethnicity course I taught. The students in 1971 had a difficult time understanding that racism permeated American culture, so I shifted to the issue of sexism permeating the culture which was easier for them to grasp, especially with the examples in Morgan's book. Word that I was using this material traveled to the only female member of the Regents. She was offended by the material and convinced the other Regents that I was propagandizing students, especially the "innocent" females in my class.[2] Although I succeeded in showing the students how sexism and racism were features of American society and culture, I was less successful in convincing the Board of Regents and the university president that my use of Morgan's material was appropriate as a teaching tool. When I refused to apologize and cease using it, I could see that even the support of my department chair would not change the minds of people more aligned with the John Birch Society than with the notion of academic freedom.[3] This coupled with a desire to return to Colorado where I had done my undergraduate degree and Nancy's family lived, led me to apply for the job of an assistant professor at the newly established campus of the University of Colorado in Colorado Springs (UCCS). I was hired and began the appointment in August, 1972.

Robert H. Hughes, who had left Northern Arizona University in 1971 as he sought increased academic freedom at the new campus, was the chair of our three-person department. In 1973, Hughes planned a way for me to offer a course in the sociology of sport in the Honors program, and then successfully propose a "Sociology of Leisure and Sport" course to the curriculum committee whose members enjoyed many outdoor leisure pursuits and thought that leisure was an appropriate topic of study. We had emphasized leisure more than sport in the proposal.

With Hughes as a mentor and advocate, I taught the leisure and sport course, which after two years was split into two courses dedicated to each of the topics, respectively. As the sociology of sport course attracted large numbers of students, and as I sought a book other than Harry Edwards' *Sociology of Sport* text (1973), Hughes encouraged me to propose a textbook and gave me release time to write the proposal and a few chapters while I taught only a sociology of sport course during the spring semester in 1975.

My thesis and dissertation advisor had been a mentor in graduate school, but Bob Hughes has been a mentor, colleague, and friend since 1972. His political abilities as department chair enabled me to do much of what I have done in the sociology of sport.

Research Trajectory

My MA thesis and PhD dissertation focused primarily on race and ethnicity, urban sociology, and social psychology. The thesis (Coakley, 1968) was a study of the impact of a 1967 race-related civil disorder on community satisfaction and social cohesion in African American neighborhoods in South Bend, Indiana, and it furthered my interest in how the civil rights movement influenced the lives of African Americans. My dissertation (Coakley, 1972a) focused on the antecedents, current contexts, and everyday life consequences of the self-identification priorities (race *vs.* religious vocation) of Black Catholic priests in the United States during 1969. Unfortunately, personal circumstances interfered with publishing articles based on these studies — something that still bothers me when I glance at those bound volumes sitting in a bookcase in my home office.

My first two publications were a social historical account of "The Negro and the Catholic Church" (Lamanna & Coakley, 1969) and "Graduate Education: A Rationale for Change" (Coakley, 1970), a call for action research and courses on progressive change in sociology programs. Apart from an article in an edited collection (Coakley, 1972b), a co-authored article on the perception of mate-selection priorities among college students (Laner & Coakley, 1974), two book reviews, and an article on gaming and simulation in introductory sociology courses, I published nothing in sociology or sociology of sport journals prior to the late 1970s.

My research during the first few years after completing the dissertation focused on local issues in and around Colorado Springs. It led to policy- and program-related research reports for agencies and organizations, including the Colorado State prison, the United States Ski Coaches Association, and the Parks and Recreation Department and the Senior Center in the city. These studies were usually linked with my teaching and I included undergraduate students as research assistants.

I had a weak publication record when I proposed and wrote a few chapters for what became the first edition of *Sport in Society: Issues and Controversies* (1978). I did not know where to send this proposal, but I met an acquisitions editor at the 1975 conference of the American Alliance for Health, Physical Education, Recreation, and Dance (AAHPERD), and he said he would take a look at it. A few months later I was shocked to receive a contract offer, and with no critical forethought about the terms of the contract, I signed on the dotted line in 1976.[4] With little professional writing experience, apart from research reports, and no major publications, my naïveté and self-confidence led me to take on the textbook project.

George Sage served as a guide in this process. I met George at an AAHPERD conference and discovered that he had been a highly successful coach for a college basketball team that regularly played the team on which I played. He remembered me, as well as a scouting report on my on-court weaknesses, and we quickly became good friends. Even though he and sociologist D. Stanley Eitzen from Colorado State University were writing a sociology of sport text at the very same time, George gave me encouragement and we shared references from our respective projects.

The publication of *Sport in Society* in 1978 gave direction to my subsequent research and publication trajectory. Although UCCS was a teaching-oriented institution with an emphasis on community service, I scrambled for resources to support my research projects and often funded my own studies. Much of this research and related scholarly work focused on socialization, especially in connection with the play, games, and sport experiences of children and young adolescents. In addition to teaching a large section of introductory sociology most semesters, I also taught courses on race and ethnicity, social psychology, popular culture, the sociology of leisure, the sociology of aging, and urban sociology, as well as the sociology of sport.

When I learned in 1980 that a Tokyo publisher wanted to translate *Sport in Society* into Japanese, and that the C.V. Mosby Company (purchased by McGraw-Hill in 1990) wanted me to write a second edition, I was caught off-guard with a full teaching load and two kids in need of parenting. As I did the revision, I began to keep meticulous track of most publications in the sociology of sport and make sure that the text accurately represented and made sense of that research for students. This, combined with my involvement in the North American Society for the Sociology of Sport (NASSS) beginning with its first conference in 1980, was the factor that led to me becoming the founding editor of the *Sociology of Sport Journal* in 1983.

Also important in my research career, 1980 marked the first time I traveled outside of North America. A trip to Germany in 1980 and to the Soviet Union in 1981 connected me with new colleagues and broadened my awareness of sports and sport scholarship and my research interests. Meeting Anita White, who earned her PhD at the University of Northern Colorado with George Sage and then founded the Sports Studies Department at the West Sussex Institute of Higher Education (now the University of Chichester), and having the opportunity to work with her in England during a sabbatical in 1985 also influenced my research. Our study of how young people made decisions about sport participation and the use of discretionary time led to presentations, publications, and a report widely used by people at the British Sports Council and leisure centers around the country.

Other research during this time in my career generally reflected my access to data — qualitative data that I collected in local self-funded projects and quantitative data collected by others who wanted me to help them with analysis of sport-related variables. Apart from the research that Anita White and I did in England I never had a research grant of more than a couple hundred dollars. My research and publications have largely been opportunistic. But the regular revisions and relative popularity of the *Sport in Society* text afforded me many opportunities to work with and learn from colleagues worldwide.

Being in Colorado Springs where the United States Olympic Committee was established in 1978 and where at least 20 national governing bodies were located also provided me with research and learning opportunities. These experiences increased my overall knowledge of sports, leisure, and physical activities. They helped me as I developed and supervised a Master's degree in Coaching Education with colleagues in the School of Education. Relatedly, I founded and directed a Center for the Study of Sport and Leisure for 10 years from 1982 to 1992 and used it as the organizational framework for developing, staffing, and supervising a physical education curriculum on a campus that never had any programs or courses related to movement, health and well-being, and the body.

These experiences put me in touch with coaches, sport managers, exercise scientists, and athletic directors in local schools, all of who expanded my knowledge beyond the social dimensions of sports and physical activities.

ABOUT SPORT

Why Does Sport Matter?

Sports are multidimensional phenomena. From a sociological perspective, they matter because they are sites for: social interaction; socialization; identity formation and affirmation; commerce and power relations; mediated messages that influence what people think and talk about; the reification of nations and national identities; the reproduction of ideologies related to race, ethnicity, gender, social class, nationality, ability, the body, competition, violence, mobility, and meritocracy; and occasionally, the expression of progressive social activism, especially in symbolic (as opposed to substantive) terms. Culturally, they matter because they are sites at which people publicly tell stories about themselves, stories that influence ideas and actions in ways yet to be fully studied and understood by those of us in the sociology of sport.

Variations in the forms and organization of sports indicate that as cultural practises they serve a diverse range of social purposes and are given different meanings from time to time and place to place. Sociological research on these variations provides valuable insights into social processes, structures, and ideologies that constitute sports. In this sense, sports also serve as windows into social and cultural life. These windows provide vantage points for observations and analysis that complement sociological observations and analyses done from other vantage points.

Overall, sports matter to the extent that they are connected with and integrated into the everyday life of individuals, relationships, and institutions. Of course, the social and cultural importance of sports and sport participation varies with social conditions and social processes. Research shows that sports are not so much a direct cause of socialization as they are a site at which people form and experience social relationships that shape the meanings given to sport-related experiences and influence their lives. This is an important point, because many people believe that sports, regardless of how they are organized and played are essentially pure and good activities that automatically lead to positive developmental outcomes at the personal and collective levels. This belief has discouraged critical thinking about sports and made it difficult to obtain funding for critical sociological research. At the same time, it has fostered exaggerated and uninformed assumptions about the social benefits of sports for individuals, schools, communities, and societies, and has led to using public and private funds to sponsor sports that fail to live up to expectations based on those assumptions. This makes critical sociological research on sports important, despite a scarcity of resources to fund such research.

How Should Sport be Studied?

As multidimensional phenomena, sports should be studied from multiple disciplinary perspectives and through the use of multiple methodologies. In the sociology of sport it is important to observe and analyze sports from multiple vantage points – not to discover ultimate truth about sports, but to understand the meanings and consequences of sports under varying social conditions for people from diverse social and cultural backgrounds.

As a critical pragmatist, I am concerned with the reliability, validity, and practical relevance of knowledge about sports. Additionally, I support various methods of producing knowledge and different theories for organizing, making sense of, and raising questions about that knowledge. Although I have done quantitative research and appreciate the importance of statistical description, relationships, and analysis, I prefer to do qualitative research. I enjoy observing sport situations in context, talking with people involved in sports, and connecting what people say with what they do. Identifying statistical patterns and relationships between variables in large populations is important and always needed in the sociology of sport, but I feel closer to the action when I do qualitative research.

Of course, the process of doing research and producing knowledge is strongly influenced by the contexts in which scholars work and the reward systems used to evaluate them. This is evident as more scholars worldwide publish research on the social dimensions of sports and physical activities. There are clear variations in the historical, conceptual, and theoretical links between sports and related phenomena, such as leisure, physical education, recreation, outdoor activities, play, games, folk festivals, tourism, and physical culture in general. This, combined with the diversity of research in the field, has attracted scholars with research interests that may not be supported by the traditional disciplines of sociology and physical education. For me, this was and remains an attractive aspect of the sociology of sport: disciplinary boundaries are more fuzzy and permeable than in sociology generally and colleagues in the field are more likely to push those boundaries.

Additionally, as the field has grown, so too have the definitions of sports used by researchers. Initially, people in the sociology of sport defined sport as "an embodied, structured, goal-oriented, competitive, contest-based, ludic, physical activity" (Loy & Coakley, 2015). This definition was useful at a time when the field was seeking recognition among more established social sciences. It was important for the object of study to be identified precisely if scholars wanted to obtain academic and scientific legitimacy. But this definition over-looked that sports are socially constructed, contested, and dynamic physical activities that are collectively created, sustained, given meaning, and changed over time. Therefore, research today may focus on tai chi practised in a Beijing park, capoeira practised in a plaza in Rio de Janeiro, parkour practised in a Paris neighborhood, windsurfing on the water of Australia's Gold Coast, or skateboarding on the concrete surfaces of neighborhoods in Oakland as much as it focuses on formally institutionalized, competitive physical activities. Research today also focuses on the body and physical culture more generally. However, research focused on the highly visible institutionalized, competitive, rule-governed physical activities in contemporary cultures often evokes the most interest and discussion in journal publications and classrooms.

Overall it is important that norms in the sociology of sport are supportive of work that pushes disciplinary boundaries so there are opportunities to learn from work done by scholars in related disciplines and encouragement for peo-ple in the field to be creative in how they conceptualize their own work.

Is Sport a Panacea for Social Problems?

Despite the long-accepted popular belief in North America and much of Europe that sports are a cure-all for social problems, this topic has not received the research attention it deserves in the sociology of sport. Maybe people enter the field with this belief and are slow to ask critical questions about it; maybe popular acceptance of the belief has undermined support for research to test it; and/or maybe the belief is so compatible with neoliberal ideas about personal responsibility as the driver of progress and change that people in the field support programs despite a lack of evidence about their effectiveness. In any case, sports have been used over the past 120 years as interventions and facilitators of development, especially in the lives of young people perceived to lack self-control and "character," as defined generally by the Protestant Ethic and specifically in cultures that value individualism.

The use of sports as a panacea is primarily a legacy of the complex class dynamics in late-nineteenth century England and the Progressive Era in the United States. For well over a century, it was widely assumed that "properly organized and controlled" youth sport programs could create in young men the energy, nationalism, and competitive spirit that would maintain personal health, fuel industrial expansion, and create strong and willing soldiers. Programs in selected team sports were used in early twentieth century US cities to Americanize immigrant children, convert unruly boys in crowded tenements into efficient and compliant workers, foster good health though exposure to the outdoors, prepare boys to serve in the military, and masculinize middle-class boys who were thought to lack political and business leadership qualities because they were raised in female-dominated households.

Fueled by anecdotal evidence, the personal testimonies of athletes, stories circulated through popular culture, and the pronouncements of physical educators and coaches, the belief that sports were a panacea became a taken-for-granted cultural truth in many Western societies. This belief goes hand-in-hand with the seldom questioned myth that sport is essentially pure and good and that all who participate in it share in that purity and goodness (Coakley, 2016). Armed with this essentialist belief, people assume that sports automatically produce positive outcomes for individuals, communities, and societies. Accordingly, parents, educators, community leaders, political officials, faith-based organizations, and a wide range of non-governmental organizations (NGOs) have allocated vast amounts of public and private resources to sports.

Even the task of global development and peacemaking has been recently assigned to sports. Because certain sports can be used to attract participants or spectators, and because participants and spectators often feel good when they share a common focus, it is assumed that sports can be used to transcend sources of structural differences, including poverty, oppression, differential access to opportunities, discrimination, and ethnic hatred and conflict in communities and societies.

Research is now questioning these assumptions and finding them in need of serious qualifications. It is also identifying the conditions, processes, relationships, and resources needed if sport programs are to be sites for effectively facilitating individual and community development. Emerging research also shows that sports do not cure social problems as much as they can be strategically organized as sites where people can be informed and empowered to engage in collective actions that lead to structural changes. As we are learning, this requires knowledge and experiences that do not magically pass onto people of any age who learn to kick, throw, hit, and catch balls, or run fast and jump high and far.

ABOUT PRACTISING SOCIOLOGY OF SPORT

Is Teaching Sociology of Sport Easy?

All teaching is a challenge. It requires taking the role of students and learning what they know and how they will perceive the learning materials and information presented in a course. This challenge is intensified in sociology of sport courses because most students have feelings and information about sports that have been shaped by the ethos and narratives of commercial sports and the associated myth about the purity and goodness of sports. This causes them to resist asking critical questions and to become defensive in the face of critical analyses of sports.

My strategy for dealing with this is to acknowledge the reality of their experiences and to discuss them in connection with the context in which they occurred. Most classes are diverse enough that students begin to see connections between context, experiences, and the integration of experiences into a person's life. This cracks emotional and cognitive doors open enough to raise critical questions. However, knowing when and how much critical information to introduce is tricky. It depends on what they have said about their experiences, the extent to which their identities are linked directly to sports, and their responses to assigned readings that raise critical issues. Of course, using current sport events and media stories in discussions is important when introducing critical analyses.

This is not easy to do because every class is different and teachers are dealing on the spot with unanticipated class dynamics. Even after teaching a basic sociology of sport course over 60 times with second to fourth year undergraduates, I still struggled to meet this challenge. Strategies that work in one class may not work in the next. The narratives that students have heard about sports are grounded in strong commercial interests and the public witness given by athletes whose lives are organized around and dependent on sports. My goal is to help them see the limitations of these narratives and statements and become willing to consider alternatives. When their experiences can be used as points of departure for doing this, it is an advantage.

Overall, I equate teaching the sociology of sport to young people today, many of whom have identities and strong memories linked to sports, with teaching the sociology of religion to young people raised in families influenced by strong religious beliefs. Therefore, it is necessary to carefully work around the faith that has prevented them from asking critical questions or considering the merits of a critical analysis. To do so would threaten the foundation on which much of their lives have been built. Sensitivity is required in this process lest future classes be small and attended only by those who already know much of what you want them to learn.

Do Sociologists of Sport Like Sport?

Most scholars in the field have had experiences that they feel give them insights into the social dimensions of sports. This is also true of scholars in many topic areas in sociology. However, the longer that scholars are exposed to critical analyses of that topic, ask critical questions in their research, and teach courses in which critical materials are included, the more likely they are to develop qualified or ambivalent feelings about the topic.

Like many of my students, my personal experiences with sports were generally positive, even though I knew that others had negative experiences or were excluded from sports due to lack of ability or opportunity. These "facts of life" became issues and problems worthy of study and action when I viewed sports through a sociological perspective. The longer I studied sports, the more I saw problems associated with them. This did not cause me to dislike them as much as it led me to see them through new eyes. In the process, I became less of a fan and more of an observer. I have always preferred to *play* sports than to watch or work at doing them, but when I watch them today I am more analytical than emotional and this often irritates people around me. My tendency to focus on relationships, social organization, and social processes does not interest others as much as it does me.

Moving from being a spectator or fan to an observer occurs over time with most scholars, although this is a topic in need of research. My hypothesis is that it takes time along with a strong commitment to observing the social aspects of sports to shed identification with favorite teams, to be less taken in by the tension excitement of a game or match, and to see and hear things extraneous to the physical actions in sport event. Although this has occurred with me, I continue to experience the joy of learning and doing physical activities. I still like to play and I lament the decline of a culture of play in highly rationalized and commercialized societies in which emotions are more tied to spectacle than to play.

Overall, I know less than I should about my colleagues on this issue. Maybe it will become a conversation topic at future conferences.

Is the Sociologist of Sport a "Public Intellectual"?

There are many ways to be a sociologist. We can produce knowledge about social worlds, synthesize and "teach" it to students, apply it in action research or social programs, and make it understandable and useful to policy makers and the general public. To become actively involved in the public sphere as "experts," opinion leaders, or agents of change is not something we learn in graduate school, nor is it something that most university-employers are anxious for us to do if our actions challenge the status quo or the interests of legislators and benefactors who support the university.

When we make sociological knowledge public we cannot escape the fact that social life is characterized by inequalities, power differences, and conflicts of interests that are meaningful and contentious. Therefore, going public with knowledge in the sociology of sport is not a simple process that automatically brings about equal and positive benefits for everyone. In fact, it is usually disruptive.

To be a public intellectual is to become a political actor. In many cases, this can have serious implications in our careers. Therefore, it is advisable to adopt protective strategies such as working behind the scenes in change-oriented organizations, allowing the organization to face the pushback created by public statements, and using the organization to increase legitimacy and influence. When an organization provides cover, it is possible to present research findings in sponsored statements and reports. This decreases the chances that an individual scholar becomes the target of responses and backlash.

An alternative strategy is to become an insider and help to shape sport-related policies and programs. Again, this requires an ability to be an effective political actor, an ability that scholars acquire only if they work at it and have knowledgeable mentors in the process. Unfortunately, this ability is not likely to be highly rewarded in most universities.

Finally, we are living at a time when access to information has exploded and many people have become skeptical of the veracity and usefulness of scientific knowledge. Science experts are increasingly identified as "elites" who are detached from everyday life. Therefore, people turn to their own social networks for information and "truth," and it becomes more difficult to effectively demonstrate the usefulness of scientific knowledge. This is a challenge that goes far beyond the sociology of sport, and it is one that scholars in all disciplines must collectively confront.

ABOUT SOCIOLOGY OF SPORT IN THE ACADEMY

Does Sociology of Sport Face Institutional/Industry Barriers?

The sociology of sport struggles for acceptance in societies where many people accept the assumption that sports are pure and good and that all who play or consume them will share in this purity and goodness. This assumption leads to the conclusion that it is not necessary to study and critically evaluate sport because it is essentially good as it is (Coakley, 2016).

Additionally, critical research done in the field often highlights problems related to the structure and organization of sports or the social worlds in which sports exist. Recommendations based on that research often threaten those who benefit from the status quo in sports. This leads some people to see the sociology of sport as controversial, which interferes with obtaining support for research. For example, I discovered this when I did research on burnout and concluded that among older adolescents it was grounded in the structure and power relations characteristic in high-performance sport organizations. But those who controlled these organizations were more willing to support and even fund research based on the assumption that burnout was caused by an athlete's inability to manage the stress associated with high-performance training and competition. For them, teaching athletes to better manage stress was preferable to changing the status hierarchy and system of control in their organizations.

Barriers in the academy itself exist, in part, because university-based knowledge production is grounded in historical and cultural traditions that assume mind–body distinctions. The enduring acceptance of the Cartesian mind–body dualism has sustained a research culture that ignores bodies or relegates them to the "repair shops" located in university medical schools, biology departments, or departments concerned with body mechanics and performance. This, of course, gives the physical sciences in kinesiology and related departments the upper hand as they make the case that their research merits priority over the research of their colleagues in social sciences. As a result, professional recognition, status, and job security flow in their direction.

The short supply of research money going to scholars proposing sociology of sport research has reduced the willingness of departments in tier-one universities to embrace scholars and courses on sports as social phenomena. Therefore, most sociologists listing sports as a primary research interest are not working in top-tier research universities where status and security depend on obtaining large research grants. Instead, they tend to have appointments in teaching-focused universities where sociology of sport courses attract students in campus competition for fund-eliciting enrollments and where securing research grants is not the highest priority evaluative criterion in promotion and tenure decisions. For example, my career would not have led to tenure in an R-1 university, and my textbook may have actually counted as a negative factor in the evaluation process.

Related to this is the fact that the United States-based American Sociological Association (ASA) does not recognize "Sports" among its 52 topic sections. Few ASA members give priority to research on sports for the reasons given above. And this continues to be why most scholars in the sociology of sport have university appointments in physical education, kinesiology, and sports studies departments than in sociology departments. But they too are facing challenges in their departments and in the promotion and tenure process.

What is the Future of the Sociology of Sport?

The future of the sociology of sport depends greatly on professional associations that provide personal support, legitimacy, opportunities for making presentations, journals for publishing research, and contexts for coming together to deal with issues facing members. Without these things, knowledge production, distribution, and application would decline precipitously in the field.

The gradual expansion of scholars in the field over the past 40 years is due to these organizations around the world. Even as commercial sport forms have grown considerably over this time, these associations have supported and given legitimacy to the careers of those doing a wide range of research on sports and physical culture. But these organizations are self-funded and self-governed, so their future is hardly guaranteed. Survival depends on recruiting qualified officers, journal editors and reviewers, board members, and general members willing to pay dues, conference fees, and journal subscriptions – and all of this is becoming increasingly difficult as neoliberal universities increase workloads and limit salary increases for faculty members.

Until recently, I have claimed that growth of the field will continue as long as scholars do research and produce knowledge that people find useful as they make decisions about the role of sports in their personal lives, families, communities, and societies. However, it has become much more complicated than that, if it ever was that simple. As many in the field are learning that it is crucial to become effective political actors in their communities and nations to create a desired future, they are also learning that the same is required in their professional lives. Without such actions and a willingness to collectively support professional associations and all that they do, the future will not involve continued growth.

CONCLUSION

I cannot imagine a more satisfying career than the one I have had as a sociologist. But I was privileged by my gender, skin color, mixed European heritage, social class, and birth year. Born two years before the first baby boomer, I benefitted greatly due to my small birth year cohort, the expansion of higher education during the 1960s, a full athletic scholarship to college (even with monthly laundry money, an on-campus job, and permission to work off campus legally), a Cold War-related National Defense Education Act fellowship that paid all graduate school expenses plus basic living expenses with stipends for spouse and children, and a job market that was expanding as I received my degrees. I chose jobs on the basis of geographical location and associated life-style, and I had the benefit of supportive colleagues, department chairs, and even a few deans and chancellors.

Due to my circumstances, I never worried or even thought about not receiving tenure, although I greatly appreciated the academic freedom that came with it. The autonomy that came with my appointment at the Colorado Springs campus of the University of Colorado allowed me to choose the sociology of sport as an area of interest, become involved in the field, and make contributions without worrying about my academic appointment. Such a career is largely a thing of the past, but 12 years after retiring I continue to write, do research, lecture here and there, and even teach a sociology of sport course when I wish.

NOTES

1. In slightly revised forms, those 10 questions would become chapter titles in the first edition of *Sport in Society: Issues and Controversies* that would be published in 1978.

2. The material was on a two-page handout and it included select items from a list of Barbarous Rituals that captured the socialization experiences of girls and women at the time. All of these were deemed offensive, including one stating, "Being a woman is … 'getting pregnant, hearing all the earth mother shit from everyone, going around with a fixed smile on your terrified face.'" This was the only "ritual" that included an obscenity. Other selections were taken from a list entitled, "Know Your Enemy: A Sampling of Sexist Quotes." The Regents objected to identifying the famous men who had made blatantly sexist statements. One I included was from legendary functionalist social theorist, Talcott Parsons, who had written, "The woman's fundamental status is that of her husband's wife, the mother of his children … "

3. The John Birch Society was a far-right advocacy group founded in the late 1950s. It was staunchly anticommunist and perpetuated conspiracy theories that were anti-Semitic, anti-African American, anti-women's liberation, anti-civil rights, and eventually, pro-white supremacist. Defined as "off the extreme right end of the political continuum" in the 1970s, it is experiencing a resurgence in the political climate of the United States in 2017.

4. This would haunt me years later as the publishing industry changed and I was bound "in perpetuity" by the contract's constricting terms.

REFERENCES

Coakley, J. (2016). Assessing the sociology of sport: On cultural sensibilities and the great sport myth. *International Review for the Sociology of Sport*, *50*(1), 402–406.

Coakley, J. J. (1968). *The effects of racial violence on the attitudes of blacks: A study of the 1967 Disorder in South Bend, Indiana*. M.A. Thesis, University of Notre Dame.

Coakley, J. J. (1970). Graduate education: A rationale for change. *Research Reports in the Social Sciences*, *1*(2), 1–8.

Coakley, J. J. (1972a). *Race and religious vocation: A study of the self-identificational priorities of Black Priests*. Ph.D. Dissertation, University of Notre Dame.

Coakley, J. J. (1972b). Sociological perspectives on the child. In F. Karlstrom (Ed.), *The child and the community* (pp. 3–20). Flagstaff, AZ: Northern Arizona University Monograph.

Coakley, J. J. (1978). *Sport in society: Issues and controversies*. St. Louis, MO: The C.V. Mosby Company.

Edwards, H.. (1969). *The revolt of the Black athlete*. New York, NY: The Free Press.

Edwards, H.. (1973). *Sociology of sport*. Homewood, IL: Dorsey Press.

Kenyon, G. (Ed.). (1969). *Aspects of contemporary sport sociology*. Madison, WI: Athletic Institute.

Lamanna, R. A., & Coakley, J. J. (1969). The catholic church and the negro. In P. Gleason (Ed.), *Contemporary Catholicism in the United States*. Notre Dame, IN: University of Notre Dame Press.

Laner, M., & Coakley, J. J. (1974). Mate selection priorities of college students: A new twist. *The Cornell Journal of Social Relations, 9* (1), 149–164.

Loy, J., & Coakley, J. (2015). Sport. In G. Ritzer (Ed.), *Blackwell encyclopedia of sociology online*. London: Wiley.

Loy, J., & Kenyon, G. (Eds.). (1969). *Sport, culture, and society*. New York, NY: The Macmillan Company.

Lüschen, G. (1970). *The cross-cultural analysis of sport and games*. Champaign, IL: Stipes Publishing Company.

Morgan, R. (Ed.). (1970). *Sisterhood is powerful: An anthology of writings from the women's liberation movement*. New York, NY: Random House/Vintage.

Scott, J.. (1969). *Athletics for athletes*. Oakland, CA: An Other Ways Book.

Scott, J.. (1971). *The athletic revolution*. New York, NY: Macmillan, Inc.

CHAPTER 4

NAVIGATING 'IN-BETWEENNESS' IN STUDYING SPORT IN SOCIETY

Agnes Elling

INTRODUCTION

In this chapter, critical issues in the development of social scientific sport research in the Netherlands and the international development of a critical sociology of sport in general and feminist sport research in particular are discussed from several experienced 'in-between' positions of the author.

ABOUT THE AUTHOR

Mentors and Influential Figures

The questions about influential people during my academic career and my research trajectory as a whole require an internal reflection on several levels of influence and 'choice'. Overall, too many people have influenced my trajectory of becoming a critical researcher in the sociology of sport and my development within the field, both at the national and international level. Some people have guided or supported me in person or through their work over a longer period of time, other personal interactions or publications were much more ephemeral, but may also have been important or even decisive sources for inspiration, advice and/or the development of my expertise and 'inner library'.

Among the first people who influenced the start of my career as a critical researcher on sport in society were the coordinators of the Masters programme

Reflections on Sociology of Sport: Ten Questions, Ten Scholars, Ten Perspectives
Research in the Sociology of Sport, Volume 10, 49–64
Copyright © 2018 by Emerald Publishing Limited
ISSN: 1476-2854/doi:10.1108/S1476-285420170000010004

'Theory and History of Human Movement Sciences' at the Free University in Amsterdam: Jan Tamboer and Onno Meier. Within the overall more medical and positivistic orientation of the study 'Human Movement Sciences', the classes on philosophy of science and more social–political reflections on the development of human movement sciences were quite different and challenging – not only in content, but also concerning the small group of 'more alternative' students that chose this programme. When Tamboer started a course on sport philosophy, it was the real start of my journey as a critical researcher into sport and society. Among the first philosophy of sport students were Ivo van Hilvoorde and Johan Steenbergen who followed a similar trajectory and also became sparring partners or co-researchers during later stages. Jan Tamboer was the supervisor of my MA thesis on physicality, gender and sexuality in sport and introduced me to a small group of scholars in the Netherlands and Flanders (Belgium) who initiated a first – more critical – research programme on Values and Norms in Sport (1993–1997) in the Netherlands, a cooperation between different universities and NOC*NSF, funded by the Dutch Ministry of Health, Welfare and Sport.

Before starting my Master's thesis, I did an internship under the supervision of Gertrud Pfister in Berlin, where I continued my first explorations on the theme of gender and sport. Since she was one of the leading scholars in Europe and also globally, I had just sent her an open application for possibilities for an internship. Gertrud invited me to work on her cross-cultural project on women's sport biographies in 1992/1993 (with Sheila Scraton, Kari Fasting and Ana Bunuel) and even arranged a place to live. She also introduced me to several German and European sport scholars.

My co-supervisor for my Master's thesis was Annelies Knoppers, who had just moved (back) to the Netherlands from North America at that time (early 1990s) and was an experienced researcher on critical (gender) issues in sport. After my studies I worked together with Annelies on several projects on gender and sport and she was the co-supervisor of my PhD thesis (2002) on mechanisms of social inclusion and exclusion in sport relating to gender and ethnicity. Although we partly differ in our approaches, there has always been a good synergy and Annelies continued to inspire me in my work, both theoretically and methodically, even though opportunities to work together became less over the last ten years.[1]

Other important people in the Netherlands regarding mentorship and the creation of job positions have been sports pedagogue Albert Buisman (Utrecht University) and my PhD supervisor Paul De Knop (Tilburg University), who were both part of the group of scholars who initiated the first critical research programmes on sport and society.[2] After my PhD thesis, the first directors of the Mulier Institute for research on sport in society (Maarten van Bottenburg and Jan Janssens) as well as the current directors Koen Breedveld and Hugo van der Poel offered me continued possibilities and support in combining more independent scholarly research with contract research, commissioned by (local) governments and other (sport) organizations. Over the last years, I also learned a lot from my interaction with medical philosopher Tineke Abma (University Medical Centre Amsterdam) and younger Dutch PhD students/scholars like Mirjam Stuij and Rens Peeters.

Apart from the international contacts during my Berlin internship with Gertrud Pfister, the first international congress I joined was the congress of the International Sociology of Sport Association (ISSA) in Oslo in 1997. It was exciting to meet so many other, more or less famous sport scholars. The ISSA network as a whole has been an influential scholarly community for 'building more international recognition', especially the executive board presidents and secretaries and the journal editors (e.g., Gertrud Pfister, Steve Jackson, Elizabeth Pike, Laurence Wenner), during the period I became a member of the extended board (2004–2011), organized the ISSA congress in 2009 in Utrecht and joined the editorial board in 2012.

Finally, I would like to name some important scholars whose work strongly influenced my trajectory. The central book for the mentioned course on philosophy of sport was *Philosophic Inquiry in Sport,* edited by William Morgan and Klaus Meier (1988) (a handbook with texts from many different scholars that initiated my intellectual capital for critically reflecting on sports in society, and more specifically on gender equality in sport). For example, through Iris Marion Young's *'Throwing like a girl'*: 'If, as Merleau-Pony argues, the basic structures of human existence − consciousness, intentionality, purposiveness, etc. − have their foundation in the body as acting and expressing subject, then the inhibition of women's development of our body subjectivity implies a profound inhibition of our humanity' (Young, p. 338).

Several other important scholars who further developed my theoretical/ methodological lenses include scholars from critical sport studies (e.g., Ann Hall, Jay Coakley, John Hargreaves, Michael Messner, Andrew Sparkes) and more broadly theorists related to embodied subjectivities/identifications and social justice (gender, race/ethnicity, sexuality) like Floya Anthias, Judith Butler, Raewyn Connell, Michel Foucault, Nancy Fraser, Arthur Frank, Irving Goffman, Jaber Gubium/James Holstein, Stuart Hall, Angela McRobbie and Maurice Merleau-Ponty.

Research Trajectory

Related to the many different people who more or less coincidently crossed my pathway over a more or less lengthy period of time, I regard the chances and possibilities concerning job positions and thematic angles as the result of an interaction of presented or given possibilities and self-chosen/managed actions and decisions.

Similar to many young people at the time as well as nowadays, I did not have a clear career perspective during the last years of my preacademic secondary school education at the end of the 1980s. After I tried to enter drama school without success, and I expected not to be able to qualify for a PE teacher programme at college level due to several dislocated shoulder incidents, I decided to study 'something with sport' at the academic level.[3] But I first wanted to spend a year abroad. I selected an au pair job in London, which I could combine with my theatre interest and continue my track and field engagement (sprint/hurdling/long jump). I was raised at a farm in the countryside and most of all wanted to experience real 'city-life' (including lesbian/gay spaces/people) during this 'in-between' year.

After this year, I started studying Human Movement Science at the Free University in Amsterdam, the capital of the Netherlands, but compared to London a relatively small city with a population of less than a million people. During my studies, I specialized in sport philosophy and also did a minor in women's studies. In this period, during the early 1990s, many books and articles were published on the topic of gender and sport. Gender studies was 'booming' and entered the so-called 'third feminist wave' with the rise of postmodernism, post-colonial studies and intersectional analyses (see also the influential scholars mentioned above).

My work may be regarded as rather eclectic or 'in-between' concerning both my theoretical and methodological positions and developments. Many different critical academics from sociology, philosophy and social psychology and interdisciplinary fields like gender studies and cultural studies have influenced my work. Compared to most other critical (feminist) sport scholars, however, my work may be somewhat more founded within or influenced by mainstream – pragmatic – human movement sciences. Despite my theoretical start in the field of critical sport studies, my own research soon became strongly empirical, being a strong advocate of mixed methods. Different, however, from many mixed methods advocates who start from a more positivistic perspective, my work is more founded within a critical, social constructivist and interpretive perspective on reality. During my career, I have always combined different 'hard' and 'soft' methodologies from multivariate analyses on quantitative data, to qualitative narrative studies, centring meaning and lived embodied experiences.

Thematically, uncovering and discussing social inequalities in sport with respect to intersecting social status positions – especially gender, ethnicity and sexuality – have been one of my key research interests and areas of expertise. This is true both in studying and *giving voice* to the often marginalized groups of women, racial/cultural/religious ethnic minorities or lesbian/gay/bisexual or transgender people in sport, and also with regard to the unmasking of more privileged and often normative higher status position groups and their cultural behavioural repertoires of men and masculinity, the ethnic majority and white western Christianity, heterosexual people and heteronormativity.

Throughout my career I have not considered myself in the first place as a feminist sport researcher, though that qualification actually fits quite right. Maybe this is related to my in-between position regarding my coming of age as a critical gender scholar and the transition from second-wave to third-wave feminism. Although I am quite critical of third-wave feminism and identify more with second-wave (sport) feminists, undoubtedly I am simultaneously influenced by a more neo-liberal, postfeminist reality. Compared to many first-generation scholars I am less of a specialist on gender and sport (e.g., Hall, Pfister).[4] My research interests and expertise have developed besides and beyond gender and intersectionality, but often include these issues. This is also related to funding possibilities in Dutch sport research.

I regard myself as a privileged person to have been part of the growth of a (critical) social scientific research expertise in the Netherlands that was nearly absent until the 1990s (cf., Knoppers, 2016). After my PhD research, I got the opportunity to do postdoctoral research on critical social issues in both recreational sporting careers and elite sporting biographies (responsible talent development, transition from elite sport) and societal values of (elite) sport (social integration, national pride) — first at Tilburg University, then at the Mulier Institute, where I have been affiliated since its foundation in 2002, and am employed since 2006. The first years I still combined research with education (Utrecht University) and also became more involved in different contract research projects by the national government, municipalities and sport federations, varying from rather quick and superficial surveys or qualitative inquiries to more longitudinal projects with somewhat more space for theory-based understanding and analyses.

To have received funding for two research projects within the first national research programme *Sport* (2013–2016), launched by the Netherlands Organization for Scientific Research (NWO), felt both as being lucky again and as a kind of recognition for my work. With a small research team — partly consisting of students and voluntary researchers — we studied media developments in women's football, part of a broader research project on the development and societal meaning of women's football, conducted in cooperation with scholars from Leiden University and Utrecht University. We analysed different angles of the sports media system: representation in mainstream media, production processes in sport media departments and 'prosumption' in social media (Peeters & Elling, 2015), building on earlier research (Elling & Knoppers, 2005; Elling & Luijt, 2009; Knoppers & Elling, 2004). The largest ongoing research project I have been involved in over the last few years ('The Meaning of Sports in Times of Health and Illness') is a cooperation with scholars at the Free University of Amsterdam and centres on sport participation and negotiated meanings by four different patient groups (diabetes, depression, breast cancer and HIV) and their health professionals. We engage in critical reflection on 'sport-illness life histories' of patients and the guidance narratives of health professionals in relation to dominant discourses on sport/physical activity

(Stuij, Elling, & Abma, 2016). Moreover, we also have been actively engaged in trying to create social impact together and formulating needed changes within health-sport practises (Abma, Stuij, & Elling, forthcoming; cf. Mansfield, 2016).

ABOUT SPORT

Why Does Sport Matter?

Sport matters since it refers to a broad range of personally meaningful leisure activities that large groups of citizens voluntarily engage in the Netherlands and throughout the globe. Moreover, it is an important societal field of self-organization (sport clubs) in the Netherlands. As in many other countries, sport has become more important in Dutch society – it has changed from a periph-eral activity to a central socio-political sector – due to a simultaneous growth at different levels (e.g., Breedveld, Elling, Hoekman, & Schaars, 2016; Crum, 1991):

- a widening of the concept of sport, including recreational activities
- a growing popularity among many different social groups
- a growing diversity in sport possibilities and sport providers (schools, local governments, commercial organizations, companies, health organizations)
- a growing instrumentalization of both recreational and elite sport
- a strong intensification of elite sport policy
- a strong intensification of (elite) sport event industry

Such structural and cultural developments in the field and societal importance of sports have legitimized a growth in social scientific studies on sport and soci-ety, including critical sociological reflection.

Recreational (club) sport became increasingly regarded as something good, especially in effectively combating major social problems related to public health and social integration/social cohesion (Coalter, 2007). There seems to be no harm in stimulating the societal surplus value of sport, as the outcome of *Sport for All* investments. However, it may become problematic, when policy attention shifts from a primary focus on making sports more accessible for all people, disregarding social status position, toward an ongoing shift in focus on the societal (economic) value. This might include a shift from a right to (not) participate in sport to a (moral) obligation to participate. For example, the Dutch Sports Federation set an aim in 2011 to increase sport participation in society from 65% to 75% in 2016 (NOC*NSF, 2011). When such goals of growth take precedence, investments are made to reach such goals by the most effective and efficient means. From a perspective of social inclusion and social justice, however, it is more important to invest in those groups of people with fewer capabilities to participate, or for whom nonparticipation is not voluntary.

Later compared to other Western societies, in the Netherlands, elite sport became a major and highly mediated business and sociopolitical field too. This was especially due to the successful Olympic Games for Dutch athletes in Sydney 2000 and the combined national Olympic committee and national sport federation NOC*NSF consequently formulated their top 10 ambition (in international medal ranking), supported by the national government (van Hilvoorde, Elling, & Stokvis, 2010). The consecutive enormous growth in governmental financial investments in the elite sport systems was legitimated by the common sense idea that international elite sport performance forms an important vehicle for (re)building national identity, social cohesion and national pride and for international prestige and economic growth.

Sport has become more important in many aspects, but the question remains whether the sport sector can fulfil all expectations and whether sport in some respects has not become *too* important. The increasing body of knowledge in the Netherlands and internationally shows that most popular beliefs and policy claims about the positive societal influences of sport participation, national elite sport success or organizing international elite sport events lack clear evidence, or may have equally substantive negative effects. What happens when governments acknowledge that sport cannot solve problems regarding public health and the broader societal participation and integration of so-called 'vulnerable groups'? Do governments then quit investing in providing accessible sport facilities and in promoting social inclusion?

How Should Sport be Studied?

As critical scholars, we have the duty to be reflective on the (changing) position and meaning of sport in broader society. But there are many different ways of doing that. Similar to journalists and policy makers, we as sociologists of sport also tend to overestimate the (negative) importance of sport for society. We often focus narrowly on sport itself, losing relations to the broader society regarding the studied issues. For example, how are issues of social in-/exclusion related to other societal fields and how are these perceived by different groups within and outside sport?

Moreover and making critically studying such issues more complex: in policy and research, 'underrepresentation' of specific groups may often straightforwardly be regarded as a problem. However, this begs the question what kind of sport participation of which social groups is taken as the norm (e.g., Elling & Claringbould, 2005)? Not only in terms of distributive equality, but also regarding the recognition of different cultural values (Fraser, 2001). Is it a problem when gay men are 'underrepresented' in mainstream competitive sports compared to straight men, or migrant women to non-migrant women? Maybe gay men and migrant women are less interested in mainstream sport activities and prefer other leisure activities. Such perceptions, however, may be equally problematic, especially when they perpetuate cultural stereotypes of certain groups, or when they are 'misused' in policy making, as happened, for example, with the findings of our first study on sport participation and sexual orientation (see also Elling & Janssens, 2009). Since we found no general differences in sport participation regarding sexual orientation, our study was used as a legitimation for dropping this as a policy issue. Disregarding large differences we found in mainstream club sport participation between self-identified straight and gay/bisexual men and clear examples of perceptions and experiences of (symbolic) exclusion by gay/bisexual men. To investigate issues of underrepresentation in mainstream competitive men's sport therefore is mainly about the extent to which certain groups of men are symbolically included and excluded (e.g., Elling & Van Sterkenburg, 2008). Fraser argues to subjecting recognition and redistribution claims to the 'justificatory standard of participatory parity' (Fraser, 2001, p. 38). The allocation of separate swimming hours to (Muslim) women – and not to white men – can be based on moral reasoning that recognizes Muslim women as a marginalized group with unequal opportunities with respect to sport participation, in combination with the policy to increase their sport and societal participation.

During my research journey in critical sport research, I have always had a kind of hate–love relation with the mainstream sociology of sport in North America. I tended to perceive the North American community of critical sport scholars as too activistic and too much focused on American elite competitive sports compared to Dutch or broader European realities in sport (research) and society. At the same time, I am aware that I owe most of my expertise and development to North American (sport) scholars. Moreover, although I still see many societal differences, I have also recognized how many socio-political changes and sport research developments in North America are – with some delay and in slightly different ways – mirrored in European countries.

Another, and maybe the most vital aspect for doing our work well, since we study people, is a continuing reflection of our own position of power as scholars over the data collection and the analyses and interpretations of the lives of the people we study (e.g., Josselson, 1996). This is always important, but even more in studies involved with deeper understanding of human bodies in particular power relations and spaces and when we find ourselves in a specific privileged social status position (Giardina & Newman, 2011). For myself, such reflections were most prevalent in several studies involving non-white/ethnic minority people and in a study on sporting experiences of transgender people (e.g., Elling-Machartzki, 2017, p. 260): 'Due to my androgynous appearance, I have personally experienced the importance of "correct" gender identification. Being born and raised as a girl and being successful in competitive sport,

I experienced biologically based performance differences between "naturally" born male and female athletes, as well as gender normative expectations and double standards. Regardless of my own (sporting) experiences as a lesbian, androgynous looking (white, middleclass) woman, I am in an outsider position to my interviewees experiences regarding gender transitioning and in a position of power to interpret their stories.' Such privileged position reflections are dynamic and contextual.

Is Sport a Panacea for Social Problems?

Sport research in general has gained popularity and status due to increasing neo-liberal policy rhetoric around positive societal values of sport related to health, good citizenship and social integration. Critical perceptions of sport are important to temper the increasing policy expectations about the positive transformative 'powers of sport'.

Both sport-for-all policies as well as our critical reflections are based on the humanist tradition directed towards eq(ual)ity, liberty and self-realization. Although we may have similar aims, our work-related tasks differ. It is our academic duty as critical scholars to reflect on both mainstream traditional sport organizations and (post)modern sporting breeding grounds that claim to create democratic and inclusive civil micro societies through sport. As sociologists of sport we try to unravel the often paradoxical processes and ambivalent social meanings within the cultural practise of sport and their mirroring or counter flowing relations to broader societal developments. Our work exposes how many sport-for-all initiatives simultaneously encompass aspects of inequality, dogmatism or assimilation. For example, projects aimed at the inclusion of ethnic minority youth may not be equally gender or LGBT inclusive and also relate to mechanisms of stigmatization, control and assimilation.

The feasibility of a universal 'good' and 'just' sport is disputed among sport sociologists due to a strongly anchored critical (postmodern) consciousness. Simultaneously most sport scholars seem to be driven by more modernist and utopian beliefs to improve sport and society at large (see Vanreusel, 2015 and several other contributions in the 50th anniversary issue of the *International Review for the Sociology of Sport*). Most if not all sociologists of sport probably recognize the (potential) positive meanings of sport participation for many people, regardless of their social status positions. However, we seem to be forced into counter positions due to often overly simplistic connotations of the 'goodness' of sport and its transforming potentials for changing the world, increasingly based on neo-liberal policies and politics.

ABOUT PRACTISING SOCIOLOGY OF SPORT

Is Teaching Sociology of Sport Easy?

In my current position at the Mulier Institute I am not involved much in teaching, apart from mentoring individual (PhD) students (the easier and often more rewarding teaching activities) and giving separate lectures about specific topics in bachelor or master level courses. I have always loved to guide smart and socially critical, but somewhat insecure students and found it much more difficult when students are (or at least present themselves as) overconfident (often also out of uncertainty, I learned).

Apart from individual differences in 'teachability', the broader social and educational context in which we teach sociology of sport issues also influences experienced teaching difficulties. Teaching a group of third-year sociology students in general seems easier than teaching students in their third year of physical education or human movement sciences. However, in all cases we have to find the right ways to ask the proper questions and trigger critical reflection among the students. Moreover, as in all teaching it is as important to combine certain 'quality standards and procedures' in studying sport sociological issues as to inspire to move beyond such standards.

And when we may sometimes have the idea that our lectures or courses on sociology of sport issues do not seem to land on any fertile ground at all, it may help to remember how we ourselves got inspired or 'converted' by critical thinkers, who may also have been outsiders within their dominant educational and/or cultural-political environments. Those may have been real persons or particular questions, examples or images from 'people you read'. For example, I remember quite vividly how a picture in Coakley's (1994, p. 245) *Sports in Society*, with somebody skiing and two other persons discussing whether Swiss people would have a specific gene for skiing – was very insightful on hegemonic ideas about black people's 'natural' advantages in (several) sports.

Do Sociologists of Sport Like Sport?

Regarding our often critical stance, one could expect that sociologists of sport are a group of people who do not like sport. However, to be able to study the field of sport with such drive and intensity as demonstrated by many of us only seems to be possible because we do in fact like sport, sometimes a lot. And because our goal is to *improve* sport.

As critical sociologists of sport in general and maybe as feminist sport scholars in particular, we are also complicit in the construction of ourselves as a group of grumpy, embittered scholars, because our analyses do not highlight the sunny, powerful, transformative elements of sport, but its (multiple) shadowy sides, relating to the reproduction or construction of social injustice.

In current Western, democratic societies, critical sport sociology seems to have reached a more difficult position in society at large due to different developments, similar to other critical academic disciplines like gender studies. For example, in many societies, mechanisms of in-/exclusion have become less clear-cut and more ambiguous. Also in sport, formerly excluded groups have to certain extents become quite well-represented in mainstream sports. Moreover, equality, justice and diversity issues may be underlined explicitly in national sport policy documents, paying lip-service to '*doing the doing*' (Ahmed, 2007). In addition, simultaneously sport research became (somewhat) more integrated in traditional academia. Our critical observations and analyses have become more theoretical, but therefore in many cases also seem to have become detached further from policy and practise.

This certainly seems the case with respect to the study of gender equality. By interpreting power relations as Foucauldian diffuse and dynamic processes being simultaneously constructed and challenged, feminist sport scholars have developed academically, but chances of social impact may have imploded. In our critical analyses of the ascribed societal values of sport, feminist sport scholars, including myself, seem to have tipped over and positive developments towards more gender equity may not have been recognized, analysed and celebrated enough (see Elling, 2015). As critical scholars we have learned that sport is not only a site for reproduction of gender ideologies, but also for empowerment, resistance and transformation. Nonetheless, the feminist output concerning (potential) challenging and transforming meanings of sport – to what extent sport contributes to a more democratic and egalitarian society – is much smaller compared to its critical oeuvre.

As a critical scholar, I regard it as very important to analyse mechanisms of heterosexualization of women's sport, the complicity of lesbian women, how gendered, sexualized and racialized powers interact and simultaneously open up power enactment and closure among different groups of sporting women (cf., Hall, 1996). Since most involved actors engage in such hegemonic processes of heterosexualization, although by partly different (strategic) beliefs and benefits, it can be interpreted as its justification, as a natural, normal and legitimate consensus. In unravelling such mechanisms of homophobia within the practise of women's sport, we sometimes seem to forget to acknowledge and explore more in-depth its positive meanings relating to broader acceptance of lesbian women and their emancipation in society as well. Since we regard being critically reflective as our main task, it may be our 'destiny' to be regarded as 'grumpy' sociologists of sport – despite our simultaneous love for sport.

Is the Sociologist of Sport a 'Public Intellectual'?

Compared to the broader field of (more positivist-oriented) sport and human movement sciences, where often more money and higher academic prestige is involved, I think that our community of sociologists of sport is privileged because of our (potential) public role and visibility. More than our colleagues in other sport science disciplines, we relate to actual social issues that are recognized by many (marginalized) people's own experiences, interests and ideas. Since most people have at least some experience in practising sport and many people are actively engaged in either supporting their children's sport career, doing voluntary work and/or are active sport media consumers, our research is relatively often met with positive comments varying from 'wow, interesting!' or with 'thank you for doing this'. This is one of the reasons why I love my work, even though policy makers may often (due to political climates) be less positive about our critical reflections. Apart from inspiring students and (future) academics, I am grateful when research results are recognized and meaningful for those groups of people that are part of the specific field of study. For example, receiving feedback from former athletes, talent coaches or parents on how our work on transition problems when quitting elite sport and on responsible talent development is important for them in terms of recognition of the size and personal gravity of the problems (e.g., Elling & Reijgersberg, 2017).

This can be similar but also somewhat different from being a public intellectual by media or policy recognition — similar in the sense that research (e.g., on interacting and sometimes contradictory processes of social in-/exclusion) is used in (local) sport policy and practise to improve equity and social justice. Nevertheless, our position as academics often seems to be mediated in the light of framing some issues as somewhat important or as 'having been handled'. That can be quite innocent, but can also lead to research on social issues in sport being ignored or even 'misused' by either policy makers or the media. For example, in relation to gender inequality in sport, as a follow-up of an accepted motion in parliament, we were asked by the Ministry of Sport in 2016 to do an inventory about women's discrimination in sport relating to (1) differences in sport participation and (2) possible inequalities in reward and appreciation in elite sport. After gender inequality had been completely dissolved in sport policy since 2010, I was pleased to be able to integrate most of the available data and studies on gender issues. And we even stretched the assignment a bit, for example, by including some data on gender and leadership and media attention. Although we acknowledged many positive developments, we also gave substantiated evidence for putting gender back on the sport policy and research agenda. However, since general sport participation figures between men and women are equal, the minister concluded that no further (policy) actions were deemed necessary.

In the run-up to the 2016 Olympic Games in Rio de Janeiro, the sports media were quite eager in quoting a 'sociologist of sport' about gender equity issues in elite sports, since for the first time in history the Dutch Olympic team consisted of more women than men. Moreover, similar to the summer Olympic editions since 2000, women were expected to win most medals. I use such momenta to distribute 'academic knowledge' also in a somewhat activist manner. I confirm that in the Netherlands girls have about equal possibilities to participate in club sport compared to boys, when compared to many other countries. In addition, especially girls and women seem to have profited from extra investments in talent development and elite sports within a somewhat less-developed global competition. However, I also try to make use of the given space to refer to the substantial underrepresentation of women in leadership positions and in mainstream sport media coverage. The media often included statements on the low number of women in highest board or coaching positions in their items, but often left out the marginalization of women's sport in mainstream sports media coverage.

Many sociologists of sport may navigate strategically between academic and public recognition in trying to create social value and impact for improving sport and society.

ABOUT SOCIOLOGY OF SPORT IN THE ACADEMY

Does Sociology of Sport Face Institutional/Industry Barriers?

Institutional and industry barriers faced by the sociology of sport may not differ much compared to many other critical academic disciplines. It may be similar to broader socio-political developments like social justice that, on the one hand, seem to develop progressively and, on the other hand, are continually counteracted, sometimes also more harshly than before. We have witnessed a growth in the recognition of the sociology of sport, both within studies related to sports and within broader academia. Sport has become a more serious field of academic study. Simultaneously, there is an ongoing dominance of medically based, positivist science, with Randomized Controlled Trial studies as the 'golden standard'. Some of the discursive or financial constraints we face, however, may also enable us to remain critically reflective of our supposed academic freedom, agency and independency.

Such diverging and converging developments occur both in the social scientific study of sport in the Netherlands as a whole, as within the Mulier Institute. Over the last ten years the Mulier Institute has gained a reputation in the Netherlands (and to some extent in Europe) of being a high-quality research institute for the study on sport in society. However, governmental subsidies have become much more affected by quantitative monitoring and evaluation of governmental policy programmes, with ample space for 'deeper understanding' and we have financially become more dependent on contract research.

Since research funding for the first multi-annual research programmes on sport and society in the Netherlands since 1994 came from the government, included projects have been rather closely related to priority policy issues like health, social integration and elite sports development. Nevertheless, the projects themselves were relatively independent with much academic freedom. The launching of the first Dutch broad national scientific research programme on Sport (2013–2017) can be regarded as a positive sign, indicative of the recognition of sport as a valuable research topic. It also suggested a more independent research perspective compared to project research commissioned by (local) governments or sports organizations as is the case with most studies conducted by the Mulier Institute. Interestingly and worryingly, however, compared to the antecedent research programmes, simultaneously this programme is much more influenced by a neo-liberal political environment, with a dominant functionalistic perspective on *vitality* and *performance* and less space for critical reflection. In our project *Sport in Times of Health and Illness,* we consciously and continuously had to relate ourselves to this hegemonic perspective in framing our proposal and research outcomes (Abma et al., forthcoming) – For example, by composing a group of consortium partners who were able and willing to invest (in time/money) to realize the 30% co-financing that was required for being eligible for funding opportunities. I certainly do not oppose the idea of building consortia of academics, policy makers and practitioners and of stimulating researchers to invest in knowledge utilization, in creating social impact (valorization). However, it does not seem to be recognized that forming alliances, attaining co-financing and creating value and impact may be extra difficult for social critical studies to realize, with smaller chances to be funded (cf., Buikema & van der Tuin, 2013).

What is the Future of the Sociology of Sport?

As a consequence of the growing (instrumental) importance of sport in modern societies and the neo-liberalization of universities and academic research, sport may become a more relevant issue within general academic disciplines, including general sociology. This may mean that the sociology of sport will become even more diversified and less tied to the traditional critical and activist core of the (North American and international) community of sociologists of sport. The central issue of methodology that I focused on in another contribution on challenges faced by the sociology of sport, with a pledge for re-integrating quantitative methods (Elling, 2015), is embedded within a more broadly felt necessity for the development of critical (feminist) sport research. Recently, we made a large contribution to the academic body of knowledge on changing and continuing social inequalities in sport. Somehow we simultaneously seem to have lost connections to really changing sport practises.

Despite the existing barriers to do so and the serious threats for ongoing independent and critical sociological reflections on sport, I believe our community is more alive than ever before and that we are more needed than ever before too.

NOTES

1. She has now retired and we are currently working on a book project on gender and leadership in sport in Europe.

2. Values and Norms in Sport (1993–1997) was followed by Values and Norms in Sport II (1998–2001) and Qualities of Sport (2002–2006). These programs did not have full time PhD positions, but initially offered part time research projects on a yearly basis.

3. Different from many other countries in the world, in the Netherlands, the educational programme for becoming a physical education teacher is only taught at colleges (bachelor level) and human movement studies at university do not involve sports practise.

4. And I define myself in the first place as an academic instead of an activist, which may be different for some first-generation feminist sport scholars. Even though I have been active within women's /LGBT movement and may be 'activistic' through my academic work.

REFERENCES

Abma, T., Stuij, M., & Elling, A. (forthcoming). Co-creating social impact: Tensions and conflicts in sports research. *Intended Journal: Qualitative Health Research*.

Ahmed, S. (2007). 'You end up doing the document rather than doing the doing': Diversity, race equality and the politics of documentation. *Ethnic and Racial Studies*, *30*(4), 590–609.

Breedveld, K., Elling, A., Hoekman, R., & Schaars, D. (2016). *Maatschappelijke betekenissen van sport. Wetenschappelijke onderbouwing en weerslag in lokaal beleid*. Utrecht/Ede: Mulier Instituut/Kenniscentrum Sport.

Buikema, R. L., & van der Tuin, I. (2013). Doing the document: Gender studies at the corporatized university in Europe I. *European Journal of Women's Studies*, *20*(3), 309–316.

Coakley, J. J. (1994, 5th [1978]). *Sport in society: Issues and controversies*. St. Louis, MO: Mosby.

Coalter, F. (2007). *A wider social role for sport. Who's keeping the score?* London: Routledge.

Crum, B. J. (1991). *Over de versporting van de samenleving. Reflecties over bewegingsculturele ontwikkelingen met het oog op het sportbeleid*. Rijswijk: Ministerie van WVC.

Elling-Machartzki, A. (2017). Extraordinary body-self narratives. Sport and physical activity in the lives of transgender people. *Leisure Studies*, *36*(2), 256–268.

Elling, A. (2015). Assessing the sociology of sport: On reintegrating quantitative methods and gender research. *International Review for the Sociology of Sport*, *50*(4–5), 430–436.

Elling, A., & Claringbould, I. (2005). Inclusionary and exclusionary mechanisms in the Dutch sports landscape: Who can and wants to belong? *Sociology of Sport Journal*, *22*(4), 498–515.

Elling, A., & Janssens, J. (2009). Sexuality as a structural principle in sport participation: Negotiating sports spaces. *International Review for the Sociology of Sport*, *44*(1), 71–86.

Elling, A., & Knoppers, A. (2005). Sport, gender and ethnicity: Practices of symbolic in/exclusion. *Journal of Youth and Adolescence, 34*(3), 257–268.

Elling, A., & Luijt, R. (2009). Different shades of orange? Media representations of Dutch women medallists. In P. Markula (Ed.), *Olympic women and the media: International perspectives* (pp. 132–149). Houndmills: Macmillan.

Elling, A., & Reijgersberg, N. (2017). The Netherlands. In E. Kristiansen, M. M. Parent, & B. Houlihan (Eds.), *Elite youth sport policy. A comparative analysis* (pp. 29–46). London: Routledge.

Elling, A., & van Sterkenburg, J. (2008). Respect: Ethnic bonding and distinction in team sports careers. *European Journal of Sport Sociology, 5*(2), 153–167.

Fraser, N. (2001). Recognition without ethics. *Theory, Culture and Society, 18* (2/3), 21–42.

Giardina, M. D., & Newman, J. I. (2011). What is this 'physical' in physical cultural studies? *Sociology of Sport Journal, 28*(1), 36–63.

Hall, A. (1996). *Feminism and sporting bodies: Essays on theory and practice*. Champaign, IL: Human Kinetics.

Josselson, R. (1996). On writing other people's lives. Self analytic reflections of a narrative researcher. In R. Josselson (Ed.), *Ethics and process in the narrative study of lives* (Vol. 4, pp. 60–71). London: Sage.

Knoppers, A. (2016). Sociology of sport: The Netherlands. In K. Young (Ed.), *Sociology of sport: A global subdiscipline in review* (pp. 245–263). Bingley: Emerald.

Knoppers, A., & Elling, A. (2004). 'We do not engage in promotional journalism': Discursive strategies used by sport journalists to describe the selection process. *International Review for the Sociology of Sport, 39*(1), 57–73.

Mansfield, L. (2016). Resourcefulness, reciprocity and reflexivity: The three Rs of partnership in sport for public health research. *International Journal of Sport Policy and Politics*, doi:10.1080/19406940.2016.1220409

Morgan, W. J., & Meier, K. V. (Eds.). (1988). *Philosophic inquiry in sport*. Champaign, IL: Human Kinetics.

NOC*NSF. (2011). *Sportagenda 2016*. Arnhem: NOC*NSF.

Peeters, R., & Elling, A. (2015). The coming of age of women's football in the Dutch sports media, 1995-2013. *Soccer and Society, 16*(5/6), 620–638.

Stuij, M., Elling, A., & Abma, T. (2016). Conflict between diabetes guidelines and experienced counselling in sports and physical activity. An exploratory study. *European Journal of Public Health*, 1–3. (Advance access) doi:10.1093/eurpub/ckw156

van Hilvoorde, I., Elling, A., & Stokvis, R. (2010). How to influence national pride? The Olympic as a unifying narrative. *International Review for the Sociology of Sport, 45*(1), 87–102.

Vanreusel, B. (2015). Assessing the sociology of sport. On utopianism and pragmatism. *International Review for the Sociology of Sport, 50*(4–5), 623–627.

Young, I. M. (1988, [1979]). Throwing like a girl: A phenomenology of feminine bodily comportment. In W. J. Morgan & K. V. Meier (Eds.), *Philosophic Inquiry in Sport* (pp. 335–340). Champaign, IL: Human Kinetics.

CHAPTER 5

PERSONAL REFLECTIONS ON THE PAST, PRESENT AND FUTURE OF SOCIOLOGY OF SPORT

Steven J. Jackson

INTRODUCTION

It is truly an honour to be invited to contribute to this volume and to share the company of such highly esteemed colleagues. It is fair to say that writing a personal reflection about one's career and the status and future of the field is rewarding, challenging and evokes emotions and nostalgia. As I wrote this chapter I felt as if I was on a high-speed train, but one that would occasionally stop to have a focused look out the window. Many moments and events passed by during this intellectual journey including: images of sporting successes and failures, late nights in libraries, stresses about passing exams, finding a job and trying to meet publication deadlines and lastly, travelling the world. Central to all of these moments and events were the wonderful people I have met along the way: a cast of characters, noblemen and women that even Dickens would be proud to have written about. In writing this specific essay I reflected in particular about my involvement in ISSA. I am lucky and grateful for the opportunity to have met such great people including: Kari Fasting, Ilse Hartmann-Tewes, Joseph Maguire, Fabien Ohl, Chris Hallinan, Kevin Young, Elizabeth Pike, Kim Schimmel, Cora Burnett and many more. There have been many magic moments along the way. As with all personal reflections I have no doubt that I looked back through a particular set of lenses which will have no doubt have clouded my perspective – apologies in advance for any errors in fact and for overlooking any contributions that deserved mention.

Reflections on Sociology of Sport: Ten Questions, Ten Scholars, Ten Perspectives
Research in the Sociology of Sport, Volume 10, 65–86
ISSN: 1476-2854/doi:10.1108/S1476-285420170000010005

ABOUT THE AUTHOR

Mentors and Influential Figures

It is important to acknowledge from the outset that learning, knowledge and the development of one's world view is a result of lived experiences within many different contexts and interactions with a wide range of people over the course of a lifetime. To this extent, while they probably do not really know that the field of sociology of sport exists (let alone what it is), my parents, family, friends and primary and secondary school teachers and coaches, have all played a significant role in not only shaping how I see the world, including sport, but also in providing me with opportunities. As a youth I was fortunate to grow up in a safe neighbourhood with good schools and easy access to outdoor space and sports facilities where there was a critical mass of young males capable of organizing an informal game of any number of sports within a moment's notice. This may seem trivial but as I look around today at changing demographics, economic and work pressures on families and a shift from outdoor to indoor play, it is no small matter. While it is unwise to become too nostalgic about the 'good old days', in a relative sense my cohort really did have a 'wonderful life' with respect to the opportunity to participate in a range of play, games and sport. In sum, while we tend not to think of our family and friends as influential mentors there is little doubt that they play an important role in our world view, political inclinations and basic theories of how the world works.

Within more formal academic settings, I was fortunate to go through quality interdisciplinary programmes in Physical Education and Kinesiology at Western University in Canada and the University of Illinois, Urbana-Champaign. At Western I had the opportunity to take a wide range of sociocultural courses in sport sociology, history and psychology. In particular, the sociology of sport courses from Peter Donnelly and Klaus Meier provided stimulating environments within which to explore the social significance of sport. In my second year of undergraduate study I recall Peter Donnelly beginning each lecture with a recent news story in order to demonstrate that the theoretical issues we were talking about had links to real-life events – a simple but effective strategy. Likewise, I recall a particular lecture from Klaus Meier that focused on how to define 'sport'. While the lecture referred to key works related to how play, games and sport have been conceptualized by various scholars in the fields of history, philosophy and sociology, the really interesting thing was not the content per se but the process we went through – it was ultimately an exercise in learning how to think critically about how to develop and defend an argument. It remains one of the first lectures I offer within my own sociology of sport courses. As graduation approached at Western, with the encouragement of Earle Zeigler, Klaus Meier, Bert Carron and other professors I applied and was accepted into graduate school at the University of Illinois, Urbana-Champaign.

The completion of a Master's and PhD at the University of Illinois occurred at a particularly fortuitous time. Not only were there a number of highly esteemed sociocultural scholars within the Department of Physical Education (later Kinesiology), including John Loy, Susan Greendorfer, Alyce Cheska and Guenther Luschen, we had access to courses in other departments taught by leading scholars including: Norman Denzin, Clark McPhail and Larry Grossberg. On reflection I realize how lucky I was to have an advisor like John Loy who, despite his own reservations about particular theoretical perspectives, compelled us to take external courses from scholars whose positions he did not necessarily agree with. The courses taken with these teachers guided my thinking as did reading the work of sport sociologists like Jay Coakley, Richard Gruneau and Eric Dunning. In a wider sense the work of Stuart Hall (1932–2014) has certainly influenced my thinking and writing. Amidst all the great work undertaken within the field of cultural studies – Hall's work was the most accessible, intuitive and has always resonated with me. Perhaps it was his collaborative approach to addressing problems and writing about them that appealed including works such as: *Resistance Through Rituals* (Hall & Jefferson, 1976); *Culture, Media, Language* (Hall, Dobson, Lowe, & Willis, 1980); *Politics and Ideology* (Hall & Donald, 1986); *The Hard Road to Renewal* (1988); *New Times* (Hall & Jacques, 1990) and *Doing Cultural Studies* (Du Gay, Hall, Janes, Mackay, & Negus, 1997). Here, I defer to Morley and Schwarz (2014) whose posthumous tribute highlights the attributes and achievements of Stuart Hall:

> Hall was always among the first to identify key questions of the age, and routinely sceptical about easy answers. A spellbinding orator and a teacher of enormous influence, he never indulged in academic point-scoring. Hall's political imagination combined vitality and subtlety; in the field of ideas he was tough, ready to combat positions he believed to be politically dangerous. Yet he was unfailingly courteous, generous towards students, activists, artists and visitors from across the globe, many of whom came to love him. Hall won accolades from universities worldwide, despite never thinking of himself as a scholar.

Beyond the faculty and the great facilities available, Illinois also offered a rich postgraduate environment attracting students in the sociocultural area that have become leaders in our field. Mary Jo Kane, Cynthia Hasbrook, David Andrews, Genevieve Rail, Jeremy Howell, Jong Young Lee, Pirkko Markula, Toni Bruce, Bob Rinehart, Jim Denison and Ken Hodge are just a few of the people whose path I had the fortune to cross. Over the last 20 years I have been lucky to have collaborated with David Andrews on a number of projects related to celebrity (Andrews & Jackson, 2001; Andrews, Lopes & Jackson, 2016; Jackson & Andrews, 2012), globalization (Jackson & Andrews, 1996, 1999) and advertising (Jackson & Andrews, 2004, 2005) and we continue to work together. Subsequent to Illinois, I secured a position at the University of Otago, New Zealand. This shift presented a number of challenges but these were far outweighed by the opportunities on offer. Perhaps due to its geographically isolated location, New Zealand offered the opportunity to gain a new perspective on various topics of interest including globalization and national identity. What has been striking about observing the field of sociology of sport internationally over the past few decades is how and why New Zealand sociology of sport has not only survived but thrived (Hallinan & Jackson, 2016; Thomson & Jackson, 2016).

Perhaps the most influential factor during my time at Otago has been the postgraduate students. I have been truly blessed that such a diverse group of gifted individuals chose to work with me as a supervisor. While undoubtedly modest in comparison to some scholars located in larger institutions, the diversity and extent of work by, and collaborative publications with, postgrad students is truly humbling (Anderson & Jackson, 2013; Beissel, 2015; Chang, Sam & Jackson, 2015; Cody & Jackson, 2016; Gee & Jackson, 2010, 2011a, 2011b, 2017; Grainger & Jackson, 2000, 2005; Jackson & Sam, 2007; Jackson & Scherer, 2013; John & Jackson, 2011; Kobayashi, 2012a, 2012b; LeBlanc & Jackson, 2007; Piggin, Jackson, & Lewis, 2007, 2009a, 2009b; Sam & Jackson, 2004, 2006, 2015, 2017; Scherer & Jackson, 2007, 2008a, 2008b, 2010, 2013; Silk & Jackson, 2000).

Research Trajectory

Reflecting on one's career and research trajectory tends to be a process filled with mixed emotions. It is easy in hindsight to be critical of oneself or others about the kinds of topics and approaches one was drawn to but ultimately the key is that you learn from your experiences and accept that making mistakes is an essential and inevitable part of the process. On that note I begin this section with a brief discussion of the research undertaken during my graduate degree. I recall attending a social function at John Loy's house in the early days of my Master's degree when the topic of potential thesis topics emerged. One of the ideas that came up was a Durkheimian analysis of major sporting events and their relationship with suicide rates − the premise being that such ceremonial occasions created not only opportunities for social solidarity but also anomie. My Australian friend Wally Karnilowicz beat me to punch indicating that he would do undertake that for his thesis. As a consequence, my search for a thesis topic continued and I ended up undertaking a replication and extension of Grusky's (1963) and later Loy and McElvogue's (1970) work on occupational achievement and racial segregation in sport − stacking. In the beginning it was all very new, interesting and exciting − collating and analysing data that would add to the body of knowledge in a well-established line of research within the sociology of sport. However, it did not take long to realize that this type of functionalist research was falling out of favour within the field. Nevertheless, I learned a lot through the process and have realized that, while some may dismiss such research because it is not 'in vogue', we should be grateful to those who are willing to invest their time to undertake such empirical research if for no other reason but that it provides evidence which is often the basis for social change. For example, consider Peter Donnelly's observations on the impact of Loy and McElvogue's 1970 study:

> Their research led others to the systematic monitoring of the race of individuals appointed to leadership positions in professional and university sport, to annual 'report cards', and to policy changes such as the National Football League's (NFL's) introduction of the 'Rooney Rule'. In other words, a piece of sociology of sport research helped to 'make a difference' in terms of racial equity in American sport. (Donnelly, 2015, p. 421)

Here, we can see that a study seeking to understand and explain a particular social phenomenon at a particular time became the inspiration and foundation for others that ultimately helped develop a substantial body of knowledge that led to social change. In this light, the outcomes of a modest Master's thesis (Loy & Jackson, 1990) now sit comfortably.

Returning to the University of Illinois after a semester of teaching at the University of British Columbia and some travelling I commenced my PhD study. One of the hot topics of the time was identity and I was interested in understanding spectator/fan identity (Jackson, 1988). Highlighting the impact of context and one's peers I recall a particular serendipitous moment that changed the trajectory of my research for years to come. I was watching ABC coverage of the opening ceremony of the 1988 Calgary Winter Olympic Games with David Andrews and Jeremy Howell when one of the broadcasters stated: 'there you have it ladies and gentlemen, that is the defining difference between Canadians and Americans – Canadians don't J-walk and they don't block up their streets with cars' (implying that they are polite drivers). I began to laugh and was then questioned about what was so funny to which I responded 'Didn't you hear what he just said?' To which they responded: 'Well, is it true?' This led to some pondering and an acknowledgement that there was some truth to the characterization of Canadians as obedient and polite but was this just a stereotype or did it hold some validity? Ultimately, I began looking at those Olympics in much more detail, comparing and contrasting how American television was attempting to represent its northerly neighbour and at the same time how Canada was trying to portray itself to the world. Here, I drew upon the work of Stuart Hall and others who emphasized the idea of 'identity out of difference'. It became very clear that both the American (ABC) and Canadian (CBC) broadcasters were engaging in this process and this prompted me to further explore Canadian history, culture and identity particularly in relation to the United States (Jackson, 1998a). Following several conference presentations related to the topic I recall being politely confronted by David Andrews and Jeremy Howell encouraging me to change my thesis topic which I eventually did. As a result, I examined a series of three sport events within the context of the 1988 Canadian crisis of identity: The Calgary Olympics, the Gretzky marriage and trade and the rise and fall of Ben Johnson (Jackson, 1994, 1998a, 1998b, 1998c). Thus, my early work focused on the role of the media in constructing forms of national identity.

Central to the media-related work has been the use and adaptation of the circuit of cultural commodification (Du Gay et al., 1997; Johnson, 1986/1987). The circuit provides a useful framework and system for exploring the production, representation, consumption and regulation of media commodities. Through a range of collaborative projects we have used the model to explore projects on Sport, Culture and Advertising (Jackson, 2015a; Jackson & Andrews, 2005), Corporate Nationalism (Jackson, 2001, 2004, 2013a, 2013b; Jackson, Batty, & Scherer, 2001; Jackson & Hokowhitu, 2002; John & Jackson, 2011; Scherer & Jackson, 2007, 2008a, 2008b, 2010, 2013), media violence (Grainger & Jackson, 2000, 2005; Jackson & Andrews, 2004) and the sport—alcohol nexus (Cody & Jackson, 2016; Gee & Jackson, 2010, 2011; Gee, Jackson, & Sam, 2013, 2016; Jackson, 2014; Wenner & Jackson, 2009). Beyond this research, largely by coincidence and good fortune, I have been able to collaborate on a range of other topics including sport mega-events, sport diplomacy and foreign policy (Esherick, Baker, Jackson, & Sam, 2017; Jackson, 2013a, 2013b; Jackson & Haigh, 2008, 2009), sport policy (Piggin et al., 2007, 2009a, 2009b; Sam & Jackson, 2004, 2006, 2015, 2017), sport migration and citizenship (Chang, Jackson, & Sam, 2015; Chiba & Jackson, 2006; Lee, Jackson, & Lee, 2007) and match-fixing (Tak, Sam, & Jackson, 2017). What is common to all of these is that they are collaborative, combine theoretical and empirical work, and have social policy implications.

ABOUT SPORT

Why Does Sport Matter?

As the title of Dunning's (1999) book suggests — sport matters. Indeed, sport should matter to everyone because regardless of whether they are interested or participate in sport — it directly or indirectly affects their lives. We can think about sport operating on a range of levels from the personal to the community to the national and international level.

At a personal level sport forms a key part of many people's self and collective identity, including my own. Indeed, sport has operated as a kind of physical cultural 'passport' that provided access to particular peer groups, teams, events and experiences. Much to my own surprise I had the fortune and honour to represent my second country — New Zealand — at the international level in the sport of ice hockey as both a player and a coach. Here, I witnessed firsthand how having even a modicum of skill in even a minor sport provided expedited access to dual citizenship.

Beyond this personal example, sport matters historically, culturally, economically and politically. Indeed, Ulrich Beck, in his book *The Brave New World of Work*, describes sport as 'the most important thing in the world' (2000, p. 62). Let us consider a few brief examples which illustrate the broader social significance of sport before offering some specific examples of its economic and political importance. First, while sport has long had religious overtones, the recent decline of some forms of Christianity has forced leaders to find new ways of attracting and retaining members. In 2004, Pope John Paul II, in conjunction with his call for the establishment of a sports department at the Vatican, proclaimed that: 'the church ... is called upon without doubt to pay attention to sports, which certainly can be considered one of the nerve centres of contemporary culture and one of the frontiers for new evangelization' ('Pope promotes sports for Christianity', 2004). More recently, and in a papal first, Pope Francis recorded a Spanish-language video message shown to fans attending the 2017 Super Bowl. According to a Vatican spokesman the pope, an avid sports fan who often refers to its potential to bring about social change, told the audience that: 'Great sporting events like today's Super Bowl are highly symbolic, showing that it is possible to build a culture of encounter and a world of peace...By participating in sport, we are able to go beyond our own self-interest and in a healthy way we learn to sacrifice, to grow in fidelity and respect the rules' ('Pope jumps on board Super Bowl party', 2017).

Another way of demonstrating the uniqueness and social significance of sport is to consider the phenomena of sport migration and citizenship. The highly competitive world of sport drives the demand for athletic talent and this offers opportunities to secure a professional career with private franchises. However, in some cases athletes are recruited specifically for the purpose of representing a new nation as a new (or dual) citizen and this is changing the way we think about national identity and citizenship. Here sport is unique as it may be the only job or career where labourers are recruited as citizens specifically for their short-term potential to enhance the nation's international standing (Jackson, 2013a, 2013b; Jackson & Haigh, 2008). At its extreme, there have been cases of entire teams of athletes effectively being sold from one country to another — for example, the sale of members of the Bulgarian weightlifting team to Qatar leading to labels such as 'athletic mercenaries'. The reasons for such recruitment and investment in athletic talent may be complex but at its most basic level we know that sport serves as an important source of collective identification and is perhaps one of the most powerful and visible symbols of national identity and nationalism.

Beyond these examples, consider the economic and political significance of sport. Economically, consider the cost of bidding for and hosting sport mega-events such as the Olympics. The estimated cost of the 2016 Rio games was $US4.557 billion, which was $US1.6 billion over budget, equating to a 51% cost overrun. Notably, the 2016 games were actually quite reasonable considering that research shows that between 1960 and 2016 the average cost of operating a summer Olympic games was $US5.2 billion with average cost over-runs of 176% (Flyvbjerg, Stewart, & Budzier, 2016). It is also worth contemplating the economic value of sport within promotional culture. There is perhaps no better way of demonstrating the value of sport than advertising spend for the Super Bowl. Overall spending for the 2017 Super Bowl was $US385, with the average 30-second advertisement estimated at $US 5 million which equates to $US166,000 per second (McCrystal, 2017). More broadly, the global sponsorship market grew from $US3.9 to $US26 billion between 1984 and 2002 (Lagae, 2003), rose to $US37.9 billion in 2007 and looks to top $US51.1 billion in 2012. While these figures refer to all forms of sponsorship, it is worth noting that 'sport' was the fastest growing sector in North America in 2011−2012, accounting for 69% of all sponsorship or approximately $US12.97 billion (IEG, 2012). There are many reasons for such extensive investment in sport (Jackson, 2013a, 2013b; Jackson & Andrews, 2012) which include the fact that it: attracts large audiences, translates well across cultural and linguistic borders, features real people demonstrating the limits of the body, serves as an important source of identity and is associated with positive images of health and nationhood (Rowe, 1996).

Collectively these points highlight the social and economic significance of sport. However, beyond these there are also some unique features of sport that make it a strategic site for politics and here I offer two brief examples. First, there are 206 national Olympic committees in the IOC − 13 more countries than there are national members of the United Nations (193). This fact, in and of itself, demonstrates the significance and potential strategic value of sport as an instrument of international relations. As a second example, consider sports' connections with another global phenomenon: terrorism. According to Louis Mizell, former special agent and intelligence officer with the US State Department, 171 sport-related terrorist attacks have been logged between the 1972 Munich Olympics and 2005. Thus, although sport has on occasion served as a vehicle for peaceful political resistance it can also serve as a potent instrument of terror (Jackson & Haigh, 2008). This point is confirmed by Simon Kuper in his book *Soccer Against the Enemy*, where he highlights some fascinating and frightening links between sport, terrorism and masculinity and the intensifying value of global sport spectacles as sites for gaining the world's attention:

> Terrorists have long been enchanted by soccer. But the main allure of soccer to terrorists is the game's global reach. Terrorism is a form of public relations. The aim is to spread the greatest fear with the least effort. To do that, terrorists seek out the most public places and events. That means sport. (Kuper, 2006, p. 293)

Recent terror attacks including the 2013 Boston marathon bombing, the 2015 assault on the Stade de France and the 2016 violence in Turkey confirm that sport remains a priority target given its visibility and popularity. It suffices to say sport matters or should matter to everyone. It directly or indirectly impacts on almost every aspect of our lives as part of our socialization including access to participation for a healthy, active lifestyle and admiration of celebrity athlete role models. It offers us insights into various forms of discrimination related to social class, gender, race, age and sexuality. Moreover, state investment in elite sport, including taxpayer-funded stadia for privately owned teams, should cause us to reflect upon what our priorities are and to ask critical questions.

How Should Sport be Studied?

Acknowledging that there are others who are far more astute and experienced it would be unwise to even presume to lecture others about how they should study sport. That said, there are some basic tenets that are the basis of all good sociology that are likely to enhance the quality and impact of one's research. As a starting point it is important to make sport 'strange', that is, to step back and look at it as a curious social phenomenon. Second, it helps to adopt a sociological imagination that, according to C. Wright Mills (1959, p. 6): 'enables us to grasp history and biography and the relations between the two within society'. In many ways this simple statement provides an important platform for identifying social problems and approaching them sociologically. It calls upon us to see social problems through a more complex lens making connections between our private lives, the public sphere and the socio-historical context within which these relationships occur. This is more difficult than it sounds but as a cultural practise and institution sport can serve as a strategic site of sociological analysis in part because it offers a treasure trove of data. For example, most nations have official sport policies related to a number of state sectors (health, education, national identity, youth and family, foreign affairs and diplomatic relations). In addition, sport events offer detailed records about competitions including who competed and the results. And, beyond official state policy documents and event records, sport has long been a key subject for the media. In combination sport-related documents and data allow for not only comparative analysis over specified historical periods but also between and across different cultural contexts.

As another strategy that can contribute to quality research, consider some of the innovative sport-media research that has been undertaken since the late 1980s. Over the past three decades, sociology of sport scholars with an interest in media (cf., Gruneau, 1989; Harvey, Law, & Cantelon, 2001; MacNeill, 1996; Silk, 2001; Silk & Amis, 2000; Wenner, 1989) have employed various formulations of Richard Johnson's (1986) circuit of culture and commodification and its later adaptation by Du Gay et al.'s (1997). The circuit of culture and commodification illustrates the key relationships between the production, representation, reading/consumption and regulation of media commodities including sport events and sport advertising. The benefit of this model is that it encourages us to: (a) see the 'life' of a sport commodity, advertisement or brand as it moves throughout the circuit; (b) acknowledge the relationships between, and the multidirectional nature of, key moments in the circuit, that is, seeing things as a process rather than as isolated events; (c) helps us to conceptualize what we often cannot see in reality, making visible the invisible or, in Johnson's (1986/1987) terms, helps illustrate the relationship between public and private; and (d) locates sport commodities and brands within particular socio-historical and political economic contexts (Jackson, 2013a, 2013b). Finally, beyond these benefits, the model also shows how various forms of regulation enable or constrain how both private and state sport-related initiatives influence people's real lives, and, in some cases help identify potential sites of resistance. Ultimately, such models are just tools that facilitate how we think about social issues and problems and how they might be examined. In order to remain relevant, they need to be continually assessed, critiqued and adapted in order to move us forward.

Is Sport a Panacea for Social Problems?

The quick and short answer to this question is clearly 'no' — sport is not a panacea for all social problems — but neither is it the cause of all problems. Sport is neither inherently good nor bad — it is, and can only be, as positive a cultural practise and institution as we, as a society, are willing and able to make it. Perhaps the easiest way of thinking about this is to simply state that sport not only reflects what is going on in society but actively plays a role in reproducing both the positive and negative aspects that emerge. This moves the discussion and debate beyond functionalist approaches that contribute to popular adages such as 'a kid in sport is a kid out of court'. Our challenge, as researchers and practitioners, is to ensure that we operate as ethically and professionally as possible based on the best information available. But we are also responsible for undertaking research that provides evidence (however, we might define it) and argument to influence policy makers. This is no easy task and one only needs to look at the field and profession of Physical Education as a prime example. It seems to defy logic that within an increasingly health conscious and obesity-obsessed era daily health and physical education are on the decline in schools in many countries. Politicians and education policy makers have failed students and society. But the field also has to accept some of the responsibility — it has simply not worked hard enough to justify itself as a priority in the curriculum. Of course not all physical education is constituted by sport but it is worth considering what role sport in the curriculum has played or could play to ensure quality, inclusive, positive experiences that help promote lifelong learning and enduring healthy, active lifestyles.

As another example, consider the explosion of sport for development and peace initiatives being promoted globally. In 2001, UN Secretary General Kofi Anan launched the United Nations Office on Sport for Development and Peace (UNOSDP). According to its website:

> Sport has a unique power to attract, mobilize and inspire. By its very nature, sport is about participation. It is about inclusion and citizenship. It stands for human values such as respect for the opponent, acceptance of binding rules, teamwork and fairness, all of which are principles which are also contained in the Charter of the United Nations. (www.un.org/sport)

Yet even the United Nations recognizes that:

> Sport is not a cure-all for development problems. As a cultural phenomenon, it is a mirror of society and is just as complex and contradictory. As such, sport can also have negative side effects such as violence, corruption, discrimination, hooliganism, nationalism, doping and fraud. To enable sport to unleash its full positive potential, emphasis must be placed on effective monitoring and guiding of sports activities. (www.un.org/sport)

Certainly the premise of using sport to achieve a range of positive outcomes in the world is a good thing but as an increasing amount of scholarship reveals — we have to move beyond public relations rhetoric and sport celebrity charity initiatives that are often more about self-aggrandizement than in effecting genuine, sustainable social change. Ultimately, we need cooperative efforts whereby local citizens are able to help researchers, field workers, policy makers and politicians identify the unique needs and solutions so that programmes are developed, delivered, monitored and evaluated with the aim of achieving real results.

ABOUT PRACTISING SOCIOLOGY OF SPORT

Is Teaching Sociology of Sport Easy?

No doubt everyone who has had the opportunity to teach a sociology of sport class will have a different response to this question. On the one hand it would seem easier to teach a sociology of sport class compared to a chemistry or mathematics class because students have some background knowledge and experience with sport, it permeates global media and features a steady stream of both celebrity athletes and social controversy. So, as a teacher one can draw upon existing research about a particular topic and find contemporary examples, including images, documentaries and YouTube clips that help illustrate the phenomena.

Conversely, the very fact that everyone has had experiences with sport, is sometimes very passionate about and has invested in it, can pose a challenge with respect to adopting a critical perspective. For many, sport is just a part of leisure time, a separate reality where they escape the stress of work, school and the challenges of everyday life. To this extent trying to engage in critical discussions about sport can be met with considerable resistance. Add to this the fact that in primary and secondary school, sport content is generally a part of the Physical Education curriculum which is itself a low priority with respect to the current knowledge hierarchy. All of that said it would seem that most sociology of sport academics feel privileged to be able to teach subject matter informed by their own research, about which they care deeply and through which they hope to make a difference in people's lives.

Do Sociologists of Sport Like Sport?

From my own experience most, but certainly not all, sociology of sport scholars have a real passion for sport as a participant, a spectator or both though there may be vast differences in the types of sport and physical cultural practises that interest people. Moreover, most have a genuine sense of self-awareness about the contradictions of enjoying something that one also critiques. However, this is not really a major issue for most of us and is easily reconciled. We did not create the existing sporting institutions, structures and systems but we acknowledge our responsibility for any complicity in reproducing inequalities and accept that it is our duty to address them. One way of doing this is by undertaking critical research that we can not only share with our students – the next generation of scholars and practitioners – but also policy makers. Yet, this can be difficult for scholars who must balance their personal and political agendas, forge important relationships with key stakeholders in order to facilitate their research, all the while maintaining a critical distance in order to ask challenging questions and offer insightful critique. As Bairner (2009, p. 126) observes: 'Our relationship with the areas of activity that we wish to critique is complex'.

Is the Sociologist of Sport a 'Public Intellectual'?

Given that, like all other academics, sociology of sport scholars are generally publicly funded and are both able and obligated to serve as critic and conscience of society, we are, almost by definition, public intellectuals. To be clear this does not mean we have more right to speak compared to others (though perhaps more opportunities and, though dwindling, more protections), nor does it mean that we are experts simply because we have three letters after our name and work in ivory tower institutions. Conversely, we do not need to be media celebrities nor march and carry protest signs for every worthy cause in order to qualify as a public intellectual. Ultimately, the core activities of our work: research, teaching and community service are important and, where possible, we should work to make links with real social issues and problems. This is not to say that blue sky research and the pursuit of grand theories need to be abandoned but rather that a conscious effort is made to engage with colleagues and the community when and where the opportunity arises. In his discussion of the role of academics Piketty (2014, p. 3) refers to the unique opportunity we have as citizens who:

> ... can help to redefine the terms of the debate, unmask certain preconceived or fraudulent notions, and subject all positions to constant critical scrutiny... [T]his is the role that intellectuals, including social scientists, should play, as citizens like any other but with the good fortune to have more time than others to devote themselves to study.

Even more forthright Donnelly comments on the role and responsibility for sociology of sport scholars calling on them to give serious consideration to the focus of their research (2015, p. 422):

> Given the widely recognized problems of the modern world .... the work of sociologists of sport should make a difference. There are many intriguing topics to study in the world of sport and physical culture, but we should ask ourselves if the questions are relevant in terms of problems such as the sustainability of sport (addressing problems relating to climate change, environment, and the cost of sports and events). The sociology of sport is also able to address, from the perspective of sport and physical culture, other problems such as poverty and social inequality; conflict and conflict resolution; participation, the social determinants of health and the spread of non-communicable diseases; the human rights and labor rights of athletes and those engaged in the industries supporting sport and physical culture; and the democratization of participation, of participants and of governance.

By and large many sociology of sport scholars are doing their best to fulfil their obligations as public intellectuals although this has not been easy given both the marginalized nature of our field and general scepticism and suspicions held about academics (Nixon, 1991). Moreover, the problem is becoming increasingly difficult with the context of a neo-liberal education sector obsessed with performance measurement (Bairner, 2009; Cooky, 2017), and where corporate funded contracts limit what researchers can say even if it is in the public interest. And, it is important to acknowledge the role that universities and academics themselves play in stifling dissent, protest, resistance and engaging as a public intellectual by making writing accessible. Although it is slowly changing, remnants of intellectual elitism endure such that writing for the general public in a manner and through outlets that are accessible is looked down upon within some academic circles. If we are to succeed as public intellectuals and as catalysts for the social change that we so desire, we need to find a way to simultaneously: engage in theoretical debates with our colleagues, speak and write in a language that reaches the wider community and offer persuasive evidence to policy makers that progressive alternatives are in the interests of the majority.

ABOUT SOCIOLOGY OF SPORT IN THE ACADEMY

Does Sociology of Sport Face Institutional/Industry Barriers?

Like sociology and the social sciences in general, sociology of sport continues to face enormous institutional, industry and even state barriers. Over the past two decades we have witnessed a virtual war on particular forms of knowledge with the prioritization of Science, Technology, Engineering and Mathematics (STEM) subjects. This war has ranged from mild debates to major restructuring of university divisions and departments, to the extreme of intellectual cleansing where entire subject areas are eliminated with the stroke of an administrator's pen. Combine this with the rising dominance of the neo-liberal university where the only knowledge that counts is that which makes a profit and it is difficult not to question the purpose and future of universities. Governments are deliberately attempting to undermine and eliminate universities as the last bastion of independent research and one of the few remaining places where individuals are entitled to act as critic and conscience of society. The rise of charter schools and dramatic changes to state funding policies whereby private providers are entitled to equal access to public tertiary education funding is clear evidence of an agenda to transform universities into training schools in the service of capitalism. With that broad, perhaps rather sobering introduction it is worth noting three specific examples of the kinds of challenges university academics face today: (1) neo-liberalism and the academic performance measurement imperative, (2) colonization and commodification of knowledge and (3) linguistic imperialism. In turn, I will comment briefly on the barriers to research for sociology of sport scholars.

Although the 'publish or perish' mantra has long been a part of university life, the emergence of a new performance management and measurement paradigm has shifted the goalposts. The UK has the Research Excellence Framework (REF), Australia has the Excellence in Research Australia (ERA) and South Africa and many other countries have some form of a National Science Foundation (NSF) evaluation. In New Zealand we have Performance Based Research Funding (PBRF) a system introduced by the government in the early 2000s to ensure a quality return on their research '*investment*'. Every single academic in the country is ranked A, B, C or R (which means zero), and each department and university is ranked based on the number of As, Bs, Cs along with the number of PhDs produced and the amount of external research income generated over a five-year period. Unfortunately, while the government can legitimately argue that the overall quantity and quality of research has improved, PBRF has resulted in a range of gaming strategies including the reclassification of academic staff including the introduction of short-term contracts, the elimination of some departments and an unknown impact on the quality of teaching. The financial cost of operating this rather arbitrary measurement machine (notably the results cannot be compared with any other country) is enormous and the human cost incalculable. Such measurement systems are likely to remain and, if left unchecked will further erode the capacity of universities to fulfil their mandated role.

Directly linked to the neo-liberal turn in education has been the colonization and commodification of knowledge and publishing. A few large publishers now control a large segment of the sport-related publishing industry and this gives them enormous power. Here, there are two concerns: the changing nature of commercial publication and censorship. Traditionally, authors published their work and libraries and academics purchased annual subscriptions to journals to gain access. While this traditional approach remains, publishers are now offering the online purchase of individual articles and, even individual chapters of authored books all at premium prices. With respect to censorship, increasing concerns about lawsuits has made some publishers and editors reluctant to approve manuscripts that are overly critical of organizations such as the IOC and FIFA or even to allow for controversial quotes that have emerged from interviews with public figures. Arguably, it is more important than ever that we avoid being censored or worse, engage in self-censorship. Beyond this we need to reflect on our collective roles as scholars and our place within the production, distribution and consumption of knowledge. Consider the following: as researchers we engage in hours of planning, grant writing, gaining ethical approval, data collection and analysis, writing and submitting to journals, then revising and resubmitting our manuscripts for publication. But, in addition to these tasks, many academics are also involved in reviewing and editing manuscripts as service to Editorial Boards. Ultimately, we labour, we produce and often we end up buying back the products of our own labour from private, profit-making publishers. Despite all his personal faults and theoretical limitations, Karl Marx may have been right about capitalism, labour exploitation and the ownership of the means of production (Jackson, 2013a, 2013b).

With all of these wider issues as a contextual backdrop let me offer a few comments about the current and future challenges for sociology of sport. The field has always struggled (but survived) in large part because of its subject matter. Those who worked in Physical Education departments were often categorized as being in the toy department of academia — 'P.E.' and sport were much the same thing and certainly held a low rank within university knowledge hierarchies. Likewise, scholars whose home was in sociology departments did not fare much better often finding themselves isolated and marginalized. Sadly, not much has changed and even in departments where sociology of sport courses attract large numbers of students, they tend to be valued only for the income generated.

The enduring marginalization of the field is evident in many ways. As previously mentioned 'sport'-themed courses tend to attract large numbers of students yet few dedicated sociology of sport positions are emerging. Increasingly, such courses are service courses linked to sport-management programmes or general interest sociology courses. From a research perspective, many academics reveal stories about the challenge of securing research funding compared to their medical and bioscience colleagues even when they are effectively doing the same kind of research.

What is the Future of the Sociology of Sport?

It is both difficult and dangerous to predict the future but let me offer a few observations about the current state of the field and how we might proceed in order to survive and succeed. In many respects there is much to be optimistic about if we consider the growth in national and regional sociology of sport associations, the number of sport-related journals, the increasing interest in sport by both other academic disciplines and state sector departments and the energy, enthusiasm and quality of emerging young scholars. With respect to professional associations, in addition to ISSA which celebrated its 50th anniversary in 2015, we currently have NASSS (North America), JSSS (Japan), KSSS (Korea), EASS (Europe), ALESDE (Latin America), TSSS (Taiwan) and a range of other emerging associations in China, India and the Philippines. If we can collaborate amongst ourselves and with related organizations such as the International Sociology Association (ISA), the International Council for Sport Science and Physical Education (ICSPPE) as well as national and regional sociology and Kinesiology associations there is enormous potential to gain important allies that will enable us to achieve more (Jackson, 2015b, 2015c).

In addition to the relatively strong presence of sociology of sport associations, scholars now have more options to publish their work than ever before. This includes many of the traditional sociology journals as well as a range of sport-related journals (e.g., the *International Review for the Sociology of Sport, Sociology of Sport Journal, Journal of Sport and Social Issues, Sport in Society, European Journal for Sport in Society, Leisure Studies, Soccer & Society, Football Studies* along with allied journals such as *Quest, Research Quarterly, International Journal of Sport Policy, Journal of Sport Management, Leisure Studies, Sport, Education & Society, Body & Society*). There has also been a virtual explosion of book series, largely edited collections, and more recently open access forms of online publishing. Furthermore, it has been promising to see the growing interest in 'sport' by other fields of study including: anthropology, geography, urban planning, media and communication studies, gender studies, literary studies, indigenous studies, political science, economics, tourism and even dance and theatre studies. While this is wonderful news and may signal growing acceptance of sport as a seriously scholarly endeavour, one concern is that many scholars in these fields appear to be dabblers who are 'discovering' sport for the first time. By discover I mean that they believe that they have an original idea and that they are the first scholars work-ing on a particular topic. Unfortunately, this often results in the publication of work that ignores significant bodies of literature from our field that would have greatly enhanced their contribution.

Adding to the momentum of scholars from other fields taking a genuine interest in sport various state sectors of government are now recognizing its sig-nificant and strategic role in society. Most nation-states have a Ministry of Sport that develops policy regarding both elite and mass sport and also have related Ministries such as Education and Health where sport operates as a port-folio. However, beyond these departments, state sectors including Tourism, Youth and Family, Foreign Affairs and even Immigration are increasingly aware of and developing policies related to sport. This may provide new sources of both research topics and funding. Equally important it may offer an opportunity to make important links where sociology of sport research can help influence social policy in order to make a difference.

All of this holds much promise for the future of sociology of sport but there are dangers — both external and internal. As previously noted externally there is the genuine external threat of the neo-liberalization of universities that has enormous implications for science and society. Internally, within our field there are a number of things we must be aware of and take caution. First, we must consider the implications of what we might call academic cults of identity politics. Over the past three decades, sociology of sport (and its parent disci-pline), has rightly become more inclusive than ever with respect to a diverse range of theories, methods and political activism. However, over time what has emerged are increasingly narrow and polarized positions where discussion and debate is stunted or ceases, any critique offered is interpreted as a threat, and people only associate with like-minded people to the point where 'you are either with us or against us'. Notably, Ingham and Donnelly (1997) raised sim-ilar concerns about the North American Society for the Sociology of Sport in the late 1990s:

> Scholarly formations, such as NASSS, thus lose their collective identity and become merely stages for the presentation of subject positions or, at best, for the presentation of subject positions to those who 'share' ... similar experiences ... The common welfare disappears and the desires of small ... congeries prevail (1997, p. 395) ... Identity validation is not, therefore, self-transformation. Self-reflexivity requires more than attending *at:* It requires attending *to* not only those who think as 'I'; but who differ from 'I'. In a political, cultural, and 'theoretical' climate that celebrates the 'I', is it now possible to construct a 'We'? (1997, p. 395)

Our challenge, is to be a community of scholars that is open to new ideas and theories but with a respectful duty to scrutinize them without engaging in censorship. For our own survival we have to be more than small pockets of like-minded individuals and, in this regard, it has been pleasing to see recent proactive efforts to listen, engage and cooperate.

CONCLUSION

Writing this chapter has been an interesting trek down memory lane. It offered an opportunity to stand in the present and to look both backwards and forwards. Hopefully this has not become too nostalgic but perhaps it would inevitably be so. Yet, there is no glossing over the challenges that lie ahead and there are many. There appears to be a global war on the academy as one of the final bastions of freedom of intellectual thought and the right and responsibility to serve as critic and conscience of society. The sociology of sport may be one small discipline within the larger academic network of knowledge production, advocacy and activism but it has an important role to play. The pathway ahead will not be easy but we will be stronger, more visible and safer if we travel and work together.

REFERENCES

Anderson, L., & Jackson, S. J. (2013). Competing loyalties in sports medicine: Threats to medical professionalism in elite, commercial sport. *International Review for the Sociology of Sport, 48*, 238–256.

Andrews, D., & Jackson, S. J. (Eds.). (2001). *Sport stars: The politics of sporting celebrity*. London: Routledge Publishers.

Andrews, D., Lopes, V., & Jackson, S. J. (2016). Neymar: Sport celebrity and performative cultural politics. In P. D. Marshall & S. Redmond (Eds.), *A companion to celebrity* (pp. 421–439). Hoboken, NJ: Wiley-Blackwell.

Bairner, A. (2009). Sport, intellectuals and public sociology: Obstacles and opportunities. *International Review for the Sociology of Sport, 44*(2–3), 115–130.

Beck, U. (2000). *The brave new world of work*. Cambridge: Polity Press.

Beissel, A. (2015). *Sons of Samoa: The corporeal economy of American Samoa Gridiron Football*. PhD dissertation, University of Otago, New Zealand.

Chang, I. Y., Sam, M. P., & Jackson, S. J. (2015). Transnationalism, return visits and identity negotiation: South Korean-New Zealanders and the Korean national sports festival. *International Review for the Sociology of Sport*, doi:10.1177/1012690215589723

Chiba, N., & Jackson, S. J. (2006). Athletic mercenaries or sporting ambassadors?: The Rugby player migration from New Zealand to Japan. *Football Studies, 9*(2), 67–78.

Cody, K., & Jackson, S. J. (2016). The contested terrain of alcohol sponsorship of sport in New Zealand. *International Review for the Sociology of Sport, 51*(4), 375–393.

Cooky, C. (2017). We cannot stand idly by: A necessary call for a public sociology of sport. *Sociology of Sport Journal, 34*(1), 1–14.

Donnelly, P. (2015). Assessing the sociology of sport: On public sociology of sport and research that makes a difference. *International Review for the Sociology of Sport, 50*(4–5), 419–423.

Du Gay, P., Hall, S., Janes, L., Mackay, H., & Negus, K. (1997). *Doing cultural studies: The story of the Sony Walkman*. London: Sage.

Dunning, E. (1999). *Sport matters: Sociological studies of sport, violence and civilisation*. London: Routledge.

Esherick, C., Baker, R., Jackson, S. J., & Sam, M. (2017). *Case studies in sport diplomacy*. Morgantown, WV: FIT Publishers.

Flyvbjerg, B., Stewart, A., & Budzier, A. (2016). *The Oxford Olympics Study 2016: Cost and Cost Overrun at the Games*. Said Business School Research Papers, Oxford University, Oxford, UK.

Gee, S., & Jackson, S. J. (2010). The Southern Man city as cultural place and Speight's space: Locating the masculinity-sport-beer "holy trinity" in New Zealand. *Sport in Society, 13*(10), 1492–1507.

Gee, S., & Jackson, S. J. (2011). Leisure corporations, beer brand culture, and the crisis of masculinity: The Speight's "Southern Man" advertising campaign. *Leisure Studies, 31*(1) 83–102.

Gee, S., & Jackson, S. J. (2011a). The Southern Man city as cultural place and Speight's space: Locating the masculinity–sport–beer "holy trinity" in New Zealand. In M. Sam & J. Hughson (eds.) *Sport in the city: Cultural connections* (pp. 100–115). London: Routledge.

Gee, S., & Jackson, S. J. (2011b). Leisure corporations, beer brand culture, and the crisis of masculinity: The Speight's "Southern Man" advertising campaign. *Leisure Studies, 31*(1) 83–102.

Gee, S., & Jackson, S. J. (2017). *Sport, promotional culture and the crisis of masculinity*. London: Palgrave Macmillan.

Gee, S., Jackson, S. J., & Sam, M. (2013). *The culture of alcohol promotion and consumption at major sports events in New Zealand*. Research report commissioned by the Health Promotion Agency. Wellington: Health Promotion Agency.

Gee, S., Jackson, S. J., & Sam, M. (2016). Carnivalesque culture and alcohol promotion and consumption at an annual international sports event in New Zealand. *International Review for the Sociology of Sport, 51*(3), 265–283.

Grainger, A., & Jackson, S. J. (2000). Sports marketing and the challenges of globalization: A case study of cultural resistance in New Zealand. *International Journal of Sports Marketing and Sponsorship, 2* (2), 111–125.

Grainger, A., & Jackson, S. J. (2005). I'm afraid of Americans?: New Zealand's cultural resistance to violence in "globally" produced sports advertising. In S. Jackson & D. Andrews (Eds.), *Sport, Culture and Advertising: Identities, Commodities and the Politics of Representation* (pp. 192–212). London: Routledge.

Gruneau, R. (1989). Making spectacle: A case study in television sports production. In L. Wenner (Ed.). *Media, sports and society* (pp. 134–154). Newbury Park, CA: Sage Publications.

Grusky, O. (1963). Managerial succession and organizational effectiveness. *American Journal of Sociology, 69* (1), 21–31.

Hall, S., Dobson, D., Lowe, A., & Willis, P. (1980). *Culture, media, language*. London: Hutchinson.

Hall, S., & Donald, J. (Eds.). (1986). *Politics and ideology*. Milton Keynes: The Open University.

Hall, S., & Jacques, M. (1990). *New times*. Chadwell-Heath: Lawrence and Wishart.

Hall, S., & Jefferson, T. (1976). *Resistance through rituals, youth subcultures in post-war Britain*. London: HarperCollins Academic.

Hallinan, C., & Jackson, S. J. (2016). Sociology of sport: Aotearoa/New Zealand and Australia. In K. Young (Ed.). *Sociology of sport: A global subdiscipline in review* (pp. 95–110). Bingley: Emerald.

Harvey, J., Law, A., & Cantelon, M. (2001). North American Professional Team Sport Franchises Ownership Patterns and Global Entertainment Conglomerates. *Sociology of Sport Journal, 18* (4), 435–457.

IEG. (2012, January 11). Economic uncertainty to slow sponsorship growth in 2012. IEG Press Release. Retrieved from http://www.sponsorship.com/About-IEG/Press-Room/Economic-Uncertainty-To-Slow-Sponsorship-Growth-In.aspx

Ingham, A., & Donnelly, P. (1997). A sociology of North American sociology of sport: Disunity in unity, 1965 to 1996. *Sociology of Sport Journal,14*(4), 362–418.

Jackson, S. J. (1988). Toward an investment theory of sport spectatorship. *Play and Culture, 1*, 314–321.

Jackson, S. J. (1994). Gretzky, crisis & Canadian identity in 1988: Rearticulating the Americanization of culture debate. *Sociology of Sport Journal, 11*, 428–446.

Jackson, S. J. (1998a). The 49th paradox: The 1988 Calgary Winter Olympic Games and Canadian identity as contested terrain. In M. Duncan, G. Chick, & A. Aycock, (Eds.), *Diversions and divergences in the fields of play* (pp. 191–208). Greenwich, CT: Ablex Publishing.

Jackson, S. J. (1998b). A twist of race: Ben Johnson & the Canadian crisis of racial and national identity. *Sociology of Sport Journal, 15*, 21–40.

Jackson, S. J. (1998c). Life in the (mediated) Faust Lane: Ben Johnson, national affect and the 1988 crisis of Canadian identity. *International Review for the Sociology of Sport, 33*, 227–238.

Jackson, S. J. (2004). Exorcising the ghost: Donovan Bailey, Ben Johnson and the Politics of Canadian Identity. *Media, Culture and Society, 26*(1), 121–141.

Jackson, S. J. (2013a). The contested terrain of sport diplomacy in a globalising world. *International Area Studies Review, 16*(3), 275–285.

Jackson, S. J. (2013b). Rugby World Cup 2011: Sport mega-events between the global and the local. *Sport in Society, 16*(7), 847–852.

Jackson, S. J. (2014). Globalisation, corporate nationalism and masculinity in Canada: Sport, Molson beer advertising and consumer citizenship. *Sport in Society, 17*(7) 901–916.

Jackson, S. J. (2015a). Assessing the sociology of sport: On media, advertising and the commodification of culture. *International Review for the Sociology of Sport, 50*(4–5), 490–495.

Jackson, S. J. (2015b). Future challenges and opportunities for the sociology of sport. Plenary Panel Presentation, World Congress of Sociology of Sport – 50th Anniversary, June, Paris, France.

Jackson, S. J. (2015c). Sport, knowledge and power: Critical reflections and future prospects for an international sociology of sport. *East Asian Sport Thoughts, 4*, 1–24.

Jackson, S. J., & Andrews, D. (2012). Olympic celebrity: Introduction. *Celebrity Studies, 3*(3), 263–269.

Jackson, S. J., & Andrews, D. L. (1996). Excavating the (Trans) National Basketball Association: Locating the global/local nexus of America's world and the world's America. *Australasian Journal of American Studies, 15*, 57–64.

Jackson, S. J., & Andrews, D. L. (1999). Between and beyond the global and the local: American popular sporting culture in New Zealand. *International Review for the Sociology of Sport, 34* (1), 31–42.

Jackson, S. J., & Andrews, D. L. (2004). Aggressive marketing: Interrogating the use of violence in sport related advertising. In L. Kahle & C. Riley (Eds.). *Sports marketing and the psychology of marketing communications* (pp. 307–325). Fairfax, VA: Lawrence Erlbaum Associates Publishers.

Jackson, S. J., & Andrews, D. L. (Eds.). (2005). *Sport, culture and advertising: Identities, commodities and the politics of representation.* London: Routledge.

Jackson, S. J., Batty, R., & Scherer, J., (2001). Transnational sport marketing at the global/local nexus: The adidasification of the New Zealand All Blacks. *International Journal of Sports Marketing and Sponsorship, 3*(2), 185–201.

Jackson, S. J., & Haigh, S. (2008). Between and beyond politics: Sport and foreign policy in a globalising world. *Sport in Society, 11*(4), 349–358.

Jackson, S. J., & Haigh, S. (Eds.) (2009). *Sport and foreign policy in a globalising world.* London: Routledge.

Jackson, S. J., & Hokowhitu, B. (2002). Sport, tribes and technology: The New Zealand All Blacks Haka and the politics of identity. *Journal of Sport and Social Issues, 26*, 125–139.

Jackson, S., & Sam, M. (2007). 'Yes Prime Minister' and the dilemmas of sport policy. *Sport Management Review, 10*(3), 307–323.

Jackson, S. J., & Scherer, J. (2013). Rugby World Cup 2011: Sport mega-events and the contested terrain of space, bodies and commodities. *Sport in Society, 16*(7), 883–898.

John, A., & Jackson, S. J. (2011). Call me loyal: Globalization, corporate nationalism and the America's Cup. *International Review for the Sociology of Sport, 46*(4), 399–417.

Johnson, R. (1986/1987). What is cultural studies anyway? *Social Text, 16*, 38–80.

Kobayashi, K. (2012a). Globalization, corporate nationalism and Japanese cultural intermediaries: Representation of Bukatsu through Nike advertising at the global–local nexus. *International Review for the Sociology of Sport, 47*(6), 724–742.

Kobayashi, K. (2012b). Corporate nationalism and glocalization of Nike advertising in "Asia": Production and representation practices of cultural intermediaries. *Sociology of Sport Journal, 29*(1), 42–61.

Lagae, W. (2003). *Sports sponsorship and marketing communications: A European perspective.* Harlow: Prentice Hall, Financial Times.

Le Blanc, R., & Jackson, S. (2007). Sexuality as cultural diversity in sport organisations. Special issue of the *International Journal of Sport Management and Marketing, 2*(1/2), 119–133.

Lee, N., Jackson, S. J., & Lee, K. (2007). South Korea's glocal hero: The Hiddink syndrome and the re-articulation of national citizenship and identity. *Sociology of Sport Journal, 24*, 283–301.

Loy, J., & McElvogue, J. (1970). Racial segregation in American sport. *International Review for the Sociology of Sport, 5*, 5–24.

Loy, J. W., & Jackson, S. J. (1990). A typology of group structures and a theory of their effects on patterns of leadership recruitment within sport organizations. In L. Vander Velden & J. Humphrey (Eds.), *Psychology and sociology of sport: Current selected research* (Vol. II, pp. 93–114). New York, NY: AMS Press.

MacNeill, M. (1996). Networks: Producing Olympic ice hockey for a national television audience. *Sociology of Sport Journal, 13* (2),103–124.

McCrystal, R. (2017, February 5). Super Bowl Commercials 2017: Ad Costs Review, Value Before Patriots vs. Falcons, The *Bleacher Report.* Retrieved from http://bleacherreport.com/articles/2691166-super-bowl-commercials-2017-ad-costs-review-value-before-patriots-vs-falcons

Mills, C. W. (1959). *The sociological imagination.* New York, NY: Oxford University Press.

Morley, D., & Schwarz (2014, February 10). Stuart Hall obituary. *The Guardian.* Retrieved from https://www.theguardian.com/politics/2014/feb/10/stuart-hall

Nixon, H. L. (1991). Sports sociology that matters: Imperatives and challenges for the 1990s. *Sociology of Sport Journal, 8*, 281–294.

Piggin, J., Jackson, S., & M. Lewis (2009a). Telling the truth in public policy: An analysis of New Zealand sport policy discourse. *Sociology of Sport Journal, 26*(3), 462–482.

Piggin, J., Jackson, S. J., & Lewis, M. (2007). Classify, divide and conquer: Shaping physical activity discourse through national public policy. *New Zealand Sociology, 22*(2), 84–103.

Piggin, J., Jackson, S. J., & Lewis, M. (2009b). Knowledge, power and politics: Contesting 'evidenced-based' national sport policy. *International Review for the Sociology of Sport, 44*(1) 87–101.

Piketty, T. (2014). *Capital in the twenty-first century.* Cambridge, MA: Harvard University Press.

Pope jumps on board Super Bowl party. (2017, February 6). *New Zealand Herald.* Retrieved from http://www.nzherald.co.nz/sport/news/article.cfm?c_id=4&objectid=11795409

Pope promotes sports for Christianity. (2004, 3 August). *NBC*, The Associated Press. Retrieved from http://nbcsports.msnbc.com

Rowe, D. (1996). The global love-match: Sport and television. *Media, Culture and Society, 18*, 565–582.

Sam, M., & Jackson, S. J. (2004). Sport policy development in New Zealand: Paradoxes of an integrative paradigm. *International Review for the Sociology of Sport, 39*(2), 205–222.

Sam, M., & Jackson, S. J. (2015). Sport and small states: the myths, limits and contradictions of the legend of David and Goliath. *International Journal of Sport Policy and Politics, 7*(3/4), 319–327.

Sam, M. P., & Jackson, S. J. (2006). Developing national sport policy through consultation: The rules of engagement. *Journal of Sport Management, 20*, 365–384.

Sam, M. P., & Jackson, S. J. (2017). *Sport policy in small states.* London: Routledge.

Scherer, J., & Jackson, S. (2008b). Cultural studies and the circuit of culture: Advertising, promotional culture and the New Zealand All Blacks. *Cultural Studies/Critical Methodologies, 8*, 507–526.

Scherer, J., & Jackson, S. (2013). *The contested terrain of the New Zealand All Blacks: Rugby, commerce and cultural politics in the age of globalization*. Oxford: Peter Lang.

Scherer, J., & Jackson, S. J. (2007). Sports advertising, cultural production and corporate nationalism at the global−local nexus: Branding the New Zealand All Blacks. *Sport in Society, 10*, 268−284.

Scherer, J., & Jackson, S. J. (2008a). Producing Allblacks.com: Cultural intermediaries and the policing of electronic sporting consumption. *Sociology of Sport Journal, 25*, 187−205.

Scherer, J., & Jackson, S. J. (2010). *Globalization, sport and corporate nationalism: The new cultural economy of the New Zealand All Blacks*. Oxford: Peter Lang.

Silk, M. (2001). Together we're one? The "place" of the nation in media representations of the 1998 Kuala Lumpur commonwealth games. *Sociology of Sport Journal, 18*(3), 277−301.

Silk, M., & Amis, J. (2000). Institutional pressures and the production of televised sport. *Journal of Sport Management, 14*(4), 267−292.

Silk, M., & Jackson, S. J. (2000). Globalisation and sport in New Zealand. In C. Collins (Ed.). *Sport in New Zealand Society* (pp. 99−113). Palmerston North: Dunmore Press.

Tak, M., Sam, M. P., & Jackson, S. J. (2017). The politics of countermeasures against match-fixing in sport: A political sociology approach to policy instruments. *International Review for the Sociology of Sport*, doi:10.1177/1012690216639748

Thomson, R. W., & Jackson, S. J. (2016). History and development of the sociology of Sport in Aotearoa/New Zealand. *New Zealand Sociology, 31*(3), 78−109.

Wenner, L. (1989). *Media, sports and society*. Thousand Oaks, CA: Sage.

Wenner, L. A., & Jackson, S. J. (2009). *Sport, beer, and gender: Promotional culture and contemporary social life*. Zurich: Peter Lang.

CHAPTER 6

WHY STUDYING SPORT MATTERS: ONE WOMAN'S PERSPECTIVE AS A SPORT SOCIOLOGY SCHOLAR

Mary Jo Kane

ABOUT THE AUTHOR

Mentors and Influential Figures

I have been influenced by a number of people over the years from my class-room teachers in high school to faculty members when I was an undergraduate. But because the purpose of this chapter is to provide my perspectives and experiences as an academic in higher education, I want to focus on a singular individual who became my mentor in graduate school at the University of Illinois beginning in the early 1980s. I was very fortunate – though I did not know it at the time – that one of the members of my dissertation committee was Professor John Loy. I soon discovered that in the 1960s, Professor Loy was one of the founding fathers of what became an academic sub-discipline within the broader field of Kinesiology – sport sociology. Loy and Kenyon (1969) were the editors of an influential textbook, *Sport, Culture and Society: A Reader on the Sociology of Sport*. They compiled a series of chapters designed to recognize sport as a fertile ground for [empirical] study within higher education in general and the social sciences in particular. Such 'fertile ground' focused on the role and impact of sport on broader social and cultural issues ranging from the economics of professional sports to racially based occupational discrimination in Major League Baseball. A number of the graduate classes I took at Illinois, as well as research papers that were presented at academic

Reflections on Sociology of Sport: Ten Questions, Ten Scholars, Ten Perspectives
Research in the Sociology of Sport, Volume 10, 87–100
Copyright © 2018 by Emerald Publishing Limited
All rights of reproduction in any form reserved
ISSN: 1476-2854/doi:10.1108/S1476-285420170000010006

conferences and printed in peer-reviewed journals, would frequently cite the invaluable contributions made by Professor Loy to this emerging body of knowledge.

What 'invaluable contributions' did Professor Loy make to my understanding of sport as an academic field of study, one where I could pursue a professional career and hope to make my own significant contributions as a scholar and educator? Looking back, the most valuable lesson he taught me was to respect and honour the scientific enterprise; to never take shortcuts when engaged in the painstaking quest to conceptualize (and then design) an empirically based study that was methodologically rigorous and grounded within a theoretical framework. Professor Loy also taught me to begin with – and continually return to – what every scholar should ask him or herself when embarking on a new journey into science, particularly when that journey seeks to discover some new and important element of the sports world as it impacts our daily lives. I can still hear him saying, 'What's the question, meaning what's the purpose of your study?' This query was inevitably followed by, 'And what will we know when you've finished asking (and answering) your question and why does it matter?'

With these questions as my guiding principles, I began every study I have conducted, every manuscript I have written and every lecture I have given within Professor Loy's foundational framework. This approach has enabled me to unearth what is truly at play when we examine how and why sports matter so much in US culture. From the deeply personal – 'OMG, my team just blew another fourth quarter lead!' – to the broader societal impact of how, for example, the ubiquitous mainstream media have created a 'cult of sports' where we forgive the latest transgression or outrage committed by male athletes so long as they 'just win, baby'. In sum, Professor Loy gave me the tools – and the wisdom – to see that one of the most powerful social, economic and political forces in our society can (and should) be examined as part of the larger sociological endeavour. And to always ask: What is it about this particular institution that has so captured the imagination, dare I say even the soul, of the American people? Embarking on a professional career with this question as my guidepost, I came to understand and fully appreciate that I will forever be indebted to Professor Loy.

Research Trajectory

I have focused primarily on two major lines of research: (1) occupational employment trends in women's sports after the passage of Title IX in 1972; and (2) media representations of female athletes. In the former instance, this was a line of inquiry I pursued early in my career and have just recently returned to. It is well-documented that prior to Title IX, over 90% of all head coaches in women's sports were female, while today women occupy just 43% of all head coaching positions in the United States (Acosta & Carpenter, 2014; LaVoi, 2016). To address this rather alarming trend, in the early 1990s, my colleague Jane Stangl and I examined the theoretical notion (and practise) of homologous reproduction whereby those in power (e.g., white males) reproduce themselves based on their own social and/or physical characteristics and attributes (Kanter, 1977). We discovered that significantly many more male coaches were hired under male athletic directors (ADs) and that this – along with other factors such as women being a token presence as coaches in men's athletics – may well account for the increasing absence of women throughout the coaching profession (Kane & Stangl, 1991; Stangl & Kane, 1991).

More recently I returned to this topic by examining the perceptions of intercollegiate ADs to determine what factors they believed accounted for the dramatic decline in the number of women in leadership positions in the post-Title IX era. In 2015, my colleague Nicole LaVoi and I replicated Acosta and Carpenter's (1988) study which found significant gender differences between male and female ADs. For example, male ADs attributed the decline to individual factors, meaning the 'failures' of individual women such as their so-called unwillingness to apply for job openings. In contrast, female ADs attributed the decline to structural factors such as success of the 'old boys' club' and gender discrimination. Dr LaVoi and I wondered whether such gender differences would still exist almost 30 years after the initial study. We employed a nationwide sample to collect data from male and female ADs but added the extension variable of senior woman administrator (SWA). We did so because SWAs are the highest ranking females in college athletic departments and often play a major role in hiring decisions, especially in women's sports. Our findings also revealed significant gender differences in that male ADs continued to attribute the underrepresentation of female coaches to their own individual failings such as they were (supposedly) less qualified than their male counterparts. But female ADs as well as SWAs attributed women's absence in leadership positions to structural factors such as the failure of the 'old girls' club' to promote women, and both conscious and unconscious discrimination (Kane & LaVoi, 2017).

My second line of research – and the one I am most known for professionally – involves media representations of female athletes. Early in my career I relied on content analysis to determine the amount and type of coverage given to male versus female athletes in traditional sport media outlets such as *Sports Illustrated* (Kane, 1988), as well as major daily newspapers like *The New York Times* and *Washington Post* (Kane, 1996). My research publications contributed to the body of knowledge on sport, media and gender in that I discovered (along with a number of other scholars) that women were significantly underrepresented in terms of overall coverage, and were much more likely to be portrayed for their off-court physical attractiveness and femininity than for their on-court athletic accomplishments. That said, a major limitation of content analysis as a methodological tool is that it far too often relies on word counts or frequency data as the primary (or only) unit of analysis. For example, in determining that female athletes are given far less overall coverage than are male athletes, a researcher may simply count the number of times that females appear on the cover of *Sports Illustrated* in any given year. Yet if scholars rely on a 'numbers game' only, it is easy for them to overlook, or disregard altogether, the *context or significance of the image* that produced the image in the first place. Serena Williams, for example, might be the only woman who appeared on *SI*'s cover over a 12-month period, but she did so because she was named their Sportswoman of the Year.

Moving beyond these methodological limitations, beginning in the mid-2000s, my colleagues and I began to employ audience reception research to examine how images of elite female athletes are interpreted by sports fans and female athletes themselves, and further, how those interpretations impact one's interest in and respect for women's sports (Fink, Kane, & LaVoi, 2014; Kane, LaVoi, & Fink, 2013; Kane & Maxwell, 2011).

The common thread of both lines of research is twofold. First, most of my scholarly writings are framed within critical feminist theory, which assumes that society is structured around a series of inequitable relationships of power whereby women are systematically devalued and marginalized (Birrell, 2000; Hoeber, 2007). Second, and related to the first, is that both lines of inquiry are grounded in the belief — and supported by empirical evidence — that sport is a particularly critical and useful site for the reproduction and maintenance of male power and privilege (Kane, 2016). A corollary to this argument is that women's intrusion into this once exclusive and sacred male space must be resisted. Throughout my career I have explored the various ways (and significant role) that mainstream sport media play in resisting women's advancement by reproducing images of female athletes as 'sexy babes' versus highly accomplished athletes. These portrayals, in turn, become a particularly effective method for reinforcing the status quo.

ABOUT SPORT

Why Does Sport Matter?

It is stating the obvious to say that sport is one of the most pervasive and influential institutions in modern American society. Indeed, did you ever stop to consider why it's 'News, Weather and Sports?' Why not 'News, Weather and Education?' Or technology? Or literature? One important measure of the all-consuming impact of sport involves the vast resources invested in sport-related activities. In terms of discretionary spending alone, billions of dollars are spent annually on the sale of licensed sport products such as football jerseys and baseball caps (Heitner, 2014). Major TV and cable networks also spend billions of dollars to secure the rights to broadcast big-time college football (Alsher, 2016). The NFL has similar, if not greater, economic impact: At the 2016 Super Bowl, advertising rates continued to soar where the cost of one 30-second ad was $5 million (Woodyard, 2016).

Another way we can address the topic of 'why sports matter' is to examine how athletes both reflect and reinforce the best and the worst of society. For example, sports have become so essential to our way of being that athletes often personify values we hold dear as well as behaviour we find repugnant. In the former instance, the NFL has launched initiatives such as 'A Crucial Catch: Screening Saves Lives' to create awareness regarding breast cancer, while in the latter it has become a cliché but nevertheless a reality that reading the sports page often feels like reading the latest police blotter. Recent examples include high-profile athletes such as Ray Rice, formerly of the NFL's Baltimore Ravens, who was captured on a security camera punching his then fiancé in the face and knocking her unconscious. Or the issue of drunk driving as reflected in the recently released videotape of NFL wide receiver Michael Floyd sitting incoherent in his car. Police arrested Floyd and charged him with a DUI because his blood alcohol registered at 0.218% (Janetsky, 2016).

Finally, sports matter because they serve as both a socializing agent and a unifier of people (Coakley, 2015). The socialization process refers to the ways in which dominant values, attitudes and beliefs are passed from one generation to the next. Because many Americans are exposed to and engage in physical activity from an early age, sport becomes a key incubator for learning important social roles such as that of a good citizen, responsible neighbour and loyal friend. As a result, sport participation contributes to the overall stability and cohesion of the broader culture. Sport can also bring people together by creating and nurturing one's personal identity, as well as establishing a sense of social identification and group unity (LaVoi & Kane, 2014). There are numerous examples of how this is accomplished, from an overall sense of well-being at the individual level ('I'm a proud varsity athlete on the women's soccer team'), to a particular region of the country uniting behind their team (the 2016 World-Series winning Chicago Cubs!), to an entire nation rooting for an Olympic athlete (the all-time gold-medal winning US swimmer, Michael Phelps).

How Should Sport be Studied?

As noted sport scholar Jay Coakley has pointed out: 'For most sociologists, the ultimate goal is to create and distribute knowledge that enable people to understand, control, and improve ... the social worlds in which they live' (2015,

p. 21). As previously noted, for millions of Americans, one highly significant world in which they live is the world of sports. We have already discussed the enormous economic impact of sport as well as its role in the socialization process. Because sport is an all-pervasive and enormously influential institution, it should be taken seriously as a subject worthy of scientific investigation. Indeed, an analysis of sport should be subjected to the same methodological and theoretical rigour employed throughout the social sciences. Mike Messner, an equally noted sport sociologist, has argued that whether one is using a quantitative or qualitative approach, scholars will be able to more fully understand the role, meaning and significance of sport by relying on the fundamental building blocks of the scientific method: (1) develop research questions or hypotheses based on previous literature; (2) select appropriate and relevant theories and methods depending on what issues/questions are under consideration; (3) collect and analyse data; (4) use your research findings to produce connections and conclusions among phenomena and (5) disseminate your results in various academic outlets such as peer-reviewed journals and presentations at international conferences (Messner, 2002).

Another issue that comes into play when discussing how sport, as an institution of great social, political and economic power, should be studied involves the role of those scholars who examine sport as part of the scientific enterprise. Should we conduct our research as objectively and dispassionately as possible? Should we present and publish our findings in academic journals and at international conferences and let others determine how our findings should be used or interpreted? Or should we design our research in ways that challenge many of the fundamental inequities that are far too often part of the structure, ideology and practise of sport ranging from sexism and homophobia to the exploitation of male athletes engaged in professional and bigtime college sports? If the answer to this latter question is 'yes' then are we as scholars committed to using our research in the cause of social justice and change? Though I do not have any easy, magic-bullet answers to these questions, I can say that studying sport as a vehicle for social change is a far cry from where I began my career under the watchful eye of John Loy who insisted that our *only* role as scholars was to conduct the research, publish the findings and remain neutral, meaning scientifically objective, at all costs. I return to this issue in greater detail below when discussing sport sociologists as public intellectuals.

Is Sport a Panacea for Social Problems?

Given the role and influence of sport in its various forms, it certainly has the capacity to produce positive social and behavioural outcomes and thus mitigate a variety of social concerns. Numerous scholars have found that sport participation can lead to health and well-being as well as emotional, physical and psychological development (Eime, Young, Harvey, Charity, & Payne, 2013). That said, according to Merriam-Webster, 'panacea' refers to a cure-all 'remedy for [society's] ills or difficulties'. Within this definition, no single institution can provide a magic-bullet potion to eliminate our problems. But sport can address – and even significantly reduce – some of our most intractable challenges.

A recent example comes from professional football where the NFL developed a partnership with NO MORE, a non-profit organization devoted to raising public awareness about domestic violence and sexual assault. In 2014, the League began airing public-service announcements (PSAs) by celebrities during football broadcasts and in stadiums during games. This was soon followed by a ground-breaking initiative in which the players themselves – including some Hall of Famers – appeared in PSAs saying 'no more' to domestic violence and sexual assault (NFL players say NO MORE to domestic violence & sexual assault in new PSA, n.d.). This is not to suggest that this type of approach, no matter how innovative and well-intentioned, will end violence against women. But it does speak to the power and capacity of professional sports to use their extraordinarily visible platforms to mobilize public awareness and action when confronting some of our biggest social challenges.

Another example of sport potentially serving as a panacea is how youth or recreational sports can be a critical environment for positive social, psychological and health-wellness outcomes. In sheer numbers alone, the National Council of Youth Sports estimates that 60 million girls and boys participate in organized youth sports throughout the United States (Sage & Eitzen, 2013). As a result, youth sport activities have an enormous reach and impact at a national level. A common belief or objective that cuts across a multitude of youth sports programmes is that participation provides opportunities for young children to develop socially desirable characteristics and belief systems such as cooperation, teamwork and respect for others. Youth sports programmes can also instil a sense of identity and belonging that may be particularly relevant to vulnerable youth most in need of credibility and acceptance among their peers.

For all the ways that sports can contribute to the common good, or provide a counterweight to our most difficult social problems, I would be remiss if I did not point out that many critics argue that far from being a panacea, the sport experience, particularly for males engaged in highly competitive, combat-oriented team sports, exacerbate – or certainly contribute to – some of society's most egregious ills. One specific and deeply troubling example involves physical and sexual assault against women by male athletes, a subject I highlight below in the section on institutional and industry barriers.

ABOUT PRACTISING SOCIOLOGY OF SPORT

Is Teaching Sociology of Sport Easy?

I have been teaching sociology of sport courses at both the graduate and under-graduate levels within a Research 1 University for almost three decades. ('Research 1' is a classification in the United States given to institutions of higher education where scholarly activity, versus classroom teaching, is given highest priority.) I have also taught other types of courses ranging from Sport and Gender to Research Methods. Because of my interest and background in studying sport from a variety of perspectives, I have found teaching sport soci-ology courses 'easy' in that my own research keeps me current regarding the latest empirical findings. In addition, because sport is in many ways a 'mother lode' for social scientists, there is an endless amount of knowledge about – and interest in – how sport and physical activity impact our daily lives. And because most of my students are kinesiology or sport management majors, they are quite eager to learn about a topic they feel equally interested in and often consumed by.

For many of these students who are former or current athletes, some even Division I scholarship athletes, sport is an avocation. It has been my classroom experience over the years that once students are introduced to content material – ranging from sports' history of race and racism, to media coverage of women's sports, to the arms race in big-time college athletics – they are not only deeply interested in and concerned about these sport-as-microcosm issues, they also realize they can pursue a professional career in some aspect of the sporting enterprise. In sum, what's not to love about teaching sport sociology?

Do Sociologists of Sport Like Sport?

I obviously cannot speak for all sociologists, but the ones I do know run the gamut from loving sport as both a participant and a fan, to cringing in disgust at sports' ever increasing (or at least more publicly visible) 'dark side'. It has also been my experience that as more and more of this dark side is exposed – from the incredibly damaging physical and mental health consequences that routinely result from sport participation, to the outrageous off-the-field behaviour of mostly male athletes – even those sociologists who have truly loved sport (including myself) find it increasingly difficult to embrace it as we once did.

Many of my non-sports loving friends often confront me with one of these latest outrages and ask me how I can justify my interest in and love for sports. I find myself saying something along these lines: 'I can't justify what so much of the sports world has to offer these days, but there are many other aspects of sport that reflect the very best of who and what we are'. If I am lucky I get an opportunity to state my case. I remind these friends that sport can inspire individuals and even an entire nation as when we witnessed US Olympic swimmer Katie Ledecky and gymnast Simone Biles capture gold medals. Or when we read about the various ways that sport serves as a vehicle for upward mobility, especially for economically disadvantaged urban youth. For example, Sage and Eitzen (2013) cite studies indicating that attending college as a student-athlete can increase the probability of attaining high-paying, high-status jobs.

I realize that for every study or dramatic example I cite I can find equally as many examples reinforcing the notion – and reality – that supporting and even loving sports can mean checking one's moral compass at the stadium door. But in my defence, I would like to point out that during these most difficult times in America, where we find ourselves in unchartered waters and staring at the abyss, sports have given me an always present, familiar and comforting distraction. I have a feeling (suspicion?) that when I compare myself to other sociologists I am not alone in this regard.

Is the Sociologist of Sport a 'Public Intellectual'?

What does it mean to be a 'public intellectual'? And how does (or doesn't) that fit with being a scholar? The primary professional organization for sport sociologists – the North American Society for the Sociology of Sport (NASSS) – devoted its 2016 conference theme to precisely this topic. Highlighting a number of social concerns ranging from public money being diverted into private stadiums, to massive corruption within international sport organizations, to college coaches in the United States being the highest paid employees in their state institutions, conference organizers asked us to consider the role of sport sociology in general and sport sociologists in particular when confronting such notions (and practises) of widespread inequality. How can we mobilize our research findings and platforms as internationally recognized scholars in the service of public engagement? In sum, what is our role beyond investigating the institution of sport within the scientific enterprise?

For many sport sociologists, including myself, conceptualizing and conducting research begins with a commitment to make our findings accessible beyond publications and presentations. More specifically, I try to use language that is easily understood by a general audience and frame my work, particularly the applications of my findings, in ways that can be used by decision makers to inform public policy and/or generate social change. A recent personal yet professional example illustrates my point. As mentioned, my reputation as a scholar comes primarily from my research on media coverage of women's sports. Over the years I have learned that the media love writing about the media. As a result, I am frequently asked by major print and broadcast outlets (e.g., *The New York Times, U.S.A. Today;* Minnesota Public Radio) to be interviewed about my latest research findings.

This level of national attention led to an invitation in 2014 to give a paper at the annual meeting of the Associated Press Sports Editors in Washington, D.C. I accepted the invitation because these individuals wield significant power over how much, and in what way, coverage is generated. I was able to present empirical data which demonstrated that 'selling sex' in the coverage of women's sports is actually counterproductive in terms of increasing interest in women's sports (Kane & Maxwell, 2011; Kane et al., 2013). In such a 'public engagement' venue, I provided these key decision makers with research-based information about how coverage which fails to emphasize women's athletic accomplishments does not encourage fans, particularly 35- to 55-year-old females and the 'dads with daughters' demographic, to read their respective newspapers. With this particular example in mind (and there are many others), I can say unequivocally that sport sociologists can indeed be engaged as public intellectuals.

ABOUT SOCIOLOGY OF SPORT IN THE ACADEMY

Does Sociology of Sport Face Institutional/Industry Barriers?

The answer to this question in many ways relates to the discussion about sport sociologists as 'public intellectuals' who use our research in the service of social change. It also relates to the issue of framing one's research in critical theory in general and critical feminist theory in particular. When a scholar's research is grounded in the proposition that mainstream social, political and economic forces not only dominate the institution of sport, but that these same forces also contribute to the status quo of, for example, racial and gender inequality, tensions are bound to arise. One way to see such tensions play out in ways that directly confront industry barriers involves an examination of off- and on-the-field violence in intercollegiate and professional sports such as football. Numerous scholars have long argued that cultural definitions, ideologies and practises of sport create and reinforce a 'cult of masculinity' that glorifies and rewards violence and physical aggression (Coakley, 2015; Kane & Disch, 1993; Messner, 1992; Young, 2012). As Coakley points out, an outgrowth of this phenomenon is that 'violence in sports [reaffirms] a gender ideology that assumes the "natural superiority of men" [and] is based on the belief that an ability to do violence is an essential feature of manhood' (2015, p. 176). He further argues that off-the-field group dynamics in men's team sports are often associated with physical and sexual assaults against women. This is precisely why sport scholars have made the claim that football engenders a rape-like culture, and further, why some research indicates that male athletes in combat-oriented sports appear to have higher sexual assault rates when compared to their male peers who do not play sports (Coakley, 2015).

On-the-field violence is also enormously harmful to the players themselves (Young, 2004). For example, a great deal of media attention and public discourse have focused on the damaging consequences of debilitating injuries such as concussion. We now know that for decades, the NFL refused to acknowledge an association between playing professional football and brain damage such as CTE, let alone accept a cause-and-effect relationship (Reimer, 2016). With billions of dollars at stake it is not at all surprising that the 'captains of industry', from professional leagues like the NFL to educational organizations like the NCAA, have aggressively resisted the kind of empirically driven data produced – and critically analysed by – sport sociology scholars.

With respect to facing institutional barriers, we need look no further than the Academy itself. It is still often the case that academic departments in Research 1 universities base promotion and tenure decisions on criteria tied to more traditional research methods and belief systems where positivism (i.e., 'objective' research) is seen as the only legitimate way to conduct science. In such instances, sport sociologists who engage in research using qualitative methodology, and take a critical, activist approach to the interpretation and use of their findings, may find themselves confronting rather difficult odds when seeking tenure. In an interrelated vein, these same scholars may encounter difficulties when trying to get their research published in that many peer-reviewed journals continue to be much more open – meaning willing to publish – studies that are quantitative in nature and hew toward a much more positivist approach.

What is the Future of the Sociology of Sport?

From my perspective, the future of sport sociology as an academic endeavour and a professional career is a very mixed bag. On the one hand, interest in all levels and types of sport appears to be insatiable, from the participants themselves to the fans as well as the ubiquitous sport media. Interest in sport is increasingly reflected in social media as in blogging and websites such as espnW. But within higher education there has been little (if any) increase in the number of academic majors – or even emphasis areas – devoted to the sociology of sport. In addition, curricular offerings are still heavily concentrated in either Kinesiology or Exercise and Sport Science departments versus departments of Sociology.

At the 2016 NASSS conference, there were a number of panels devoted to this very topic. For example, one panel focused on ways to more directly connect sport sociology to other academic disciplines such as movement science and sport management, while another panel examined ways to make sport sociology more relevant to the discipline of sociology overall. One theme – or reality –which emerged across the panels was that an increasing number of graduate students and faculty members are also aligned with Sport Administration and Sport Management programmes. Current NASSS President Theresa Walton-Fisette recently made precisely this point: 'We've seen [NASSS] membership split away from our historic connections with Sport History and Sport Psychology. Many of our members now go to NASSM [Sport Management's annual conference] as their other main conference … This [trend] is reflected in the work that has been presented at NASSS in the past five years' (T. Walton-Fisette, personal communication, 14 January 2017). Finally, though membership in NASSS has remained relatively stable over the last decade or so, we are only talking about 350–400 members (B. Riemer, personal communication, 16 January 2017).

In spite of such a grim assessment of the current state of sport sociology within higher education overall, there are a few areas where enrolments in courses such as Sport & Society are flourishing. One such place is the University of Minnesota where I have been a faculty member since 1989. One of our most popular courses at the undergraduate level is Sport in a Diverse Society. It was recently approved as meeting a general education requirement so we have students who enrol from all across the University coming from a variety of academic majors. In the 2016–2017 academic calendar alone, 351 students took the course generating 1,053 credit hours. Another positive sign is the number of peer-reviewed journals specifically publishing research on sport from a social science perspective. Such journals include: *Sociology of Sport*, *Communication & Sport* and the *International Review for the Sociology of Sport*.

The title of this chapter calls attention to my experiences and perspectives as a scholar who has spent close to 30 years examining how and why sport matters. It has been an enormous honour and privilege to do so. And even though the statistics and trend lines I highlighted above should give one pause about the future of sport sociology, particularly in the Academy, I nevertheless want to encourage those faculty members and students who also have a great interest in and commitment to studying sport to become (or stay) engaged. Sport remains one of the most challenging, often difficult to defend, yet incredibly compelling institutions this country has ever produced. In the final analysis, studying sport truly does matter. Those who choose to do so will find more than a few equally committed fellow travellers – including yours truly – along the way.

REFERENCES

Acosta, R. V., & Carpenter, L. J. (1988). Women in intercollegiate sport. A longitudinal study – eleven year update, 1977–1988. Retrieved from ERIC database. (ED314381).

Acosta, R. V., & Carpenter, L. J. (2014). Women in intercollegiate sport: A longitudinal study. *Women in Sport and Physical Activity Journal, 9*(2), 141–144.

Alsher, J. (2016, November 15). What are the most valuable college sports conferences in 2016? Retrieved from http://www.cheatsheet.com/sports/most-valuable-conferences-college-sports-2016.html/?a=viewall

Birrell, S. (2000). Feminist theories for sport. In J. Coakley & E. Dunning (Eds.), *Women, sport, and culture* (pp. 221–244). London: Sage.

Coakley, J. J. (2015). *Sport in society: Issues & controversies* (11th ed.). New York, NY: McGraw-Hill.

Eime, R. M., Young, J. A., Harvey, J. T., Charity, M. J., & Payne, W. R. (2013). A systematic review of the psychological and social benefits of participation is sport for adults: Informing development of a conceptual model of health through sport. *International Journal of Behavioral Nutrition and Physical Activity.* doi:10.1186/1479-5868-10-135

Fink, J. S., Kane, M. J., & LaVoi, N. M. (2014). The freedom to choose: Elite female athletes' preferred representations within endorsement opportunities. *Journal of Sport Management, 28*(2), 207–219.

Heitner, D. (2014, June 17). Sports licensing soars to $698 million in royalty revenue. Retrieved from http://www.forbes.com/sites/darrenheitner/2014/06/17/sports-licensing-soars-to-698-million-in-royalty-revenue/#10dddc7741b7

Hoeber, L. (2007). Exploring the gaps between meanings and practices of gender equity in a sport organization. *Gender, Work and Organization, 14*(3), 259–280.

Janetsky, M. (2016, December 12). Cardinals receiver Michael Floyd arrested on DUI charge in Scottsdale. Retrieved from http://www.azcentral.com/story/news/local/scottsdale-breaking/2016/12/12/cardinals-receiver-michael-floyd-arrested-dui-charge-scottsdale/95338172/

Kane, M. J. (1988). Media coverage of the female athlete before, during and after Title IX: *Sports Illustrated* revisited. *Journal of Sport Management, 2*(2), 87–99.

Kane, M. J. (1996). Media coverage of the post Title-IX female athlete: A feminist analysis of sport, gender, and power. *Duke Journal of Gender Law & Public Policy, 3*, 95–127.

Kane, M. J. (2016). A socio-cultural examination of a lack of women coaches in sport leadership positions. In N. M. LaVoi (Ed.), *Women in sports coaching* (pp. 35–48). New York, NY: Routledge.

Kane, M. J., & Disch, L. (1993). Sexual violence and the reproduction of male power in the locker room: A critical analysis of the "Lisa Olson incident". *Sociology of Sport Journal, 10*(4), 331–352.

Kane, M. J., & LaVoi, N. M. (2017). An examination of intercollegiate athletic directors' attributions regarding the underrepresentation of female coaches in women's sports. Manuscript submitted for publication.

Kane, M. J., LaVoi, N. M., & Fink, J. S. (2013, February 13). Exploring elite female athletes' interpretations of sport media images: A window into the construction of social identity and "selling sex" in women's sports. *Communication and Sport.* doi:10.1177/2167479512473585

Kane, M. J., & Maxwell, H. D. (2011). Expanding the boundaries of sport media research: Using critical theory to explore consumer responses to representations of women's sports. *Journal of Sport Management, 25*(3), 202–216.

Kane, M. J., & Stangl, J. M. (1991). Employment patterns of female coaches in men's athletics: Tokenism and marginalization as reflections of occupational sex-segregation. *Journal of Sport and Social Issues, 15*(1), 21–41.

Kanter, R. M. (1977). *Men and women of the corporation.* New York, NY: Basic Books.

LaVoi, N. M. (Ed.). (2016). *Women in sports coaching.* New York, NY: Routledge.

LaVoi, N. M., & Kane, M. J. (2014). Sociological aspects of sport. In P. M. Pedersen & L. Thibault (Eds.), *Contemporary sport management* (5th ed., pp. 426–449). Champaign, IL: Human Kinetics.

Loy, J. W., & Kenyon, G. S. (Eds.). (1969). *Sport, culture and society.* Toronto: The Macmillan Company.

Messner, M. (1992). *Power at play*. Boston, MA: Beacon Press.

Messner, M. (2002). *Taking the field: Women, men, and sports*. Minneapolis, MN: University of Minnesota Press.

NFL players say NO MORE to domestic violence & sexual assault in new PSA. (n.d.). Retrieved from http://nomore.org/nflplayerspsa/

Reimer, A. (2016, March 28). The NFL's crusade to mask the dangers of head trauma looks worse than ever. Retrieved from http://www.sbnation.com/nfl/2016/3/28/11250362/nfl-concussions-cte-connection-roger-goodell-comments

Sage, G. H., & Eitzen, D. S. (2013). *Sociology of North American sport*. New York, NY: Oxford University Press.

Stangl, J. M., & Kane, M. J. (1991). Structural variables that offer explanatory power for the under-representation of women coaches since Title IX: The case of homologous reproduction. *Sociology of Sport Journal, 8*, 47–60. (Authors acknowledge equal contribution).

Woodyard, C. (2016, February 7). Super Bowl ad costs soar—but so does buzz. Retrieved from http://www.usatoday.com/story/money/2016/02/07/super-bowl-ad-costs-soar——but-so-does-buzz/79903058/

Young, K. (Ed.). (2004). *Sporting bodies, damaged selves: Sociological studies of sports-related injury*. Amsterdam: Elsevier.

Young, K. (2012). *Sport, violence and society*. London: Routledge.

CHAPTER 7

MY JOURNEY: PERSONAL REFLECTIONS ON A SOCIOLOGICAL CRAFT

Joseph Maguire

INTRODUCTION

There are dangers in looking back on life. There is a tendency to suffer from wilful nostalgia and/or to romanticize the past. Consciously, or otherwise, we select that which we wish to remember or seek to celebrate or acknowledge. Additionally, the path taken might appear too logical, thought-through and guided by some overarching plan. If that were so I would not have remained at the same university for so long. In addition, the focus tends to be on the positive figures in one biography, omitting the knaves, fools and charlatans who have also been encountered, worked with or had the misfortune to meet. Yet, why dwell on them? In looking back, however, it maybe that in doing so we lose sight of the need to see the road ahead. In fact, the opportunity presented by this retrospective account makes it clearer to me as to why I am pursuing the academic journey I am currently undertaking. Looking back makes this author realize the role and form of sleeping memories that are part of the choices of sociological topics pursued in the past and the present day. This is something I will return to in my concluding remarks.[1]

Reflections on Sociology of Sport: Ten Questions, Ten Scholars, Ten Perspectives
Research in the Sociology of Sport, Volume 10, 101–117
ISSN: 1476-2854/doi:10.1108/S1476-285420170000010007

ABOUT THE AUTHOR

Mentors and Influential Figures

I first encountered Eric Dunning in 1975, or 1976, in the university library in London. I say 'encountered', not in person, but via his edited collection *Readings in the Sociology of Sport*. The work was listed on the module course reading of Bob Pearton, one of my undergraduate tutors (he, along with Eric Dunning and myself, would later edit *The Sports Process*, 1993). In reading this collection of essays, timing and location proved crucial in ontological and epistemological terms – and also in my subsequent embrace of figurational/process sociological studies. Let me explain.

In Britain, in the mid to late 1970s sociology was rediscovering both its classical Marxist past and its roots in interpretive sociology. Such trends would find expression in social history work, new directions in the sociology of education and a critical turn in deviance and criminological studies. I was the beneficiary of this via my enthusiastic lecturers in history and education. Such trends would also find expression in sociology of sport courses taught by Bob Pearton. Thus, I was introduced to the work of classical theorists, and also to contemporary work by Brohm (1978), Hoch (1972), Rigauer (1981), and Vinnai (1973). For me, at the time, their writings made sense. Such work was certainly polemical, but, equally, the insights outlined in their writing were also consciousness-raising.

Not all of my fellow students were so predisposed to or 'switched on' by such 'radical' thinking. This might have been a consequence of a background in history – at school and university – and the curriculum being taught. It dovetailed with my 'outsider' status – an Irish Catholic reared on rebel songs and family stories of resistance. It is important to note what was present and also what was absent. As a feature of the time there was little direct attention to questions of gender or 'race', though re-reading Vinnai later, I could see clearly that his work was also a contribution to the study of masculinity. Resistance, at this time, was class and nationalism based. Yet, some early signs of what was to follow were evident – some liberal feminist work and readings on race and sport by writers such as Hargreaves (1982) and Edwards (1985) appeared. Crucially, the courses taken were not modules – you had time on your hands to 'read around'. Reading lists were to be read and there was a library to go to. Philosophy of Sport courses dovetailed with Philosophy of Education courses. Hence, encounters with Jean-Paul Sartre, Martin Heidegger, Søren Kierkegarrd and Alfred Schultz (in retrospect, I realize that such readings would influence how I would eventually write about what I termed a 'quest for exciting significance'). This, however, is to jump the biography a little too far ahead.

Questions of violence and sport would also figure as part of the courses in sociology of sport courses. Indeed, that was Bob Pearton's own research area supervised by Eric Dunning. Eric Dunning would also give occasional lectures at the University of London's Institute of Education. It was here that our paths first crossed – in 1978. I remember being impressed, but am at a loss to remember the exact topic, though it may have been on the socio-historical aspects of association football. Both tutor and future supervisor were friends and, as a feature of the then informality of British academia, and of Eric Dunning's academic habitus, I was invited along for a beer, and listen to faculty discuss sport. Yet, my first research on sport, an undergraduate dissertation, was mainly informed by a symbolic interactionist/phenomenological perspective – exploring the process of becoming and being a Physical Education teacher! Gone were the functionalist, quantitative studies of the 1960s that sought causal links between sporting participation and academic attainment (though sadly such stuff appears back in fashion). There was no figurational sociology in sight – the nearest link was the work of Bernstein (1975) and his research on class, codes and control. More broadly, the intellectual context was driven by readings in Marxist sociology of education and symbolic interactionist/phenomenological insights into sport – it was this that occupied my space of possibilities. That was about to change.

My move from London to Leicester was driven by my application for a doctoral studentship funded by the then Social Science Research Council (SSRC), though I had thought of applying to US universities for a graduate assistantship to study for a Master's degree. Leicester University possessed what was probably the most important sociology department in post-war United Kingdom. Eric Dunning and Patrick Murphy (then a Senior Lecturer in the Department of Sociology) had secured funding from SSRC to study the social roots of football hooligan violence. The studentship, under Eric Dunning's supervision dovetailed well with aspects of my academic and social background. The thesis ended up studying the long-term emergence of football hooliganism as a social problem from the late Victorian period through to the 1970s – possibly the first doctoral thesis on football hooliganism.

A more long-lasting, and profoundly more enriching impact than simply gaining the PhD, was Eric Dunning's supervision style and substance. His role as mentor involved an apprenticeship in sociological craft and the development of an academic habitus. On returning from various archive adventures Eric, patient and supportive, would offer two abiding pieces of advice that I have passed onto my own doctoral students – 'to find nothing is to find something' and 'think until it hurts'. Chapters returned were a master class in the craft of writing and of writing in a process sociological manner – avoidance both of using language that reduced processes to static variables or states, and of a thinking/writing style that gave primacy to a single variable, a priori, and thus, in advance of where the evidence led. Given ongoing debates about questions related to involvement and detachment in sociological enquiry what struck me, and has stayed with me, is that Eric Dunning was an involved scholar, committed in a Weberian sense to sociology as a vocation (Dunning, 1972, 1999). I have tried to follow in this path.

This intellectual habitus – both a way of thinking (detachment) and way of feeling (involvement) was a commitment to the sociological craft – which contemporaries of mine supervised by colleagues such as John Loy might have termed the sociological imagination. The task was an attempt to 'solve' sociological puzzles – some of which were also social puzzles (problems). Ingrained within this habitus was a disposition to be critical, to embody curiosity, to make connections across time, space, place – to see the bigger picture, now known as 'big history'. While this task was then and remains a work in progress, it was meant to be enjoyed, to take pleasure from the excitement of the research at hand and to probe what significance it has. I see this now as a form of play – a sociologica ludens akin to Huizinga's notion of homo ludens (Huizinga, 2000). My current work is a form of play from which I take pleasure but which also seeks to probe its significance to me, and to others.

In being part of the 'Leicester School' – associated with figurational/process sociology – and conducting a PhD in this context, it might surprise and enlighten some to realize the latitude offered by Eric Dunning. 'Go where you're thinking takes you' was also his mantra. Thus, while Eric was pivotal to my sociological craft and academic habitus, I read widely in Marxist theory and social history, critical criminology and the emergent cultural studies. Certainly, in my thesis all of these strands came together in helping to understand the emergence of football hooliganism as a social problem. And then, of course, work by writers such as Gruneau (1983), Hargreaves (1982), Hargreaves (1987), Whannel (1980), and Whitson (1984) and others, began to be published. The social field of sport studies was widening and deepening. Rather than gaining a post-doctoral fellowship at Oxford in criminology I took a post in sociology of sport – a turn of events that I came to see in later life as a 'sliding door'.

Drawing on the strands that made up my doctoral reading it never seemed to me that no one group could lay hegemonic claim to being critical, or that the various strands outlined were as incompatible as some suggested. For me, these various strands overlapped and were a necessary part, along with other approaches, to our understanding of sport, culture and society. That remains my view. Indeed, following my doctoral work, the two strands I pursued – what in retrospect would be seen as work on the body and globalization – encapsulated a range of approaches, all of which I saw as necessary if perhaps not sufficient. The figurational/process sociology approach became the lodestar around which I drew in other ideas, thinking and orientations (Maguire, 1999, 2005, 2013; Maguire, Jarvie, Mansfield, & Bradley, 2002).

Research Trajectory

Work on the body extended my thinking on violence and, hence, my work on the emotions, bodies, pain and injuries. Here, consciously or otherwise, I was revising aspects of Elias and Dunning's (1986) 'quest for excitement'. Drawing from readings and my own empirical research, I developed the notion that what was at stake in sport was a 'quest for exciting significance'. In hindsight, I wish I had continued this vein of research, though those I have supervised for doctoral work have pursued this further. I regret, then, that the lived experiences, contested identities and symbolic, existential dimensions of sporting lives, were not as fully explored by me as they could have been. In subsequent years, my good friend, and brilliant academic colleague, Alan Klein (1991) would often say to me that I should have accompanied him more into the anthropological field.

My early work on Americanization, bound up in debates that were current in the United Kingdom in the 1980s, also reflected questions of identity politics. This latter concern related to my own identity, biography and family history, shared in various ways and degrees by the Irish living in the United Kingdom. Hence, in moving from questions of Americanization to the broader discussion of globalization, my research considered questions of the reconfiguration of the state, the ongoing significance of the nation and nationalism, and matters relating to global flows, the role of TNCs, and the emergence of the sports—medical—industrial complex Maguire (1999, 2005, 2013). My current work, as I will indicate in the conclusion, has returned full circle (Liston & Maguire, 2016). Questions of identity, the nation and nationalism underpin ongoing research.

In retrospect, the twin themes of the body and globalization may appear part of a grand plan. There was no such thing. Interests and concerns reinforced and reflected the social currents and academic tides that I was caught up in. Yet, within this, I sought to navigate a course. At a global level, this involved presidency of the International Sociology of Sport Association (ISSA), engagement with the wider sociological community and legitimating the study of sport more broadly. At a local level, I sought to locate sociology of sport within sport and exercise sciences, reflecting a need to engage with natural sciences but also to ensure that power resources and status would allow sociology of sport to grow and flourish, not only at Loughborough University, but across the United Kingdom as a whole. This research and pedagogical strategy may have helped over the past three decades, but is now in retreat.

ABOUT SPORT

Why Does Sport Matter?

In comparison with art, sport might seem unimportant or mundane. These are value-judgements. In the study of art, sociologists do not seek to make aesthetic judgements. And, as Georg Simmel astutely noted, the seemingly mundane can be significant (Simmel, 1978). In political, economic, cultural and social terms, sport is highly significant. Indeed, it is the very everyday ordinariness of sport that makes it so significant, so deeply intertwined with the workings of society. Let me explain why this is so with reference to the role of heroes and champions.

Homer's *The Iliad* and *The Odyssey* are two of the oldest texts surviving in western literature. They conjure up images of heroic deeds and of warriors such as Hector and Achilles. The qualities of these heroes, who were champions of their city states, are captured by Homer in a way that endures over time. Reading these legends captures the lived and embodied experience of heroism. Is there anything left to say and what does such mythology have to tell us about sport today? What is it to be a champion and why do they mean so much to us? In a simple sense, a champion is someone who is the first among all contestants or competitors and in this regard, the word refers to the ability of an individual or team to win a contest or championship. Yet, the origin of the word indicates a different usage and offers a clue as to why champions are so much more important to us than just their ability to win and why we attach such meaning to them. Its first usage, in English, emerged in the context of the medieval tournament and referred to the person who would act as a champion of others; who would defend, support or *champion* a cause.

In this sense, athletes are not simply champions of their sport, but also of their local community and nation and sometimes, humanity as a whole. An example of this *par excellence* is the late Muhammad Ali. A champion is said to possess special gifts and exude a certain charisma: they perform 'miracles' and achieve the seemingly impossible – akin to the heroes captured by Homer. Athletes, for better and for worse, are our modern heroes – symbolic representations of our cultural values and who we would wish to be. Champions are talented individuals but as heroes they are people whose lives tell stories about us, to ourselves, and also to people from other nations.

People appreciate excellence and have a desire to achieve it and, if not, then at least to share in it. The champion allows us to catch a glimpse of what we could be: by representing us they make us vicariously fulfilled human beings. They are our modern heroes because sport has become the forum in which communal self-revelation occurs. That is, modern sport is a form of surrogate religion and popular theatre in which there occurs the communal discovery of who we are. Sports stadia are contemporary venues in which we can observe champions as heroes and experience the 'sacred', moments of exciting significance, while leaving behind the profaneness of ordinary life. In this sense, society needs its champions as heroes. They perform the manifest function of achieving sporting success for themselves and their local community and nation. But they also perform a more latent role: they are meant to embody the elements that a society values most. As idealized creations, they provide inspiration, motivation, direction and meaning for people's lives. Champions as heroes act to unify a society, bringing people together with a common sense of purpose and values. That is how *modern* sport developed. Pioneers of the nineteenth century linked sport to muscular Christianity: unselfishness, self-restraint, fairness, gentlemanliness and moral excellence. This was itself supplementing traditional notions of chivalry: honour, decency, courage and loyalty. These qualities are some of the very attributes associated with the long-retired footballer Sir Bobby Charlton (England World Cup winner in 1966 and team member of the winning Manchester United European Cup team of 1968) as well as more recent champions.

Despite the sense of nobility that Bobby Charlton embodied, there are, how-ever, threats to the manifest and latent functions of champions as heroes. This stems from issues associated with authenticity and integrity. The status of the champion relies upon the authenticity of the contest. If the contest is tarnished by corruption, cheating, drug-taking or betting scandals, then the hero is diminished in our eyes. The contest is no longer either a mutual quest for excellence or societies forum in which communal self-revelation occurs. This lack of authenticity also occurs when the sport becomes too make-believe, is rigged or becomes too predictable. And the tentacles of the sports—medical—industrial—complex entangle us in geopolitical intrigue and moral dilemmas. Elite sport produces 'champions' but not all are heroes.

The champion as hero also, as noted, embodies the elements that a society holds most dear. But, the integrity of the champion may also be undermined in several ways. The champion may be a flawed genius – either due to the fact that they suffer from hubris and feel they need not dedicate themselves to the level and intensity of preparation and performance required, and/or because their private lives intrude on their status as heroes. Here, the examples of George Best and Paul Gascoigne spring to mind. George Best who played for Manchester United in the 1960s is still regarded both as the finest Irish foot-baller ever and also as the fifth Beatle, due to his celebrity status, arguably the first footballer who crossed the sport/celebrity divide. Paul Gascoigne, played football for England – fame came early for him and the attention he received created undue media pressures. On retirement in 2002 he experienced a range of personal difficulties. Thus, our idealized image of them as athletes is shat-tered, though in the case of Best, we still mourn his death in a profound expres-sion of grief. In addition, our champion maybe less of a hero and more a celebrity – they are famous but not heroic. David Beckham may be seen in this light. If this is the case, such fame is short-lived and they fail one of the tests of a 'true' champion as hero – the test of time. In order to understand why it is that a champion mean so much to us, and what impact they have, we have to consider the role sport plays in society.

Sport is both a separate world, and a suspension of everyday life, yet is also highly symbolic of the society in which it exists and embedded in wider politi-cal-economic and socio-cultural currents. In the context of sport, we can both experience a form of exciting significance that we rarely, if ever, encounter in our daily lives, and also conduct a symbolic dialogue with fellow participants and spectators that reveals things about ourselves and others. We are laid bare in sport in ways which we cover up in everyday life. Sport is a modern morality play that reveals fundamental truths about us as individuals, our societies and our relations with others. Sport, then, moves us emotionally and matters to us socially. That sport performs these functions relates to several reasons that dovetail with and highlight the role of champions.

One of the principal features of sport is the arousal of pleasurable forms of excitement. People appear to have a need to experience various kinds of spontaneous, elementary, unreflective yet pleasurable excitement in increasingly rule governed and risk-averse societies. In sport, whether as a participant or spectator, people quest for this controlled decontrolling of emotions. Here, emotions flow freely and do so in a way that elicits or imitates the excitement generated in real-life situations. Sports, then, are mimetic activities that provide a 'make-believe' separate setting that allows emotions to flow more easily. This excitement is elicited by the creation of tensions that can involve imaginary or controlled 'real' danger, mimetic fear and/or pleasure, sadness and/or joy. This controlled decontrolling of excitement allows for different moods to be evoked in this make-believe setting that are the siblings of those aroused in real-life situations. Our champions are identified with – in terms of their technical accomplishments but also in terms of the emotions they, and thus, we, go through, in terms of the well-played game or thrilling contest.

Tie-breaks in tennis, penalty shoot-outs in football and sudden death play-offs in golf evoke a range of emotions, so much so that by the end of the contest we are emotionally drained. And, unlike a well-performed play or well-acted film, we know that what we were witnessing in sport is real and that the outcome was not determined beforehand. Sometimes, our champions fulfil their own and our dreams but, on other occasions, the tragedy of defeat must be endured. A champion, such as Roger Federer, on entering Centre Court at Wimbledon can observe a plaque that displays Rudyard Kipling's poem *If*. The poem notes, that when you meet triumph and disaster you have to meet those impostors just the same. In dealing with triumph, and defeat, in Wimbledon finals Federer has arguably embodied such sentiments.

Only when sports are associated with matters of deep cultural and personal significance do they become important to fans. Major sporting events are thus mythic spectacles where fans are provided the opportunity for collective participation and identification that serves as a means of celebrating and reinforcing shared cultural meanings. It is precisely because sports are a 'separate world' that they are able to celebrate shared cultural meanings that are expressed through and embodied by champions. The anthem, the emblem and the flag associated with sporting contests highlights how champions represent the nation. The England World Cup team of 1966 became world champions but also have had a collective heroism attached to them. Their success has stood the test of time – it still moves England fans. But it is perhaps the iconic images of Bobby Moore, then England captain, who died young from cancer, that remain etched in people's minds. This gives a clue to the fact that the symbolism of sport, and the role played by the champion, is even deeper than mere nationalism and patriotism. Bobby Moore symbolized something more than winning.

If social life can be conceived of as a game through which identities are established, tested and developed then sports can be viewed as idealized forms of social life. Its rules and codes of play (such as in golf etiquette) allow for a fair contest and a true test of ability. The 'true' champion, playing an authentic match, with integrity, is the best expression of this. It is in this context that it is possible to establish an identity with greater consensual and authentic certainty then in social life itself. We insist on the authenticity and integrity of the contest − on the strict formal rules and their fair enforcement − because we want any differences of worth between us to be based on merit. In real life our class, race, gender or religion interfere and rig the game of social life and its outcomes. As such, its victors and losers are profane deceptive illusions. But, on the field of play, sport outcomes are sacred, they are real and authentic. That is also why champions seek to beat fellow champions: that is the true test. Honour and respect are not achieved by knowing in advance that you will beat inferior opponents. The on-field handshake between Bobby Moore and Pele (widely regarded as the best male footballer ever) during the 1970 World Cup match between England and Brazil symbolizes such honour and respect. The 'hand-of-god goal' scored by the Argentinian Diego Maradona, wonderful player though he was, does not. His patriotism expressed by this goal reflected his national status but undermined his stature as a broader hero.

Sport is thus a symbolic dialogue: it symbolizes the strict requirements of how a dialogue should be conducted. Sport, then, involves a dramatic representation of who we are and who we would like to be. The stadium is a theatre in which we experience a range of pleasurable emotional and exciting significance: the excitement of the played-game, uncertain as to its outcome but its significance lying in what we have invested in it emotionally, morally, socially. Our champions as our heroes express both the myths, and revered social values of a society, and the sports ethic that underpins involvement in sport. They have to take risks, to exhibit the hallmarks of bravery and courage and show integrity. That is why we remember them, as we do Hector and Achilles. That is why sport matters.

How Should Sport be Studied?

The question of how sport should be studied is, in part, related to the nature and scope of the enquiry, as a part of the mainstream, sociological discipline, or as part of sport and exercise sciences. What form of sociological explanation you work with will also orientate your enquiry. My approach, drawing on figurational/process sociology, but also engaging with other areas and approaches in sociology, can be outlined in the following way. In examining 'art as collective activity', Becker (1982/1984) highlighted how a specific artistic expression is located within a *network* of suppliers, performers, dealers, agents, managers, critics and consumers. These networks are marked by a series of conventions, taboos, power struggles and commodity chains. Each is essential to the operation of the network and the production of art. Sport performances are no different. Art Worlds then consist of those people whose activities are necessary to the production of art. In examining how these people interact, Becker refers to the 'co-ordination of activities', the use of 'conventional understandings embodied in common practise' and the 'established network of co-operative links among participants' (Becker, 1982/1984, pp. 34–35).

Becker's idea of networks links very well with how I see the set of interdependencies that contour and shape social, and sporting, life. Thus, following Becker and Norbert Elias, I study 'Sport Worlds' as networks, or figurations, of interdependent groups of people. Four key 'points of departure' can be used to sensitize us to the networks that contour Sport Worlds. These points are: (1) human beings are interdependent; their lives evolve in, and are significantly shaped by, the social figurations they form with each other; (2) these figurations are continually in flux, undergoing changes of different orders – some quick and ephemeral, others slower but perhaps more lasting; (3) the long-term developments taking place in human social figurations have been and continue to be largely unplanned and unforeseen; (4) the development of human knowledge takes place within human figurations, and forms one important aspect of their overall development.

These points of departure provide some general lines of orientation to make sense of Sport Worlds, within which Becker's insights into Art Worlds also help to focus on the specific case of sport. For Becker, Art Worlds have five distinguishing characteristics, the first of which, as noted, is the role of networks in their production. Second, the boundaries that surround Art Worlds are permeable – it is difficult to discern what art is, and what is not, without reference to other worlds. And, the production of what is defined as art is dependent on these other social worlds. Third, while the people involved in Art Worlds try to distinguish their world from others, they too have 'intimate and extensive relations' with people from those other worlds. Fourth, Art Worlds are sustained by conventions, but innovations and challenges also occur. Finally, Art Worlds have degrees of relative autonomy from interference by other groups and social worlds. While Becker over-emphasizes the co-operative dimension of Art Worlds (or, conversely, downplays the power struggles that make up such worlds), he effectively questions the extent to which artistic expressions are 'free' and autonomous.

Considered in this light sport can be studied as a form of collective action, involving a host of different people, connected in particular networks, and creating particular forms of sport products and performances.

Attention can be paid to the 'conventional understandings' that mark sport subcultures and govern sport practises. And it is necessary to critically examine the extent to which Sport Worlds are 'relatively autonomous' from the political and economic context in which they are situated. In the 'established networks' linking Sport Worlds to other social worlds, it is necessary to focus both upon the process of co-operation and on the process of confrontation. Co-operation and confrontation, such as that between allies and foes, characterize the networks that shape Sport Worlds. As sociologists examining sport, we are just like our colleagues who examine art, religion, medicine and work — we are all studying how people cope with the problems of interdependence.

Is Sport a Panacea for Social Problems?

Searching for relevance, impact and short-term problem solving can lead you to believe that sport acts as a social glue, a form of social capital and/or a panacea. To re-orientate the debate is necessary. We have to rethink the subject and the subject matter. Sociologists of sport should make their own 'problems', not 'take' the problems defined for them by advocates of sport worlds. Indeed, we need to consider what is a social problem — both its objective conditions and its subjective definitions. It seems clear that those in positions of power and those who advocate for sport management and business curricula do not want sociologists of sport to view the present state of sport worlds as reflecting the sports–medical–industrial complex. The evidential base that sport acts as a panacea is lacking; moreover, this is the wrong question to ask. Indeed, sport may contribute to, exacerbate and create new social problems. The notions of a panacea of relevance and impact are signs of an ideological involvement and magical mythical thinking. A greater degree of detachment is needed.

In order for the sociology of sport community to have a better chance to assess the functions and meanings of sport in the lives of individuals and the communities that they form, it must: build on knowledge for its own sake, contribute to theory and concept development, generate knowledge about and for humankind as a whole, tackle small- and large-scale issues and concerns at local, national and global levels, decide who's side it's on, adopt a 'destroyer of myths' outlook, and develop a critical analysis of power, structures and control. Sadly, sociologists of sport are caught up, to varying degrees cross-culturally, in a competitive career and subject struggle to show their masters at university, national and global levels that their brand of academic practise is what counts. Emancipation from this situation is no easy matter.

ABOUT PRACTISING SOCIOLOGY OF SPORT

Is Teaching Sociology of Sport Easy?

I suspect that my teaching at my home university was not representative of the experience of colleagues more broadly. Over 28 years, I have taught highly qualified students, many of whom were also elite athletes. To assess this experience, it is important to consider the student and the teacher. At the beginning of my career in teaching, it was possible to see before me a student-athlete. Now, anecdotally, and given what we know about the professionalization of elite sport, its growing seriousness and competitiveness, those who I have taught recently have become more like athlete-students.

This trend was also combined with the corporatization of higher education in the United Kingdom. Universities are now proto-businesses, competing for students who now pay fees that are among the highest in the Western world. The structure of degrees has changed; short, discrete, knowledge-packaged learning forms part of the modules students are expected − and demand − to complete. Now more outcome-oriented, students expect and require that degrees enhance their employment opportunities. Into this changing scene, we can also insert the resurgence of advocates of bio-science within sport science.

Yet, within sport and exercise sciences, albeit unevenly across the globe, social sciences and humanities had grown in size and influence. This was evident in an increase in academic positions, curriculum content, publishing and research. These trends reinforced my own biographical experiences outlined earlier. That state of play has now changed. Now, sociology of sport is caught up within the 'vices' of bio-science and sport management/business. The redesign of degree programmes, and the competing claims for modular time, weighting and significance, weighs heavily against sociology of sport. This makes the teaching of sociology of sport more challenging but, within the classroom, no less enjoyable, thrilling and worthwhile.

As a result of the liberal education I received, for me, teaching was and is a 'subversive activity'. Keeping abreast of contemporary events, drawing on the richness of empirical examples and guiding students to sociological theory all informed my teaching. My task was not to promote a single way of interpreting sport, but to help students arrange questions about sport in the right order. Was that easy? No. Was it enjoyable? Yes. In a lecture or tutorial, when students make the connections: that completes your day more so than the debates one sometimes has with colleagues.

Do Sociologists of Sport Like Sport?

'Given what you write, you must not like or have played sport'. Such observations have been a refrain throughout my career. Yet, the question is not simply about whether sociologists of sport like sport, or have done sport, but: do they need to? After all, in studying crime − murder for example − criminologists need not like the murderers nor do they have had to have been one. That is not to say, in some *verstehen* sense, that you do not need to involve yourself, immerse yourself in the culture and see things, as far as you can, as the participants see themselves.

Yet, what I liked about sport when I was young is not what I like now. My vantage point is different. I know more, and my role is now more diffuse − participant, member, spectator, coach, parent, observer, activist and sociologist. The desire to see a well-played game, to see the exciting significance of a rugby victory for Ireland over England, to protect your children in playing sport and to observe that there needs to be a critical analysis of the global sport power elite and the inequalities of the sports−medical−industrial complex are not mutually exclusive.

There is, however, something 'rotten' at the heart of global sport. University presidents are in awe of the athletics department, former sportsmen and women seek power and connive in the drug and corruption abuses of their sport, and the sports−medical−industrial complex's tentacles reach into all levels of the sport community. At university level, this compromises the mission of the university, contributes to its rebranding as a world-class firm but marginalizes critical thinkers within the institution. We do not have to like sport, or like the trends we observe in sport; our task is to capture things as they really are. For sociologists of sport that task has become harder in recent times.

Is the Sociologist of Sport a 'Public Intellectual'?

Given the trends outlined above, the sociologist of sport *must* engage as a public intellectual. Concerned less with being a brand intellectual, and chasing short-term impact and relevance, sociologists of sport must critically evaluate the status quo and, through their teaching and research, inform students, media personnel, politicians and sport administrators. They must speak truth to − and with − authority. Alternative facts, fake news and intellectual relativism go hand-in-hand to erode the capacity of the sociologist of sport to see how things really are.

Sociologists of sport face two challenges. The first is about deconstructing the status quo, and challenging current orthodoxies. The second is about establishing under what conditions adequate knowledge about sport can be generated and disseminated in various public realms. For Ingham and Lawson (1999, p. 19), the social-trustee, civic science and professionalism approach requires that academics should 'integrate their formal roles with that of their own citizenship'. As public intellectuals academics have to become sensitive to the production, dissemination, curriculum development and application of the knowledge they provide. The same issues apply whether we are providing knowledge for students, athletes, coaches, administrators, the media, governmental agencies or Trans National Corporations (TNCs). A series of questions have to be addressed including: How wasteful is the present system? Who are the winners and the losers in global sport – both on and off the field of play, at different levels of sport and in different modes of movement culture? What are the costs, as well as the benefits to the system being constructed – for the individual, the community and the society as a whole?

Answers to these questions lie in an analysis of the specific position sociologists of sport have with sports science and the sports–medical–industrial complex. A shift from a human performance model to a human development model in sport and exercise sciences would not only provide emancipatory knowledge for sport communities and societies as a whole, it would also release the sports science community from the tentacles of achievement sport. Thus, 'involved advocacy' of a human development model – with its emphasis on justice, citizenship and equity is required. Social-trustee, civic science professionals must act 'as stewards of the just society' and act to 'protect and support free spheres of action and public social spaces' (Ingham & Lawson, 1999, p. 19).

These observations need to be extended and linked to a consideration of environmental concerns, green issues and the development of notions of sustainable sport. In so doing, sociologists of sport would be engaging in forms of 'committed service'. My fear, however, is that the academic and cultural conditions are becoming less conducive to the generation of such knowledge. Nevertheless, this should not stop us, as a community of scholars, from making the case.

ABOUT SOCIOLOGY OF SPORT IN THE ACADEMY

Does Sociology of Sport Face Institutional/Industry Barriers?

Sociology of sport made significant progress over the last 50 years. Its knowledge base expanded. The known function, meaning and significance of sport became more rooted in reality-congruent knowledge. Institutionally: undergraduate, masters and PhD courses and programmes developed, and publications increased exponentially. Organizationally: developments included the emergence of the ISSA and regional organizations, which – to varying degrees – flourished. Such developments were always uneven, in quality, range and depth. Whatever progress this represents, sociology of sport may have reached a high tide mark and now, it seems, it may be beginning to ebb and retreat.

In part, it was ever thus. From its initial development within departments of physical education and sport science, the sociology of sport has suffered from what Bourdieu (1990) termed 'double jeopardy'. That is, sociology of sport is marginal to the interests and concerns of mainstream sociology. It is also loathed and feared in equal measure by the sport community. In the academic game of whose knowledge counts, sociology of sport was never able to move beyond the margins and constitute part of the essential knowledge of either sociology or sport studies. However well we conduct an analysis of power, we appear less able at gaining and maintaining positions of power. Why so?

I am struck by a seemingly paradoxical feature. On the one hand, there exists the supportive nature of colleagues across many different countries who welcome you to conferences irrespective of theoretical persuasion. On the other hand, and despite being a relatively small, outsider group, we continue to be internally fractious, deconstructing our subject matter and boundary identities, and indulging in paradigmatic rivalries. The world passed us by and thus, positions were lost and our knowledge marginalized. In the eyes of the established, but also students, our status was diminished.

This was not all of our own making. As indicated earlier, changes in academia and in the subject area of sport and exercise science has resulted in the resurgence of the influence of power of the sports−medical−industrial complex. The academy demands relevance, and application to industry. The business of sport is a medical−industrial−complex that requires knowledge that yields results, profits and medals. Sociology of sport advocates find it increasingly difficult to compete in such an academic marketplace. I hope I am wrong.

What is the Future of the Sociology of Sport?

In considering the future of the sociology of sport, its knowledge base is arguably needed now more than ever. Local and global sport worlds are beset by, and contribute to, a range of social, economic and political issues. Questions of ethics combine with issues concerning governance and democracy; the fault lines within and between societies surface along with environmental dilemmas. Elite sport performance also raises profound questions of what it is to be human. These are the known knowns and known unknowns. Yet, there are also problems which the sociology of sport community has not yet grasped internally or externally. These might be said to be unknown unknowns.

Despair, however, is not an option. Utilizing the knowledge of elders − those who have or will soon to retire − would help. Engaging further with sociology and colleagues across the social sciences and humanities would enhance research and provide possible safe harbours for the continuing existence of the sub-discipline. Fostering beacons of hope via centres of excellence, and appreciating rather than denigrating colleagues, would also move things in the right direction. Conference themes that explore dilemmas and challenges would also provide a forum for new ideas, from a different generation living their lives as academics today.

The barriers are real and remain potent, and are growing more so. But, sociology of sport must still make the case for its importance and relevance. For my own part, my current and future work lies, as noted at the outset, in an exploration of identity, nationhood and nationalism, in the context of global sport. This is where my passionate detachment currently lies. Hence, in conjunction with Dr Katie Liston (University of Ulster), our research concerns Ireland, the British Empire and sport. In doing so, we seek to understand our own biographies and those of others; and, at the same time, to contribute to mainstream sociological knowledge, and the sub-discipline of the sociology of sport. In some small way, it may help a broader understanding between the peoples of the British Isles. That is where our future lies. We shall see.

NOTE

1. I would like to record my appreciation to Kevin Young for the invitation to contribute to this volume.

REFERENCES

Becker, H. (1982/1984). *Art worlds*. Berkeley, CA: University of California Press.

Bernstein, B. (1975). Class and pedagogies: Visible and invisible. *Educational Studies*, *1*(1), 23–41.

Bourdieu, P. (1990). Programme for the sociology of sport. In P. Bourdieu (Ed.), *On other words: Essays towards a reflexive sociology* (pp. 156–167). Oxford: Polity Press.

Brohm, J.-M. (1978). *Sport: A prison of measured time*. London: Ink Links.

Dunning, E. (Ed.) (1972). *Readings in the sociology of sport*. London: Cass.

Dunning, E. (1999). *Sport matters: Sociological studies of sport, violence and civilisation*. London: Routledge.

Dunning, E., Maguire, J., & Pearton, R. (Eds.) (1993). *The sports process: Essays in comparative and developmental sociology*. Champaign, IL: Human Kinetics.

Edwards, H. (1985). *The revolt of the black athlete*. Ontario: Collier-Macmillan Limited.

Elias, N., & Dunning, E. (1986). *Quest for excitement: Sport and leisure in the civilising process*. Oxford: Blackwell.

Gruneau, R. (1983). *Class, sport and social development*. Amherst: University of Massachusetts Press.

Hargreaves, J. (Ed.) (1982). *Sport, culture and ideology*. London: Routledge and Kegan Paul.

Hargreaves, J. (1987). *Sport, power and culture: A social and historical analysis of popular sports in Britain*. London: Polity Press.

Hoch, P. (1972). *Rip off the big game: The exploitation of sport by the power elite*. New York, NY: Anchor Books.

Huizinga, J. (2000). *Homo Ludens: A study of the play element in culture*. London: Routledge.

Ingham, A., & Lawson, H. (1999, June). Prolympism and globalization: Knowledge for whom, by whom? Paper presented at the German Association of Sport Science, Heidelberg: Germany.

Klein, A. (1991). *Sugarball: The American game, the Dominican dream*. New Haven, CT: Yale University Press.

Liston, K., & Maguire, J. (2016). Sport, empire and diplomacy: 'Ireland' at the 1930 British empire games. *Statecraft and Diplomacy*, *27*(2), 314–339.

Maguire, J. (1999). Global sport: Individuals, societies, civilisations. Oxford: Polity.

Maguire, J. (2005). *Power and global sport*. London: Routledge.

Maguire, J. (2013). *Reflections on the sociology of sport: 'Walking the line'*. London: Routledge.

Maguire, J., Jarvie, G., Mansfield, L., & Bradley, J. (Eds.) (2002). *Sport worlds: A sociological perspective*. Champaign, IL: Human Kinetics.

Rigauer, B. (1981). *Sport and work*. New York, NY: Columbia University Press.

Simmel, G. (1978). *The Philosophy of Money*. In T. Bottomore & D. Frisby (Ed. & Trans.). London: Routledge & Kegan Paul.

Vinnai, G. (1973). *Football mania*. London: Ocean Books.

Whannel, G. (1980). *Blowing the whistle: The politics of sport*. London: Pluto Press.

Whitson, D. (1984). Sport and hegemony: On the construction of the dominant culture. *Dialectics and Humanism, 11*(1), 5−19.

CHAPTER 8

CARIBBEAN SPORT SOCIOLOGY: THE ONGOING JOURNEY

Roy McCree

INTRODUCTION

My interest in the sociological study of sport started in the late 1980s, when sport was not as commercialized and studied as it is today. This period also coincided with a spate or spurt of publications on sport drawn mainly from history (Mangan, 1986, 1988; Manley, 1988), political science (Allison, 1986) and particularly sociology (Gruneau, 1983; Gruneau & Cantelon, 1982; Hargreaves, 1982, 1986; Horne, David, & Tomlinson, 1987; Lawrence & Rowe, 1986; Mandle & Mandle, 1988; Williams, Dunning, Murphy, 1984/1989) as the study of sport started to be taken more seriously. In this chapter, I reflect on some of my experiences working in this field over the last 30 years and comment on a range of issues relating to the significance of sport, the teaching of the sociology of sport, public sport sociology, the challenges of the subdiscipline, as well as its future as a field of endeavour.

ABOUT THE AUTHOR

Mentors and Influential Figures

In 1987, the first stage of my intellectual journey in the sociological study of sport started as an undergraduate student at the University of the West Indies (UWI), St. Augustine Campus. It took the form of a coursework project which

Reflections on Sociology of Sport: Ten Questions, Ten Scholars, Ten Perspectives
Research in the Sociology of Sport, Volume 10, 119–133
Copyright © 2018 by Emerald Publishing Limited
All rights of reproduction in any form reserved
ISSN: 1476-2854/doi:10.1108/S1476-285420170000010008

examined the rise and fall of three sport teams in my home community as part of an undergraduate course dealing with social research methods. A short version of this study was subsequently published four years later in the *Arena Review* as part of a special issue on Caribbean Sport (McCree, 1990). This publication on sport represented my first ever publication not only on sport but on anything. This initial study was followed up by my examination of several attempts to professionalize the sport of soccer in Trinidad and Tobago between 1967 and 1982 as part of MSc in sociology also at the UWI (McCree, 1995a). A short version of this study was also subsequently published in 2000 in the *International Review for the Sociology of Sport* (McCree, 2000). In this same year, I entered the PhD programme in sociology at Leicester University which I completed in 2005 under the astute supervision of Patrick Murphy at the then Centre for the Study of Sport in Society (CSSS). It was here that I was first introduced to figurational sociology and the figurational sociology of sport under the supervision of Murphy.[1]

Before my Leicester experience, however, my deep interest in the study of sport would have been influenced and assisted along the way by several scholars both local and foreign. Locally, three individuals stand out: sociologists Lloyd Brathwaite and Dom Basil Matthews and CLR James, all of whom are from Trinidad and Tobago. Brathwaite is a former Principal of the UWI at St. Augustine who established himself as a premier sociologist in the post-war Caribbean, particularly in relation to the study of the family, race relations and education (Ryan, 1991). He was also the first sociologist to write on sport in the Caribbean although it did not figure prominently in the wider corpus of his sociological writings. In addition, I was also fortunate to be one of his undergraduate students in the 1980s, as well as his Research Assistant in the early 1990s, just before his death in 1995. Dom Basil Matthews was also a sociologist and a former Catholic priest (McCree, 1995a). Although he wrote the first known history of soccer in Trinidad and Tobago in 1965 (Matthews, 1965), unlike Brathwaite, he distinguished himself as a football administrator in his capacity as president of the National Football Association and as principal of one of the leading high school teams in local soccer in Trinidad and Tobago in the 1960s (St. Benedicts College). As for the incomparable James, his majestic *Beyond a Boundary* published in 1963, coincidentally, the same year I was born, continues to inspire and motivate my ongoing commitment to the sociological study of sport ever since I first read it in 1985.

Internationally, some of the other significant formative influences on my work and interest in the sociology of sport are drawn mainly from Canada (Richard Gruneau), the United Kingdom (Maureen Cain, David Silverman, John Hargreaves) and the United States (Alan Ingham, Michael Malec, Jay and Joan Mandle), a few of whom I have met personally. For the United States, Professor Michael Malec of Boston College deserves special mention for two major reasons. Firstly, in his role as editor of the 1990 special issue of the *Arena Review* dealing with Caribbean sport as well as the book which followed it in 1995 (Malec, 1995), he created the opportunity to obtain my first publication in the sociology of sport. Secondly, since those early publications, Professor Malec has come to serve as a sort of mentor over the years since we have kept in touch both personally and professionally as members of the North American Society for the Sociology of Sport (NASSS). This close association was to culminate in my visit to Boston College in 2014 as a visiting scholar in the Department of Sociology, facilitated by Professor Malec. The 'Mandle's' (Mandle, 1994; Mandle & Mandle, 1988) pioneering work on basketball in the Caribbean was published at a time when I was still a graduate student at the UWI and eagerly searching for sociological work on Caribbean sport, as part of my review of the literature, which was quite sparse and almost non-existent (McCree, 1995a). Their work peaked my interest even more because their first book on basketball, published in 1988, was based on Trinidad and Tobago, and even included the organization of basketball in my home town. The 'Mandles', whom I met with personally at a couple of Caribbean conferences, played an important role in diversifying the study of sport in the Caribbean away from cricket at a time when the West Indies cricket team was still all the rage globally, and when local interest in the NBA was also at an all-time high in the 1980s and 1990s (Mandle, 1994; Mandle & Mandle, 1988).

The late Alan Ingham, together with Canadian Richard Gruneau, both of whom I never met, were also major intellectual influences on my early work in the sociology of Caribbean sport. However, I was introduced to the work of both men in a rather fortuitous if not circuitous manner when I started work on my MSc dissertation. In 1988, I first wrote to Ingham on the advice of one of my graduate teachers, British sociologist, Professor Maureen Cain. Before this, I had never heard of Ingham. Although Professor Cain did not have any particular interest in the study of sport and had never even met Ingham herself, she assumed the role as mentor in trying to facilitate my sociological research into sport. In addition, she was also instrumental in getting me to visit Goldsmith's College in 1990, as part of an exchange programme with the then British Council. Another notable scholar who facilitated this visit was Professor David Silverman who hosted me at his home for two weeks. Silverman was then a Senior Lecturer at Goldsmith's College who has become known for his work on qualitative research (Silverman, 1985, 1993). Both Cain and Silverman were to give me feedback and encouragement on my early study of sport in Trinidad part of which was subsequently published (McCree, 1990, 1995b). As part of this visit, I also got the opportunity to meet with John Hargreaves, who was also at Goldsmith's College at the time, and to make a presentation to his graduate students on the work I was doing then on Caribbean athletic migration. Hargreaves (1986) had only recently published what can be considered one of the early seminal books in the sociology of sport, *Sport, Power and Culture: A Social and Historical Analysis of Popular Sports in Britain*. The six-week visit allowed me to acquire this book as well as other relevant work in the area of sport sociology,[2] which was also very limited in nature, even for Britain at the time. But returning to Ingham, in a 1988 letter to me, he suggested 16 references, which were among the major books on sport at the time, although three of them did not actually deal with sport. Fortunately, among the list, was Richard Gruneau's classic, *Class, Sports and Social Development* (1983) as well as his own unpublished doctoral dissertation, *American Sport in Transition: The Maturation of Industrial Capitalism and Its Impact Upon Sport* (1978), both of which proved invaluable in shaping my MSc dissertation, theoretically and methodologically. Ingham ended his letter to me as follows:

> Finally, if you have not read Raymond Williams's *Sociology of Culture and Marxism and Literature*, you should find his theme of 'residual, dominant, and emergent' very helpful. I do not know Maureen Cain but I hope that you convey my best wishes to her, also my thanks for encouraging you to pursue a sociology of sport project. I wish you well. (Ingham, 1988, p. 3)

After doing as Ingham advised, Williams' (1977, 1981) notion of 'residual, dominant and emergent' in relation to the workings of culture and ideology became a central component of the theoretical framework of my graduate dissertations in the sociology of sport both at UWI (McCree, 1995a) and at Leicester University (McCree, 2005). Thanks to these various individuals, my early and later work in the sociology of sport benefitted immeasurably.

Research Trajectory

Over the past three decades, as intimated earlier, my work has not focused on any one particular sport or issue. On the contrary, it has embodied a sort of thematic, sporting and theoretical pluralism since it has examined multiple sports, namely, athletics, basketball, boxing, cricket, soccer as well as multiple issues relating to the conflict between professional and amateur sport, nationalism, governance, athletic migration, gender, media, community sport, sport policy and sport participation (McCree, 2016, p. 350). This variety is perhaps attributable to my home town (Point Fortin) which had at one time a national reputation in multiple sports, notably athletics, soccer and basketball (McCree, 1990, 1995b).

Theoretically, my work has drawn on a range of concepts and theories some of which may seem at variance with each other. These include Gramscian hegemony, Gruneau inspired Neo-Marxism, cultural imperialism, globalization, structuration theory, figurational sociology, networks, invented traditions, the expectancy value model of sport participation as well as 'residual', 'premergent' and 'emergent' cultural forms. While this eclectic theoretical mix can be seen as offering more interpretive richness, on the other hand, it remains open to the possible charge of being confusing, too broad and lacking a main or core focus. This can perhaps be explained by my subscription to theoretical pluralism and an aversion to any species of reductionism or meta-narrative. This diversity, however, is underpinned by one common thread: the examination of the way(s) in which human actions or human agency in sport have been constrained as well as facilitated by particular political, economic, social and cultural processes as well as ideas at both the micro, macro, local and global levels.

However, methodologically, my work has not been as diverse since it has been dominated by qualitative research which has involved the use of mainly the life history approach; *verstehen*, phenomenology, interviews, documents and textual analysis. But in addition, it has also made use of Weber's typology of various modes of human action (viz. instrumental, value rational, affectual, traditional) to examine the nature of actor's behaviour or orientations in sport (Ingham, 1978; McCree, 1995a).

ABOUT SPORT

Why Does Sport Matter?

While there may be little or no consensus on the definition of sport, what is irrefutable is that, historically, sport has been implicated in several related social, cultural, political, economic and even technological processes which make it ripe for and relevant to the scientific study of human society. In this regard, social science in general and sociology in particular have had as their primary object of study: the role of particular economic, political, cultural and social institutions or practises in shaping or reshaping social life, people and *vice versa*. More specifically, in the study of human society, the social sciences have focused particularly on issues such as exploitation, oppression, inequality, discrimination, identity formation (e.g., ethnic, sexual, gender, class, national, body image), socialization, freedom, empowerment and capital accumulation. In this context, the study of sport is more than relevant since as a particular social institution or practise, it has been directly and indirectly implicated in these various processes that have come to (re)define the human condition. Relatedly, it is generally well-known that sport can facilitate social change at the same time that it can also facilitate particular modes of domination and hierarchy, be it along the lines of race, colour, ethnicity, gender, class, age, region or ability. The study of sport is relevant therefore, not only because it can help us to see and understand social wrongs but it can also be used to help correct or eliminate them and so make the world a better place. In other words, a major value or objective in the study of sport is not just to use it as a prism through which to understand the structure(s), culture(s) and dynamic(s) of society, but to show how it has been used as a mechanism to challenge them as well as to help bring about social change. As a throwback to Marx's critique of Feuerbach, the sociology of sport seeks not just to interpret sport or the world but to help change them.

In addition, the commercialization of sport and the growth of a global sport industry have added even more to the contemporary value of sport and its relevance both as an institution and as an area of study. This global industry, which is driven by professional sports, merchandizing, the media, the hosting of international sport events, in particular mega events such as the Olympics and the FIFA world cup was estimated to be worth US1.5 trillion dollars in 2015 (Plunkett Research). Relatedly, sport tourism has also emerged as a major sector within the tourism industry as many countries, particularly those in the Caribbean heavily dependent on tourism, seek to diversify their tourism product away from the traditional matrix of sand, sea, sun and sex. In this regard, the sport tourism market has been valued around US800bn which represents 10% of the international tourism market (UNWTO, 2016). Sport matters, therefore, on multiple fronts as a source of wealth, employment, economic development, identity, equality and, as a vehicle for social change.

How Should Sport be Studied?

This question raises conceptual, theoretical and methodological issues. There is no particular way to study sport since as with the study of other social phenomena, this is a function of the particular discipline, researcher, research questions and the particular research situation (funding, time, access to field). But however it is studied, the study of sport must be based on a recognition that it has been socially constructed to serve particular interests and has been shaped by as well as shapes other social, economic, political, technological, cultural and environmental conditions or processes. But, while recognizing the dialectical nature of the relationship between sport and other processes or institutions, it must also be recognized that sport is an institution *sui generis* with its own peculiar history, myths, stereotypes, beliefs and characteristics (e.g., sport and politics should not mix, sport does not merit academic study and is not a means to test or generate theories and hypotheses or understand the interpretive nature of reality; athletes are intellectually challenged despite evidence to the contrary; sport builds character; sport is play or recreation not work; the exaltation of role models, heroes, heroines and records). In addition, in terms of formal theory, the study of sport should also make use of the rich array of theoretical approaches in order to avoid monocausal or unidimensional explanations that focus solely on say economics, race or gender while also being cognisant of issues of intersectionality as well as the intimate linkages between the local, regional and global in sport. In relation to methodology, the study of sport allows for the use of both qualitative and quantitative approaches to the study of social phenomenon although my work has focused more on the former approach.

Is Sport a Panacea for Social Problems?

Historically, sport has been constructed as a paragon of virtue that can help lead to peace, unity, harmony, good character and good health. The emergence of sport for development as a distinct area of study through the creation of academic courses, a specialist journal as well as its incorporation as an integral component of sport policies around the world, have served to underline this traditional conception of sport. In addition, the establishment of an Office on Sport for Development and Peace (UNOSDP) by the United Nations as well as a Special Advisor to the Secretary General of the UN on this subject since 2001 have served to further reinforce this functionalist conception of sport as a possible solution to a wide range of social problems (UNOSDP, 2015). As part of these developments, the UN has hosted since 2009 an International Forum on Sport for Peace and Development (UNOSDP, 2013), while the 2010 Millennium Summit Declaration recognized that '… sport, as a tool for education, development and peace, can promote cooperation and solidarity, tolerance, understanding, social inclusion and health, at local, national and international levels' (UN, 2010, p. 13). Although the UNDOSP was closed in May 2017, the UN will still be involved in sport for development initiatives through partnering with the International Olympic Committee as it continues to promote the value of sport in helping to achieve wider development goals (Play the Game, 2017).

While some of these utopian views of sport can be seen as an expression of functionalist fantasy, there is no doubt that sport has been used in real and symbolic ways to facilitate social solidarity and peace (Ekholm, 2013; UNDOSP, 2015). Relatedly, involvement in sport has become a popular component of strategies to help deal with non-communicable diseases like diabetes, cardiac problems and obesity (Coalter, 2007). However, while research has clearly confirmed the importance of sport activity, it must also be noted that sport can also be a source of health problems or even death through over training and substance abuse (Coakley, 2015). In addition, research has also shown that there is no necessary relationship between sport, and the reduction of crime, violence and conflict (Ekholm, 2013; Miller, Melnick, Barnes, Sabo, & Farrell, 2007). On the contrary, sport itself has been seen as a source of these problems through the existence of hooliganism, racism, player violence, match fixing, bid rigging and drug abuse (Coakley, 2015; FRA, 2010; Young, 2012). However, notwithstanding its contradictory effects, it is undeniable that sport can offer a major platform or vehicle for public education and public mobilization around particular issues as well as giving a voice and visibility to many subaltern groups.

ABOUT PRACTISING SOCIOLOGY OF SPORT

Is Teaching Sociology of Sport Easy?

I first started teaching the sociology of sport in 1997 at the UWI but this took the form of just one module in a larger course on Caribbean Civilization and lasted only two years. Since 2001, however, I have been teaching a full course on the sociology of sport, which I developed myself, as part of the undergraduate degree in sport management at the UWI. The course consists of seven modules dealing with defining sport, the history of sport, sociological theories of sport, commercialization, media, social structure, gender and deviance. For the first five years of the BSc in Sport Management, the course was limited to only students doing their major in sport management but, over the last 10 years, it has been opened up to students doing general management and other degree programmes at the University. In this regard, the course has attracted students from the fields of communication studies, economics, international relations, nutritional sciences, psychology and sociology. However, in the period 2006–2016, these students have amounted to just 11 (3.7%) of the 294 students who have done the course during this period, and only four of whom were actually sociology students. The course remains dominated therefore, by management students.

It is not easy teaching the sociology of sport to students doing any form of management studies and those with no background in sociology as a whole. In such a situation, you have to teach two courses in one as you first have to expose them to the particular sociological theory or concept, then examine its application in sport. And since sociology is not one of the most valued subjects, this can be challenging. Apart from lacking a background in sociology, many students are also theory averse although this is not unique to them or to sociology. This is evident in the fact that over the past 15 years, the least attempted question for the final examinations in the sociology of sport, as well as the coursework has been the one dealing specifically with theories in sport (e.g., functionalist, Marxist, interactionist) while the most attempted or popular questions have been deviance, the media and gender although these also contain theoretical issues.

Within this context, as communications technology has developed over the years, I have made use of sport films, you-tube videos and relevant sport documentaries as part of my teaching strategies in order to encourage and sustain student interest in the course. Some of the more notable films I have used include the *Gladiator*, very useful for examining sport in Roman society, *Million Dollar Baby*, for both gender and disability in sport and *Chariots of Fire*, used to examine the early professional–amateur conflict in modern sport. In turn, students are also allowed to make use of videos and films in doing their class presentations which have helped significantly in encouraging and sustaining their interest in the course.

Do Sociologists of Sport Like Sport?

A cursory glance at the biographies of many authors in the sociology of sport suggests that many have been involved in sport as either a fan or participant or both. I also belong to this category, for my study of sport over the last 30 years can be seen as a reflection of my fervent interest in sport itself as both a fan and a participant, particularly in athletics, cricket and soccer at the high school, community and university levels. I even had the opportunity to captain the cricket and soccer teams. Taking part in sport and studying sport however, are not necessarily related although participating can give you possible insights into the workings of sport which can then possibly feed into your understanding or application of particular theories, methodologies and policy issues.

Is the Sociologist of Sport a 'Public Intellectual'?

The role of the sociologist and the relevance of sociology to society has been a subject of much controversial discussion in both Europe and North America (Burawoy, 2005; Clawston et al., 2007; Cole, 2001; Patterson, 2014; Turner, 2006). At the core of the debate, is the extent to which the sociologist should be a 'public intellectual' or be 'publicly engaged' in various social issues and the broader public policy process in particular. The same discussion has replicated itself in the context of the sociology of sport and its own marginalization within sociology itself (Bairner, 2009; Donelly, 2015; Donnelly, Fraga, & Aisenstein, 2014; Ingham & Donelly, 1990; Jarvie, 2007; McDonald, 2002). And so much so that the main theme of the 2016 conference of the NASSS was: 'Publicly Engaged Sociology of Sport'.

This issue would of course hinge on how we define 'public intellectual' or 'public engagement'. In his fourfold classification of sociology and sociologists into the professional, policy, critical and public oriented, Burawoy (2005) distinguished the latter by its communication with persons or publics outside of academia, which may include minorities, workers, women etc. However, he noted further that this type of engagement may assume two forms: (i) an elitist or top down type of engagement where the sociologist remains largely invisible while examining major social issues and (ii) a more participatory or advocacy type of engagement in which the sociologist becomes actually involved with the organization or groups in question through actually protesting or lobbying for change. The latter type of public sociologist is more akin to the Gramscian type organic intellectual who becomes involved in public advocacy, and action which may assume a political character. Burawoy noted however, that his four categories are neither 'water tight' nor 'mutually exclusive' since they may overlap and even feed into each other (Burawoy, 2005), thus amounting to a kind of heuristic tool within which to (re)locate the sociologist.

In the sociology of sport, there have been some noteworthy individuals who can exemplify this notion of the public intellectual in the activist and political sense. They include American Harry Edwards (Lypsyte, 1988) and Canadian Bruce Kidd (Kelsall, 2013) who were both united in their opposition to racism and sexism in sport and society. Being a public sociologist, however, does not necessarily mean pounding the pavement. Apart from this hard-core variant, it can also be expressed in softer ways that may include being a media commentator, sport policy advisor or just talking to athletes, parents and coaches about the perils of drug abuse. The public sociologist, therefore, may be seen along a continuum of action that varies from the hard-core to the soft-core.

ABOUT SOCIOLOGY OF SPORT IN THE ACADEMY

Does the Sociology of Sport Face Institutional/Industry Barriers?

Drawing on my experience at the UWI over a quarter of a century, I can safely assert that the perception or position of the sociology of sport within the academy is not fundamentally different from that of sociology on the whole, which is one of general devalorization linked perhaps to a dominant view that sociology is not as marketable as say management, economics or psychology and, as such, does not have a clear career path after graduation.

In this general context, one can state that the sociology of sport faces a very mixed future in the academy due to ongoing challenges and some promising developments or possibilities. The major challenges or barriers previously identified were the absence of sport-specific research funding, the lack of a cadre of sport sociologists who can offer leadership, more courses and attract more students, the persistence of old ideas which dismiss sport as an area of study, its marginalization from the traditional teaching, research and development agenda as well as a general failure to understand the importance of sociological research in sport to either sport development or sport for development (McCree, 2016, pp. 352–353). In addition, neither the subject of sport sociology nor the sport management programme in which it has developed over the past 16 years has ever been promoted nationally or regionally which has contributed further to its invisibility or marginalization. No wonder then that in a 2016 survey of my sociology of sport class, of the 19 students who took the survey, out of a class of 27, all reported never having heard of the sociology of sport before their entry into university. Furthermore, in the 30 years that I have been doing the sociology of sport, one problem that has stood out is what I call the 4D experience. This experience describes the reaction I get whenever I indicate to someone that I am studying sport or did my PhD on the subject: dismay, discomfort, disgust and dismissiveness. It is as if you are doing something wrong or discussing a taboo subject like sex and sexuality. The historically dismissive and perhaps changing view of sport within the local academy can be possibly captured in a congratulatory remark of one my colleagues on my recent promotion to Senior Fellow when he stated: 'Respect and congratulations to you Roy! The recognition of the specialty contribution of your research area, by our UWI, is a welcome development my friend' (Underline added).

Unfortunately, this mind-set exists not just within the academy but also within the wider society regardless of age, level of education, class, gender, ethnicity and whether one plays sport or not. The idea that sport does not merit academic or intellectual study runs deep and remains dominant in spite of attempts to the contrary and, in spite of its social, political and increasingly economic value. This situation can be likened to Bourdieu's 1988 observation that the sociology of sport is 'scorned by sociologists and despised by sports persons' (cited in Washington & Karen, 2001, p. 187) although this thinking is not limited to the sociological study of sport. Commenting on the commonality of the experiences faced by sociologists of sport in 23 countries across Africa, Australasia, Europe, South America and North America, Young (2017, p. xix) noted that 'Authors speak of incessant battles for recognition, for legitimacy, for funding and for resources and … disciplinary and campus struggle'. The contempt for the sociology of sport as well as the study of sport on the whole therefore, can be seen as a historical universal which remains a major barrier to change everywhere.

What is the Future of the Sociology of Sport?

In view of the various economic, organizational, historical and developmental challenges faced by the sociology of sport both within the academy and without, one can be rather pessimistic about its future. However, for several reasons, the situation is not all doom and gloom. This cause for cautious optimism stems from the following six factors:

(i)   The emergence of a couple local academics with an expressed interest in the sociological (Rampersad, 2011, 2014) as well as anthropological study of sport (Kerrigan, 2012, 2016).

(ii) The introduction of students to the sociology of sport at the high school level as part of a restructured physical education programme since 2009 (Caribbean Examinations Council, 2014).

(iii) The introduction of undergraduate and graduate sport degree programmes at other campuses and universities throughout the Anglophone Caribbean which provide structured opportunities for the teaching of sport sociology (McCree, 2016).

(iv) The emergence of sport policies, sport tourism and the use of sport for development which can create opportunities for the conduct of sociological research in relation to a range of issues in relation to sport participation and the socioeconomic benefits of sport (McCree, 2016).

(v)   The author's intention to lobby for a greater array of courses which would relate to the sociology of sport either directly or indirectly, in the following areas: sport and social theory, gender and sport, disability and sport, sport media, sport for development, youth sport and the sociology of coaching. The absence of such lobbying or advocacy has been a major drawback to the expansion of both the sociology of sport and sport studies in general, in the local academy.

(vi) The plan to forge alliances or partnerships with other stakeholders notably, physical education teachers and other tertiary institutions where sport sociology is taught as a component of other programmes. Such alliances have also been completely absent in the development of the subject thus far in the Caribbean region.

Consistent with an international pattern (Donelly, 2015), the sociology of sport has not developed on its own accord in the Caribbean academy but as a part of programmes in both physical education and more recently, sport management. However, if it is to grow further and become institutionalized as a subject of study in the academy, its practitioners must broaden its thematic appeal, consolidate on its existing disciplinary links and reach out to other relevant stakeholders in the field of sport, sport tourism and sport for development. As a consequence, while there may have been some gains along the way, and while I have been able to travel to many places and meet many people, there is still a very long way to go along this arduous Caribbean sociology of sport journey since the rate of progress has been abysmally slow.

NOTES

1. Murphy belonged to a team of researchers at the CSSS who became renowned for their pioneering work on football hooliganism in Britain and Europe in the 1980s and 1990s (cf., Murphy, Williams, & Dunning, 1990; Williams, Dunning, & Murphy, 1984/1989).

2. Millennials and others should keep in mind that before the era of buying books online, it was not an easy task to access certain books and journals, particularly on sport, when you were based in the developing world since they were normally not available locally. Trips abroad therefore offered a major opportunity to do so.

REFERENCES

Allison, L. (Ed.). (1986). *The politics of sport*. Manchester: Manchester University Press.

Bairner, A. (2009). Sport, intellectuals and public sociology: Obstacles and opportunities. *International Review for the Sociology of Sport, 44*(2-3), 115–130.

Burawoy, M. (2005). For public sociology. *American Sociological Review, 70*, 4–28.

Caribbean Examinations Council. (2014). *Caribbean advanced proficiency examinations: Physical education and sport syllabus*. Kingston: Caribbean Examinations Council.

Clawston, D., Zussman, R., Misra, J., Gerstel, N., Stokes, R., Douglas, L., & Anderton, L. D. (Eds.). (2007). *Public sociology: Fifteen eminent sociologists debate politics and the profession in the twenty-first century*. Berkeley, CA: University of California Press.

Coakley, J. (2015). *Sport in society: Issues and controversies*. Columbus, Ohio: Irwin Mc Graw-Hill.

Coalter, F. (2007). *A wider social role for sport: Who's keeping the score?* New York, NY: Routledge.

Cole, S. (2001). *What's wrong with sociology?* New Brunswick, CT: Transaction Publishers.

Donelly, P. (2015). Assessing the sociology of sport: On public sociology of sport and research that makes a difference. *International Review for the Sociology of Sport, 50*(4−5), 419−423.

Donnelly, P., Fraga, B. A., & Aisenstein, A. (2014). For a public sociology of sport in the Americas: An editorial call on behalf of a socially engaged scholarship on sport and physical education. *Movimento, 20*, 9−20.

Ekholm, D. (2013). Sport and crime prevention: Individuality and transferability in research. *Journal of Sport for Development, 1*(2). Retrieved from https://jsfd.files.wordpress.com/2013/12/sport-and-crime-prevention.pdf

FRA. (2010). *Racism, ethnic discrimination and exclusion of migrants and minorities in sport: A comparative overview of the situation in the European Union*. Vienna: European Agency for Fundamental Rights.

Gruneau, R. (1983). *Class, sports and social development*. Amherst: University of Massachusetts.

Gruneau, R., & Cantelon, H. (Eds.). (1982). *Sport, culture and the modern state*. London: University of Toronto Press.

Hargreaves, J. (Ed.). (1982). *Sport, culture and ideology*. London: Routledge and Kegan Paul.

Hargreaves, J. (1986). *Sport, power and culture: A social and historical analysis of popular sports in Britain*. Cambridge: Polity Press.

Horne, J., David, J., & Tomlinson, A. (Eds.). (1987). *Sport, leisure and social relations*. London: Routledge and Kegan Paul.

Ingham, A. (1978). *American sport in transition: The maturation of industrial capitalism and its impact on sport*. Ph.D. Dissertation, University of Massachusetts.

Ingham, A. (1988). Personal Correspondence. February 8.

Ingham, A. G., & Donelly, P. (1990). Whose knowledge counts? The production of knowledge and issues of application in the sociology of sport. *Sociology of Sport Journal, 7*, 58−65.

James, C. L. R. (1963). *Beyond a boundary*. London: Hutchinson.

Jarvie, G. (2007). Sport, social change and the public intellectual. *International Review for the Sociology of Sport, 42*(4), 411−424.

Kelsall, C. (2013). Bruce Kidd. *Athletics Illustrated*. Retrieved from http://athleticsillustrated.com/interviews/bruce-kidd/. Accessed on February 6, 2017.

Kerrigan, D. (2012). White supremacy versus gangsterism on the small-goal football field. *Anthropology Now, 4*(3), 7−14.

Kerrigan, D. (2016). Languaculture and grassroots football: "Small goal" in Trinidad. *International Review for the Sociology of Sport, 51*(6), 735−751.

Lawrence, G., & Rowe, D. (Eds.). (1986). *Power play: The commercialisation of Australian sport*. Sydney: Hale and Iremanager.

Lypsyte, L. (1988). An outsider joins the team. *New York Times*, May 22. Retrieved from http://www.nytimes.com/1988/05/22/magazine/an-outsider-joins-the-team.html?pagewanted=all. Accessed on February 6, 2017.

Malec, M. (Ed.). (1995). *The social roles of sport in the Caribbean*. Amsterdam: Gordon and Breach Publishers.

Mandle, J. (1994). *Caribbean hoops: The development of West Indian basketball*. Amsterdam: Gordon and Breach Publishers.

Mandle, J., & Mandle, J. (1988). *Grass roots commitment: Basketball and society in Trinidad and Tobago*. Parkersburg, WV: Caribbean Books.

Mangan, J. A. (1986). *The games ethic and imperialism: Aspects of the diffusion of an ideal*. New York, NY: Viking.

Mangan, J. A. (Ed.). (1988). *Pleasure, profit, proselytism: British culture and sport at home and abroad 1700−1914*. London: Frank Cass.

Manley, M. (1988). *A history of West Indies cricket*. London: André Deutsch.

Matthews, B. D. (1965). The evolution of football in Trinidad and Tobago, 1908-1962. Presidential Address delivered at the Hotel Normandie, Port of Spain, Trinidad, December 12.

McCree, R. (1990). Whither jets, hawks and civic? The organisation of sport in a community in Trinidad: The case of Point Fortin, 1970–1986. *Arena Review*, *14*(1), 86–100.

McCree, R. (1995a). *Professionalism and the development of club football in Trinidad, 1967–1986*. MSc Dissertation, The University of the West Indies, St. Augustine.

McCree, R. (1995b). Whither, jets, hawks and civic? Conflict, continuity and change in the organization of sport in a Trinidad community: The case of Point Fortin, 1970-1993. In M. Malec (Ed.), *The social roles of sport in Caribbean societies* (pp. 173–196). Newark, NJ: Gordon and Breach Publishers.

McCree, R. (2000). Professional soccer in the Caribbean: The case of Trinidad and Tobago, 1969–1983. *International Review for the Sociology of Sport*, *35*(2), 199–218.

McCree, R. (2005). *Athletic migration, globalization and identity formation: The case of McDonald Bailey, 1944–1954*. PhD Dissertation, University of Leicester, UK.

McCree, R. (2016). Sociology of sport: English-speaking Caribbean. In K. Young (Ed.), *Sociology of sport: A global subdiscipline in review* (pp.343–359). Bingley, UK: Emerald Group Publishing Limited.

McDonald, I. (2002). Critical social research and political intervention: Moralistic versus radical approaches. In J. Sugden & A. Tomlinson (Eds.), *Power games: A critical sociology of sport* (pp. 100–116). London: Routledge.

Miller, K., Melnick, M. J., Barnes, G. M., Sabo, D., & Farrell, M. P. (2007). Athletic involvement and adolescent delinquency. *Journal of Youth Adolescent*, *36*(5), 711–723.

Murphy, P., Williams, J., & Dunning, E. (1990). *Football on trial: Spectator violence and development in the football world*. London: Routledge.

Patterson, O. (2014). How sociologists made themselves irrelevant. Retrieved from http://www.chronicle.com/article/How-Sociologists-Made/150249/.

Play the Game. (2017). UN secretary general closes UNOSDP. May 11, 2017. Retrieved from http://www.playthegame.org/news/news-articles/2017/0309_un-secretary-general-closes-unosdp/. Accessed on August 22, 2017.

Plunkett Research. Sports & recreation business statistics analysis, business and industry statistics. Retrieved from http://www.plunkettresearch.com/statistics/sports-industry/. Accessed on February 4, 2017.

Rampersad, A. (2011). The social and cultural consequences of cricket world cup 2007: Poor spectatorship in Trinidad and Tobago. In L. A. Jordan, B. Tyson, C. Hayle, & D. Truly (Eds.), *Sports event management: The Caribbean experience* (pp. 171–182). London: Ashgate.

Rampersad, A. (2014). Ethnicity, national identity, and cricket in contemporary Trinidad and Tobago. In J. Nauright, A. G. Gobley, & D. K. Wiggins (Eds.), *Beyond C.L.R. James: Shifting boundaries of race and ethnicity in sport* (pp. 239–252). Fayetteville, Arkansas: University of Arkansas Press.

Ryan, S. (Ed.). (1991). *Social & occupational stratification in contemporary Trinidad & Tobago*. St. Augustine: Institute of Social and Economic Studies.

Silverman, D. (1985). *Qualitative methodology and sociology*. Aldershot: Gower Publishing Company.

Silverman, D. (1993). *Interpreting qualitative data: Methods of analyzing talk, text and interaction*. London: Sage.

Turner, B. A. (2006). British sociology and public intellectuals: Consumer society and imperial decline. *British Journal of Sociology*, *57*(2), 169–188.

United Nations. (2010). *Millennium summit declaration*. New York, NY: United Nations. Retrieved from http://www.un.org/en/mdg/summit2010/pdf/mdg%20outcome%20document.pdf

UNOSDP. (2013). *3rd International Forum on Sport For Peace and Development: Creating a common vision*. New York, NY: United Nations. Retrieved from https://stillmed.olympic.org/Documents/Olympism_in_action/Peace_through_sport/Rapport_NY_ENG_WEB-2.pdf

UNOSDP. (2015). *Annual Report 2014. United Nations Office on Sport for Development and Peace*. Geneva: UNOSDP. Retrieved from https://www.un.org/sport/sites/www.un.org.sport/files/ckfiles/files/UNOSDP%20Annual%20Report%202014%20web(1).pdf

UNWTO. UNTWO International Conference on Tourism and Sports: Technical Note, Vietnam, 24 September, 2016. Retrieved from http://cf.cdn.unwto.org/sites/all/files/pdf/technical_note_8. pdf. Accessed on February 3, 2017.

Washington, E. R., & Karen, D. (2001). Sport and society. *Annual Review of Sociology*, *27*,187–212.

Williams, J., Dunning, E., & Murphy, P. (1984/1989). *Hooligans abroad: The behaviour and control of English fans in continental Europe*. London: Routledge.

Williams, R. (1977). *Marxism and literature*. Oxford: Oxford University Press.

Williams, R. (1981). *Culture*. London: Fontana Press.

Young, K. (2012). *Sport, violence and society*. New York, NY: Routledge.

Young, K. (2017). Introduction. In K. Young (Ed.) *Sociology of sport: A global subdiscipline in review*. Bingley: Emerald.

CHAPTER 9

THE SOCIOLOGY OF THE TASTE FOR SOCIOLOGY OF SPORT

Fabien Ohl

INTRODUCTION

Social and intellectual trajectories are interwoven and, like others, I am a 'sociologist (who) is socially situated' (Wacquant, 1989). Keeping this in mind may help to go beyond hagiography and engage a reflexive analysis. I will engage this notion with attention to the question of mentors and influential figures that I will explore in relation to the specific context of my education and the situation of sociology of sport in the scientific field. I will then focus on my personal social trajectory, and the social context that influenced it to inform my research trajectory.

ABOUT THE AUTHOR

Mentors and Influential Figures

Initially, I registered both in sociology and sport science when I started university, but I put my studies in sociology on standby mainly because I did not expect to find a job as a sociologist. I was more confident in finding one as a physical education (PE) teacher. Later, I restarted studying sociology at the Masters level parallel to my work as a teacher.

Many academics are lucky and proud to have an important figure, usually a prestigious professor, as a mentor. Unfortunately, I have to confess that it is

Reflections on Sociology of Sport: Ten Questions, Ten Scholars, Ten Perspectives
Research in the Sociology of Sport, Volume 10, 135–152
Copyright © 2018 by Emerald Publishing Limited
All rights of reproduction in any form reserved
ISSN: 1476-2854/doi:10.1108/S1476-285420170000010009

not so in my case. I met a diversity of colleagues, in both sociology and in sport sciences, but none of them was really a mentor per se — it was, rather, influential sociologists who inspired my work, through my own readings and sometimes indirectly thanks to other sociologists in my cohort.

One of the first sociology courses at university was a surprise. Michel Maffesoli, a well-known French sociologist (Maffesoli, 1996), was teaching in a small room, sitting at the only table in the middle of the room with most of the students sitting on the ground. And Maffesoli was like a dandy, with a big hat in a 'Three Musketeers' (Alexandre Dumas) style presenting smart analysis of society that seemed mainly based on his feelings. This was not what I expected! I discovered sociology of sport thanks to a PE teacher, Guy Gravier. Gravier was not a researcher but he shared his knowledge nonetheless. In France, there were very few researchers in sport sciences until the 1980s. The real integration of sport sciences into university and research took place in the mid-1980s, and this helped to create a new generation of researchers in France. The only professor in sociology of sport at my university, in Strasbourg, was Bernard Michon. Michon had a fascination for the work of Pierre Bourdieu. He was a good speaker, selling very well a burlesque type of sociology. He was using Bourdieu's theory, especially the articulation between capital, habitus and field, in a very mechanical manner. However, that motivated me to learn more about Bourdieu's sociology. My Masters and Doctoral supervisor was Christian de Montlibert, a sociologist not focusing much on the sociology of sport. But he was close to Bourdieu and had an impressive sociological knowledge that afforded him a sharp and smart analysis. He was very inspiring, but unfortunately reluctant to share his time with his PhD students.

I had the chance to start my PhD in the mid-1980s in connection with a generation of sociologists such as Christian Pociello (Pociello, 1981), Jacques Defrance (Defrance, 1989), Catherine Louveau (Louveau, 1987) and Jean-Paul Clément (Clément, 1995), who more or less started their academic career in the most favourable moment of the institutionalization of sport sciences in France. Bourdieu's sociology had a strong influence on this growing field, but it was not homogeneous. For example, Georges Vigarello (Vigarello, 1988) and André Rauch (Rauch, 1982) also played key roles in the sociohistorical approach inspired by Foucault.

The circulation of international research was limited in the 1980s, although Dunning and Elias' (1986) book was translated into French. In general, French sociology of sport had few connections with the growing international research in the sociology of sport — these two worlds were relatively separated. And I did not connect to the international networks through sociology. As I was working on consumption, I had to be involved in the growing field of sport management which provided the opportunity, in France and also elsewhere, to maintain or develop sociological studies in the 1990s (Ohl, 2015). Sport management networks were encouraged by Erasmus programmes and strengthened the very positive connections with international academic networks. I switched to the International Sociology of Sport Association (ISSA) later, at the end of the 1990s. Thanks to ISSA, I discovered a new academic world. It was like getting fresh air! It was less entangled in conflicts between theoretical schools and I met colleagues from diverse countries and backgrounds. Most of them seemed very open and supportive. However, these friendly feelings may certainly have been accentuated because, as a non-native English speaker, one is perhaps unable to perceive all the nuances. Though, that gives the feeling of a kind of enchanted world of research compared to France. An enchantment that was, of course, naive. English is the vector of the globalization of research, and even if most of the colleagues, at least at the ISSA, were mindful of this, that was also a soft move in favour of a domination of research by Anglo-Saxon academics.

Research Trajectory

I was raised in a French middle-class environment, in tune with and aware of my cultural capital. My interest in sociology arose at the end of the 1970s both when I was at high school and engaged in a sporting career, in conjunction with an uncle, a sociologist in Paris, and with other sociologists in my circle. But I am aware that these influences would not have been effective had I not been located in a social position under tension between diverse influences.

My family has a higher cultural than economic capital. My left-wing parents influenced my sensitivity to social inequality and to social justice. However, our family networks were also connected with wealthy and very right-wing people. For instance, my father hunted in a region of France where such leisure pursuits were very expensive. Furthermore, I was also living in a small privileged district of a popular neighbourhood, and school friends were from the lower classes. So, I shared experiences with diverse sets of people from lower, middle and upper-classes. I would not say that my habitus was 'divided', which was the case of Bourdieu (a sociologist who had a strong influence on my research – Bennett, 2007), but there is no doubt that I felt the tensions between different social class values and behaviours. It certainly fed my awareness and sensitivity to issues such as social class, inequality and domination, three topics at the core of Bourdieu's work.

However, I was never a political activist. I was involved in sport and that was my priority. I was competing in kayak racing as member of the French national team. At the time, being an athlete did not have an elevated social status in the French cultivated middle class I belong to. I was afraid of seeming to have a limited intellectual ability, because being a sportsman was sometimes seen as the opposite of someone 'clever'. In the 1970s, sport was not a valued subject in France for intellectuals, nor was it for the highbrow newspapers, for example. At this time in France, valuing outdoor sports was correlated with a disdain for the sport of football. Most of my friends doing wild-water kayaking were extremely resistant to football. It was perceived as brainless, violent, corrupted and unfair. Doing a minor outdoor sport went hand-in-hand with the celebration of the wilderness, increased the value of masculinity through this high-risk occupation, and the pride of being an amateur, and not corrupted by the notion of sport-as-business. As we were training very hard, we were also annoyed by the weak social recognition of our performance. The media mostly focused on football players who, to tell the truth, I perceived as the icons of the consumer society.

I grew under the influence of the famous 'May 68' events which had an important impact on French society. These included massive worker strikes and the government was defeated. It was a period of a kind social and cultural effervescence that had an important impact on the way some of the young French generation perceived culture, politics and power, and also sport. I was only 7 years old in 1968, but I strongly felt it in the 1970s, because I am the youngest in my family and directly influenced by siblings and family who experienced it more directly. Although this narration of the event is biased, my selective history of May 1968 (Sommier, 1994) is based on my perception as a social actor. This time had a strong influence on what I did, what choices I made and how I perceived both sport and sociology.

Thus, when I started high school, I was open to the mood of the seventies, fighting for freedom, against capitalism, against consumption. I was the third of three children, and as a consequence I was more influenced by the hippy mood of the 1960s–1970s than other people of my age. At this time in France, being an intellectual had great status. And the intellectual field in France, with important figures such as Sartre, Baudrillard, Foucault and Bourdieu, completed by international figures from the Frankfurt school, the Italian anti-psychiatry of the Palo-Alto research on communication, all had influences on me. This was true even in high school where I wrote my first paper on sport, in conjunction with the 1978 World Cup of soccer. It was a critique of FIFA (Fédération Internationale de Football Association) because the World Cup endorsed General J. Videla, dictator of Argentina at this time. My comments on the FIFA 1978 World Cup were inspired by Jean-Marie Brohm's book (Brohm, 1978) and his papers published in '*Quel corps*', a critical journal published from 1975 to 1997.

Thus, the combination of my social trajectory, my position in the field of sport and the events of May 1968 certainly explain my contempt for football and my perception of it as a form of alienating mass culture. My early adoption of a critical view of culture, including sporting culture, was typically the social judgment denounced by Bourdieu in his famous book *Distinction*. It means that the genesis of an interest for the sociology of sport was based on social stereotypes, expressing my own lifestyle and perception of society. In other words, I expressed 'incorporated principles of classification' (Bourdieu, 1984) that were themselves classifying acts. And, furthermore, sociology seemed to be a smart and legitimate manner to be critical – not quite a noble motivation and not at all the best start for a sociologist!

In conjunction with the combination of my social experiences, my research topics generally aim to understand the specific local environment and the situation in the field of research in the 1980–1990s. I was at secondary school for my early presociological steps (the aforementioned critique of the ideology of the 1978 FIFA World-Cup). Then, during the first years of study, I was under the influence of a combination of the Frankfurt School and Baudrillard, who Georges Ritzer consider as '*the* leading postmodern social theorist' in the introduction of the translation of one of Baudrillard's book (Baudrillard, 1998). Thus, I kept my interest for consumption and applied it to sport for my PhD research. But the theoretical background was under the influence of Bourdieu's local and national enthusiasts. I studied, in a largely quantitative fashion, how people doing sports consume goods and services. The aim was to explain economic behaviour, thought to be the outcome of a so-called homo-economicus, through sociological variables. And my PhD provides a look at the symbolic economy of sport, which was observed to be of greater importance than incomes to understand the sporting goods and services used. I later developed this topic trying to understand sport consumption (e.g., Ohl, 2003, 2004, 2005).

I also extended this topic in three main directions. The first was to use sociological knowledge for sport marketing (Desbordes, Ohl, & Tribou, 2001). This may seem like a strange choice for a sociologist, but it was also a way to use sociology for sport-management lectures. I felt some tension at this point because sociologists often denigrate marketing research, but colleagues in this field also publish good research. Furthermore, some results of marketing research are applied and need to be consistent to face the reality and complexity of markets and consumer behaviours. I learned much from it, especially the importance of empirically-based research. For example, there was a gap between my sociology of sporting tastes, mainly based on cultural and economic capital, and what people really consume. I recalled one of the '4 Ps' of the marketing learning – you only consume something you have access to. As a sociologist, I learned from marketers, especially the non-academic ones. But it may be possible that my social background increased my tolerance to and for marketing. However, I completely stopped this research as I had the chance to be hired in a position that was only in sociology, and was more focused on other sociological topics.

The second topic was on media consumption. Under the influence of my initial critiques of football mega-events, I kept an interest in the critical analysis of mass media. After having observed the relationship between media and consumption, it was important to analyse the supply. This is why I studied how local sport journalists produce their newspapers, under the influence of their 'passion', their social background and their position within the field of journalism (Ohl, 2000b). I was also attracted to Goffman's focus on interactions and I analysed journalistic writing as the description of social interactions

(Ohl, 2000c), which led me to discover Suzan Birrell's research (Birrell, 1981). And under the influence of colleagues such as David Rowe and Toni Bruce, I continued with research more focused on gender, with Lucie Schoch, who was my PhD student at the time (Schoch & Ohl, 2011).

The third topic, and the most important to me, is doping. This research continues. I started to work on this subject when I moved to the University of Lausanne, situated near the IOC (International Olympic Committee) head offices and most of the International Federations. I was in the middle of this specific ecosystem which gave me opportunities to develop research on doping. Doping was a strange form of consumption to me because I am not a consumer of any drugs and I had not visited a doctor for years. I had the chance to start a new project, supported by WADA (World Anti-Doping Agency), in 2006, within an international team of researchers. We compared young French, Belgian and Swiss bicycle riders to observe their relationship to pharmacology. One of the main results was that riders did not depend on their morality per se, but on how they were supported and how the follow-up was organized (Ohl, Fincoeur, Lentillon-Kaestner, Defrance, & Brissonneau, 2015). Simultaneously, with other colleagues, I published a book on doping in professional cycling (Brissonneau, Aubel, & Ohl, 2008). All these projects combined Bourdieu's sociology and Becker's sociology of deviance (Becker, 1963).

I continued to do research on this topic and signed a contract with a UCI (Union Cycliste Internationale) manager who asked me to think of possible prevention strategies. My answer was to suggest changes in the cycling culture. That was really immodest for a sociologist − to claim to be able to change social things. But it was a challenge because I believe sociology could be more practically useful to society. The manager asked me to contribute to the changes and I collaborated with UCI from 2010 to 2016. That was the start of six years of adventure with UCI and Professional WorldTour Teams. Instead of believing that doping is mainly a *moral* issue, we developed the idea, already in the 2006 WADA study, that the support of riders is essential in organizing doping prevention. With the research team, we analysed riders as workers and we focused on their work conditions − workload, the organization of the team, how people work together, what it means to be a professional, what the constraints are, etc. (Aubel, Lefèvre, & Ohl, 2015; Aubel & Ohl, 2015). That helped us to implement new prevention strategies (Aubel & Ohl, 2014). We also accepted to audit the Astana team, which was not really a position that I recommend as a sociologist. After the audit and in combination with other episodes, we were both in a position of a 'judge' who could influence the access to the WorldTour, including the Tour de France, and experts who give advice about implementing antidoping policies in teams. But because we also wanted to publish our results, the confidence of the teams decreased.

ABOUT SPORT

Why Does Sport Matter?

I can think of many reasons why sports matter, but this is a problem. If I present all these reasons to sociologists not specialized in sport even the nonpositivists may question my lack of distance from my research subject. Obviously, I like to *do* sport. Furthermore, like many other researchers, I have an objective interest to assert that sport matters: the more it matters, the more my job is valuable. Giving importance to sport within the scientific field seems to be a claim for a specific jurisdiction, which supports the defence of an occupation thanks to a specific expertise (Abbott, 1988). As a consequence, I need to question why I believe in the sociology of sport. Is it just to protect the narrow territory of my work? Is it a kind of luxury hobby for academics from wealthy countries? To be honest, many other subjects, such as migration, religion, violence, inequality, conflict, racism, etc., appear to be more urgent to deal with. So, is the study of sport itself worthwhile? Many other topics related to major issues that societies have to face may be perceived as more important. This rationale could explain why, in the francophone area, sociologists did not give much attention to sport as a subject, at least until 2000 (Collinet, 2002).

But is it really a lack of distance that explains why sports matter for sociologists? There are many other domains, which are not major social or political issues, that also matter for sociologists. Other cultures, such as art, are important subjects for sociologists without being a 'hot topic'. Furthermore, sport sociologists do not create sport's importance as a practise, a display, a market and as an important social and political issue. The interest for sport is very broad and goes beyond the sociologist's professional interests. Sport matters because it is a fascinating narration (Birrell, 1981) − it is a ritual that helps to observe, discuss and assess human behaviours, categories and identities (Ohl, 2000c). Sport matters for good and bad reasons. Some are proud of their city or their nation thanks to athletes and teams and use sport as a kind of 'extended self' (Belk, 1988). The sense of belonging can be positive or based on the hate of others, people, cities or nations. Sport may foster social capital (Groeneveld, Houlihan, & Ohl, 2011) but also segregation, racism and exclusion. Some people use sport to shape their identity, others use it to belittle females or homosexuals. Sport matters because of its diverse social uses: it is crossed by many sociological matters, such as health, violence, globalization, gender, inequality, etc., that are of interest to sociologists. It offers a broad and rich empirical field to observe and consider. As a consequence, it is no surprise that it is of interest to sociologists and there is no sole explanation of *why* sport matters. Thus, describing briefly the main reasons why sports matter would need to present a summary of the sociology of sport in a few lines, which is not relevant. This is why I will rather explain why it matters *to me*, and why I studied it as a sociologist.

There are three main reasons why sports matter *to me*. The first, is the big gap between an enchanted and naive perception of sport, spread by many sport organizations and medias, and a less shining reality. For example, the IOC claim for the fundamental principles of Olympism ('Olympism seeks to create a way of life based on the joy of effort, the educational value of good example, social responsibility and respect for universal fundamental ethical principles') and the corruption, doping, exclusion, violence, domination, inequalities in sporting culture that can be observed. These essentialist visions of sport and the hidden ideologies behind them are not acceptable as a citizen, a sociologist or even as a sports fan.

The second reason derives from Bourdieu's lens that reveals the hidden dimension for sport cultures. It means observing sports as cultural practises, such as arts or music, that participate in the symbolic struggles between social classes in the various social fields (Bourdieu, 1984). Sports feed the formation and the reproduction of symbolic practises by which social groups try to maintain social domination (Ohl, 2000a). Valued skills, goods, practises, styles and places, such as prestigious clubs or resorts, reaffirm social differences between groups. For sociologists, it is stimulating to analyse these cultural markers and how they exert symbolic violence and naturalize social differences.

The third reason why sports matter to me is because it is a specific social space that offers a rich fieldwork for a sociologist who wants to study culture, inequality, work, gender, body, power, etc. As I am working on doping issues, close to sport organizations, it is fascinating to observe how people fight for positions of power, to gain symbolic capital, struggle with ethical issues but sometimes also cooperate, etc. I met a lot of people working for International Federations, IOC, WADA, NADOs (National Anti-Doping Agencies), laboratories and media. And it is really relevant to observe their interactions both in the visible public space, in various media, and also in the back stages of life. The issue is not only to defend 'clean athletes' or 'clean sport', as it is claimed – each actor tries to defend her/his autonomy, their specific territory, their coherence and their credibility.

How Should Sport be Studied?

It is difficult to say how sport should be studied. I can only explain how my study of sport changed over the years and what I learned from it. The main change for me was a move from classic academic research to studies more connected with sport organizations. I kept the same basic methods, but I am more involved in sport organizations. This is due to my position in Lausanne, near many international organizations. When I started to work in this local context,

I perceived sporting organizations as the ideal targets for critiques. Not only because of the many scandals along their history, but because they are big and powerful institutions. Sociology, along with investigative journalism, are among the rare voices able to produce critical analysis of their power inside or outside the organization. But I also learned that, as sociologists, we need also to be critical of our own critiques. Even with the powerful institutions we may dislike, we also have to recognize the great diversity of their outcomes. Although they can have corrupted staff and board members, some are also reflexive, devoted or critical with their work and are in-tune to key social issues. Using these sport organizations as examples of unethical behaviour is convenient; it may increase one's recognition in the academic field, etc. But to be fair, it cannot be done seriously without observing the diversity of what they do. But my less distant view of organization certainly biased my sociological position. This is why I also recommend using diverse methods and theories to maintain critical analysis in sociological research.

Is Sport a Panacea for Social Problems?

Essential perceptions of sport are widespread and incite the consideration that sport is a kind of pure culture that may be corrupted by social problems. It is common, especially in sport organizations, to argue that violence, corruption, drugs, etc., in sport come from values that are opposite to those of sport. And, for example, there is a belief that doping prevention must target youngsters, so that the supposed positive values of sport will be in place for their whole life. But, for me, educating pupils is just nonsense. Young people do not learn about doping at school, but in clubs, within teams, with coaches, physicians and teammates. Researches show that external values are not corrupting sport, sport organizations produce a kind of 'positive deviance' (Hughes & Coakley, 1991) and athletes conform to their expectations. It means that sport also creates social problems and, as a consequence, it cannot be claimed that sport is a panacea for social problems.

However, sport can also reflect social problems. The permeability of sport organization to violence, drugs, corruption or sexual abuses also depends on the social and political environment. There is no doubt that the 2016 Russian state sponsored doping scandal was not just a question of sport. It was expressing the connection between Russian 'soft-power' strategy and sport. The intent was to use sport as a political tool; although that was fitting with national organizations (laboratory, national anti-doping agency, clubs, etc.) open to corruption, the outcome was not just due to sport.

Sport cannot be a panacea for social problems because it can both produce and express a social problem. However, the sporting field has its own autonomy and that may help to filter part of the social problems that could be expressed in sport. But the counterpart is that this autonomy works with organizations that are more transparent, that include a counter-power and that should be scrutinized by independent organizations. It is a condition for sport to be able to contribute to playing a role in society.

ABOUT PRACTISING SOCIOLOGY OF SPORT

Is Teaching Sociology of Sport Easy?

Teaching sociology of sport can be both easy and difficult. To me, it depends on the audience, on the teacher and on the interaction within the classroom. Both the audience and the teacher have their own characteristics, tastes and values, which can produce euphoric situations, embarrassment and dysphoric interplay (Goffman, 1967). Like many sociologists, I want to encourage critical thinking, sociological awareness and social justice (Grauerholz & Gibson, 2006). Most of the students I teach are from sport sciences, but some are from social sciences, psychology and political sciences. It is no surprise that I find it more difficult to have an immediate good interaction with students who are sports fans, yet who are less familiar with social sciences. Obviously, the social origins of students themselves may also play a role. Many of them want to focus on sport performances and often have the belief that performance comes from genetics, physiology, bio-mechanics and occasionally psychology. This narrow view is sometimes reinforced by the domination of bio-sciences in sport sciences. Life sciences' higher scientific legitimacy combines with a perception that they are useful to produce performance and healthy practises, which is much more ambiguous from a historical point of view.

All of this means that teaching sociology may be perceived as a kind of 'martial art'[1] in which you try to change student's perception of sport. But it needs to be a subtle one, closer to aikido than MMA (Mixed Martial Arts). It should not rely on the symbolic violence a teacher may use in a class, but on arguments and methods of convincing. Class should not be a fight but a coop-eration. A few years ago, a student spoke to me during a course to complain. I was too critical, which meant to him that I did not like sport at all. I was bothered, but I tried to be empathetic and I explained that, quite the opposite, that I liked sport culture, but not all of it, because of its many misuses. Now when I introduce this course, I often use this example to understand what criti-cism is and to emphasize the value of criticism to favour a more equal, fair and open sport culture. And I also use the FIFA or other scandals to underline pos-sible outcomes of the absence of critical thought in organizations.

To change the beliefs of students in sport is a challenge but it is crucial. Most of them are going to teach, to participate in public policies, to work in sport organizations, etc. It seems to me that teaching sociology of sport could modestly contribute to the changes I would like to occur in all the areas of the sporting field. And some topics are really important to address because changes in sporting culture are expected. But teaching 350 students a year is quite a small contribution. And I thought that spreading reflexive and critical thinking may be supported by new tools for distance learning such as MOOC (Massive Open Online Course), blogs and social networks. This is why I tried recently to share sociology with a broader audience. To me, sociology of sport should not just stay in the academic field. That is why I was happy to offer a MOOC on doping, in French and in English, and a Facebook page on doping, in which sociology is important.[2] It extends my audience to thousands of students. I received many very interesting learner stories from people from all over the world. Indeed, the students attending the course are from 160 countries. It is great to connect with people who face difficulties to take courses, because they do not have access to universities, they are working, or living in countries that do not provide such courses. So, it is a great way to share the sociology of sport papers and to encourage critical thinking.

Do Sociologists of Sport Like Sport?

This is a tricky question. To be perceived as an honourable sociologist, I just cannot seriously answer this question on sport without an inquiry based on a consistent methodology. Among the readers of this book, many of them may be sociologists, and they would blame me to comment on sport sociologists without an inquiry. However, I can give a very biased answer — I assume this shortcoming, based on the weak empirical evidences I collected, when attending conferences for example.

For French sociologists, I would rather say that most of them do not like sport. As for my colleagues from other countries, particularly the Anglo-Saxons, I would answer yes, because they often seem to be sport fans.

But do they all really *like* sport? The answer may be more complex. Most of the French sociologists come from sport studies and in many cases this orientation is based on a particular sporting background. But, being critical is a professional ethos that drives sociologists to express a kind of dislike for sport. Inherited from a sociological tradition, recalled by influential sociologists such as Bourdieu, there was a kind of impulse to be critical that leads to different interpretations. For some sociologists, the fight against all forms of power and domination is translated as a professional obligation to be against sport institutions, and even sometimes against sport itself. Naive discourses on sport and sport's alleged contribution to health, etc., were and are still perceived as a social position that needs to be critiqued. But it targets sport organizations more often, and the sporting events, rather than the sport practises. However, it gives the impression that some colleagues hide what they like in sport and more easily express their dislike.

In the more Anglo-Saxon sociologist style, it is clear, at least for the male, that they like to watch football, rugby, the Olympics and other games. It seems, for many of them, to assume that enjoying a good game does not mean being a collaborator of the sport system. However, many do not seem really motivated to practise sport. But I do not think they show-off their taste for media-sport to hide a rather low motivation for the practise of sport! I have the feeling that they are more distant to the type of professional injunction that existed in France.

But my regard is definitely biased. I guess that motivations for the sociological study of sport must be related to a taste or a distaste for sport. Without it, I doubt that someone would be able to work for so many years on this topic.

Is the Sociologist of Sport a 'Public Intellectual'?

Sartre, Lacan, Foucault, Bourdieu, etc. were used to being identified as public intellectuals in France. But today, there are no such iconic figures in France, and no chance in the near future that a sociologist of sport could be identified as a 'Public Intellectual'; sport is simply far from being a 'serious topic'. However, there is a market for sociological public expertise that is interesting to understand to assess how sociologists of sport interact with diverse audiences, how they play a social role and find a kind of external legitimacy. I clearly participate in this market and there are various reasons that combine to explain this increasing role. For instance, it is certainly because I am at another stage of my career, even if my young colleagues are also invited, I am on the lists; I am identified and I have gained some recognition. Another reason may be the changes in the media field. Sport journalists' backgrounds have changed, they are more educated, they still have to celebrate sport, but they also like to question it (especially after the numerous scandals on doping and corruption, there is a demand for a different analysis). The third reason is local context: most of the International Federations and the IOC are in Lausanne and that favours analysis on sport. The audience is perceived as being interested in sporting issues, not only on the results, like in most places, but also in issues related to it. However, it is still not easy to know how to interact with the media. Sometimes interviews are too short to analyse complex social issues. Explanations and understanding, especially on doping, may be perceived as justifying it. Analysing dopers as deviant or as people who are following the dominant values of sport, instead of 'cheaters', may be difficult to explain in a few seconds on the TV or on the radio.

But the public role of intellectual depends on how you define the role of a sociologist. If you consider a sociologist as the one observing social debates, that is you think that distance is one of the basic foundations of sociology, it means sociologists need to be distant from what they observe. If you define sociology as a conventional science, with a classical positive epistemology, that means that you can legitimately participate in public debates and spread the scientific 'truth'. You may also be involved in sport organizations, coaching alliances, blogs, networks, etc., not claiming to tell the truth, but because part of the role of sociology is to bring critical issues to the media's attention and organization that are reluctant to question their practises. As far as I am concerned, sociology must become ever more widespread in sport if we want it to be useful.

ABOUT SOCIOLOGY OF SPORT IN THE ACADEMY

Does Sociology of Sport Face Institutional/Industry Barriers?

Do I really belong to the so-called homo-academicus category? I occupy an academic position for which I have been paid for 25 years, so no doubt I am objectively one among the particular homo-academicus species. However, for a better understanding of social and intellectual trajectories, positions must also be observed in their subjective dimensions, through the social experiences of occupations. As a consequence, there is an 'imperative of reflexivity' (Wacquant, 1989) to understand my own trajectory within the academic field. My various experiences, related to the positions held throughout my career, give a particular example of the place of sociology of sport in the structure and functioning of the academic field. Science, with its disciplines and sub-disciplines, its hierarchies, its changes, its norms, etc., is one among other social fields. It is ruled by a specific symbolic economy that necessarily must be analysed to understand my own social and intellectual trajectory. This is why the interest of focusing on my trajectory goes beyond a narcissistic exercise. It may be a way to map an area of the scientific field of the sociology of sport, and its recent changes in relation to other areas of the scientific field.

I identify at least three academic barriers. The first has to do with the social hierarchies between sport sciences and other fields of research. Before I arrived in Lausanne, in 2004, the faculty council discussed the opportunity to create a full professor position in sport sciences. The choice was to close the department or to hire academics specialized in sport. One member of the council, a professor of international relations, was completely astonished that the faculty could hire someone in sport sciences. He was asking if the option was to recruit, for instance, tennis superstar Roger Federer at the faculty! Since then, sport sciences have gained a real standing in the faculty, both for internal and external reasons. However, this particular local situation does not mean that the sociology of sport has gained recognition outside sport sciences. In most countries, the history of the sociology of sport is strongly linked to the history of institutions in charge of educating PE teachers (Collinet & Terral, 2007; Malcolm, 2014). And despite some connections with sociological departments, journals and associations, the sociology of sport is rather a peripheral topic in the field of sociology, it is ranked far behind the 'hard topics' such as social class, organizations, state, social movements, etc. As a consequence of this peripheral position within the field of sociology, most of the positions are in sports science departments and the sociology of sport has to face the domination of experimental and life sciences, that in many cases monopolize resources in the departments, because of their status as a 'real sciences' compared to the more 'subjective sciences' such as sociology (Ohl, 2015). Finally, the domination of the bio-sciences, plus an increasing pressure to find external funding, reinforces the valuation of topics that respond to social demand, especially applied health-related topics (Bairner, 2010). The financing depending on social demand increases the heteronomy of the field and reduces the autonomy of research. In addition to that, the students' demand for professionalization also favours a management orientation. This also threatens resources allocated to sociology and puts pressure to bond the sociology of sport with topics on public policies, governance or management.

Sociology, sport organizations and industry are most often separate worlds. Most of the organizations do not think it is necessary, or useful, to have sociologists scrutinizing them. So, they are not really keen on sociology, and if not, they only collaborate if sociology can be useful in the short term. This means using sociology as a practical tool, for example, when analysing sport consumers to increase audience, to bring new fans, to sell more sporting goods, etc. But most of them do not see any advantage in a critical gaze on their organization. People think that critical views do not bring income and little added value to governance. As a consequence, teams and clubs prefer to hire marketers, lawyers, accountants, etc., rather than sociologists.

In April 2015, I was invited to the Lausanne Olympic museum by *Panathlon International* for a talk on sport and money. So, as a sociologist, I expressed some criticism on the transparency of international sport organizations, on the power that the redistribution of money gives to the board, on how it is used to keep the power in some of the international federations; why some presidents can run for four or five mandates. Without giving any names, I was intimating that rules should change for the sake of the organizations; for example, a president should not be allowed to have more than two mandates. As I remember, FIFA was a sponsor of the event, and some FIFA staff members attending the event came at the end of the speech to regret that FIFA was, without being named, a target of my speech. It was a very short and friendly discussion. For them FIFA was quite transparent and did not deserve such criticism. But on May 27th, 14 FIFA officials were arrested on corruption charges. On 29 September Blatter was elected, but on 2 June, after leading the world soccer's governing body for 17 years, he resigned. I just thought that FIFA had made major mistakes; instead of hiring a plethora of lawyers and marketers, they should have hired Andrew Jennings, whose work is recognized by sport sociologists (Jennings, 2011). Then, FIFA would have been in a better situation today! Even if a sociological regard may be bothersome in the short-term, I am convinced that it is necessary. However, Jennings would certainly have refused any invitation to collaborate because he thinks that 'reporters and academics should never be guests of the powerful' (Jennings, 2011).

Of course, Jennings may be right – working with sport organization might indeed threaten the independence of researchers. And I confirm that working with the so-called 'powerful' is not easy. When the UCI manager asked me to find how to improve the anti-doping prevention strategy, I accepted the challenge. With the University of Lausanne team, we worked with the UCI for a few years to find an alternative approach to the prevention of doping in cycling (Aubel & Ohl, 2014). One of the outcomes is the implementation of organizational specifications that is now, from 2017 onwards, mandatory for the best Teams (WorldTour) to be included in the professional circuit. But it was really a challenge for sociologists because we were at a crossroads of the power games between the organizers, who control most of the economy of cycling, especially the ASO (Amaury Sport Organization) owner of the Tour de France, the teams and their riders, with whom we had to work to understand how they are producing their performance, and the UCI who needed our sociological analysis to implement new policies that not only serve the cycling powered people, at the ASO or the UCI, but who also serve the ordinary rider who has to produce performance, faces exhaustion, precariousness and stigmas because of the many doping scandals. It is a difficult and an ambiguous position because you never know how the work is going to be used by protagonists. It is definitely not an 'armchair sociology' (Dey, 2004) – it was difficult, costly and, especially when working on doping, very difficult to trust any of the informants. They all pretend to do it only for the values of sport and for the athletes, but many have a specific agenda that does not always fit with this claim.

But I will not conclude from this experience that sociologists of sport should stay far from sport organizations. First, because it was such a rich and incredible experience. The complexity of the sporting culture, the diversity of actors and games, emphasize the need for a sociologist to develop a kind of empirical humility because there is not on the one side the good sociologists and on the other the bad sporting organizations. Second, because it gives us a much better knowledge of cycling and its stakeholders that will feed research and sociological lectures. But the risks and the discomfort need to be accepted because I think, at least in the European countries that I know better, that more social sciences in public debates, policies, politics, education, as well as in business, is important. Such strategies may cause some discomfort to the gentrified armchair sociologist. But to me, sociological knowledge is much less useful if it merely serves academic careers, and is only shared in specialized congresses and journals. I am convinced that for a better and fairer sport, sociology must be shared — we cannot just stay 'between peers' if we want it to impact sport culture.

What is the Future of the Sociology of Sport?

It might sound odd to say, but the future of the sociology of sport might depend on its *success*. If it spreads to sport journalists, fans, staff organizations, federation board members, coaches, etc., more than today, it may question sociologists' professional identity and role. Howard Becker already extends the sociologist identity (Becker, 1998): for him, whatever the professional title they use, many people are in the trade of studying society. As a consequence, it is a good thing to lose the monopoly that is under academic recognition. For example, Andrew Jennings, a journalist, published only a few papers in sociological journals, but certainly did more to spread critical analysis than most of us as sociologists.

The disappearing of professional sociologists may even be a success! Sociologists of sport could just disappear thanks to these other social actors working in federations, industry, etc., that would be able to do produce their own form of *sociology*. These educated and smart people would be aware of social issues, engaging in critical thinking without the boring sociologists and their bad habit of playing a role of 'moral entrepreneur'.

However, it is very optimistic to believe that sport organizations, industry, states, etc. will give much room to independent critical knowledge. Even academics are actually at risk in some countries because of their independence. And it seems very optimistic to hope that other social actors, such as journalists or sport organization staff, would be able to have the time, resources and conditions that would allow independent, reliable and consistent sociology. Many media, especially newspapers, have to face economic pressure and have less resources for investigations. To be realistic, the sociology of sport will continue to have difficulties to spread, and at best, will try to survive in sport sciences departments. A wish for the sociology of sport could be that, like in any other research field, it stays diverse and divided. It is important to keep this fragmentation as a part of a scientific field, with its debates, agreements and struggles.

NOTES

1. 'La sociologie est un sport de combat- Pierre Bourdieu', a Pierre Carles movie on Bourdieu's sociology, 2001.
2. https://www.coursera.org/learn/doping/
   https://www.coursera.org/learn/dopage/
   https://www.facebook.com/groups/MOOCdoping/.

REFERENCES

Abbott, A. D. (1988). *The system of professions: An essay on the division of expert labor.* Chicago, IL: University of Chicago Press.

Aubel, O., Lefèvre, B., & Ohl, F. (2015). Les équipes cyclistes "professionnelles" face aux nouvelles injonctions au professionnalisme. *Sociologie du Travail, 57*(4), 470–495. doi:10.1016/j.soctra.2015.09.006

Aubel, O., & Ohl, F. (2014). An alternative approach to the prevention of doping in cycling. *International Journal of Drug Policy, 25*(6), 1094–1102.

Aubel, O., & Ohl, F. (2015). De la précarité des coureurs cyclistes professionnels aux pratiques de dopage: L'économie des coproducteurs du WorldTour. *Actes de la recherche en sciences sociales, 209*(4), 28–41. doi:10.3917/arss.209.0028

Bairner, A. (2010). Sport, space and memory: Extending the sociology of sport. *East Asian Sport Thoughts: The International Journal for the Sociology of Sport, 1*, 21–37.

Baudrillard, J. (1998). *The consumer society: Myths and structures.* London: Sage.

Becker, H. S. (1963). *Outsiders. Studies in the sociology of deviance.* New-York, NY: The Free Press.

Becker, H. S. (1998). *Tricks of the trade: how to think about your research while you're doing it.* Chicago, IL: University of Chicago Press.

Belk, R. W. (1988). Possessions and the extended self. *Journal of Consumer Research, 15*(2), 139–168.

Bennett, T. (2007). Habitus Clivé: Aesthetics and politics in the work of Pierre Bourdieu. *New Literary History, 38*(1), 201–228. doi:10.1353/nlh.2007.0013

Birrell, S. (1981). Sport as ritual: Interpretations from Durkheim to Goffman. *Social Forces, 60*(2), 354–376.

Bourdieu, P. (1984). *Distinction: A social critique of the judgement of taste.* Cambridge, MA: Harvard University Press.

Brissonneau, C., Aubel, O., & Ohl, F. (2008). *L'épreuve du dopage: Sociologie du cyclisme profession-nel.* Paris: Presses Universitaires de France.

Brohm, J. (1978). *A prison of measured time. London*: Ink Links.

Clément, J.-P. (1995). Contributions of the sociology of Pierre Bourdieu to the sociology of sport. *Sociology of Sport Journal, 12*(2), 147–157.

Collinet, C. (2002). Le sport dans la sociologie française. *L'Année Sociologique, 52*(2), 269. doi:10.3917/anso.022.0269

Collinet, C., & Terral, P. (2007). Conflicts and competition for influence: The history of PETE in France. *Sport, Education and Society, 12*(1), 59–72. doi:10.1080/13573320601081559

Defrance, J. (1989). Un schisme sportif [Clivages structurels, scissions et oppositions dans les sports athlétiques, 1960–1980]. *Actes de La Recherche En Sciences Sociales, 79*(1), 76–91.

Desbordes, M., Ohl, F., & Tribou, G. (2001). *Marketing du sport.* Paris: Economica.

Dey, I. (2004). Grounded theory. In C. Seale, G. Gobo, J. F. Gubrium, & D. Silverman (Eds.), *Qualitative research practice* (pp. 80–93). London: Sage.

Dunning, E., & Elias, N. (1986). *Sport et civilisation, la violence maîtrisée.* Paris: Fayard.

Goffman, E. (1967). *Interaction ritual: Essays in face to face behavior.* Chicago, IL: Aldine Pub.

Grauerholz, L., & Gibson, G. (2006). Articulation of goals and means in sociology courses: What we can learn from syllabi. *Teaching Sociology, 34*(1), 5–22.

Groeneveld, M., Houlihan, B., & Ohl, F. (2011). *Social capital and sport governance in Europe.* New York, NY: Routledge.

Hughes, R., & Coakley, J. (1991). Positive deviance among athletes: The implications of overconfor-mity to the sport ethic. *Sociology of Sport Journal, 8*(4), 307–325.

Jennings, A. (2011). Investigating corruption in corporate sport: The IOC and FIFA. *International Review for the Sociology of Sport, 46*(4), 387–398. doi:10.1177/1012690211408845

Louveau, C. (1987). *Talons aiguilles et crampons alu, les femmes dans les sports de tradition masculine.* Paris: INSEP/SFSS.

Maffesoli, M. (1996). *The time of the tribes: The decline of individualism in mass society*. London: Sage.

Malcolm, D. (2014). The social construction of the sociology of sport: A professional project. *International Review for the Sociology of Sport, 49*(1), 3–21. doi:10.1177/1012690212452362

Ohl, F. (2000a). Are social classes still relevant to analyse sports groupings in "postmodern" society? An analysis referring to P. Bourdieu's theory. *Scandinavian Journal of Medicine and Science in Sports, 10*(3), 146–155.

Ohl, F. (2000b). Le journalisme sportif, une production sous influence: l'exemple de la presse quotidienne régionale. *Regards Sociologiques, (20)*, 109–128.

Ohl, F. (2000c). Les commentaires journalistiques sur le sport ont-ils un sens? *Recherches En Communication, (14)*, 185–214.

Ohl, F. (2003). Les objets sportifs: Comment des biens banalisés peuvent constituer des référents identitaires. *Anthropologie et Sociétés, 27*(2), 167. doi:10.7202/007452ar

Ohl, F. (2004). Goût et culture de masse: l'exemple du sport. *Sociologie et sociétés, 36*(1), 209–228. doi:10.7202/009589ar

Ohl, F. (2005). Staging identity through consumption. Exploring the social uses of sporting goods. In S. J. Jackson & D. L. Andrews (Eds.), *Sport, culture and advertising: Identities, commodities and the politics of representation* (pp. 241–262). London: Routledge.

Ohl, F. (2015). Assessing the sociology of sport: On sport organizations and critical knowledge. *International Review for the Sociology of Sport, 50*(4–5), 553–557. doi:10.1177/1012690214548492

Ohl, F., Fincoeur, B., Lentillon-Kaestner, V., Defrance, J., & Brissonneau, C. (2015). The socialization of young cyclists and the culture of doping. *International Review for the Sociology of Sport, 50*(7), 865–882. doi:10.1177/1012690213495534

Pociello, C. (1981). *Sports et société: Approche socio-culturelle des pratiques*. Paris: Vigot.

Rauch, A. (1982). *Le corps en éducation physique. Paris*: PUF.

Schoch, L., & Ohl, F. (2011). Women sports journalists in Switzerland: Between assignment and negotiation of roles. *Sociology of Sport Journal, 28*(2), 189–208.

Sommier, I. (1994). Mai 68: Sous les pavés d'une page officielle. *Sociétés Contemporaines, 20*(1), 63–82. doi:10.3406/socco.1994.1365

Vigarello, G. (1988). *Techniques d'hier... et d'aujourd'hui: une histoire culturelle du sport*. Paris: Ed. Robert Laffont.

Wacquant, L. J. D. (1989). Towards a reflexive sociology: A workshop with Pierre Bourdieu. *Sociological Theory, 7*(1), 26. doi:10.2307/202061

CHAPTER 10

APPROACHING SPORT FROM HISTORICAL AND SOCIOLOGICAL PERSPECTIVES: THE LIFE AND WORK OF A FEMINIST SCHOLAR

Gertrud Pfister

INTRODUCTION

I was very pleased and proud but also a little worried when I received the invitation to write a chapter for this book because I am not a "clear-cut" sociologist, and I also felt that I do not have good answers to all the questions. However, I have a rather unique approach to many issues in the broad area of sport and exercise because of the mixture of my interests and qualifications. As a "sportswoman," a feminist, a sport historian and a sociologist, a teacher and researcher living in Germany, Denmark, and the United States, I can provide specific approaches to and insights into developments and current issues related to sport, its developments, institutions, participants, and practises. And I fully agree with Joseph Maguire's statement about the importance of a collective social science and humanities approach "explain[ing] the meaning and significance of sport at local, national and global levels" (Maguire, 2011, p. 872). Relations between history and sociology have been − for a long time − an issue of discussions and even controversy between scholars working in these fields. However, there seems to be a growing consensus among scholars them both disciplines are enriching and complementing each other (e.g., Malcolm, 2005, 2015). An excellent example of the benefits of the use of both approaches in feminist research may be found in Jennifer Hargreaves book "*Sporting*

Reflections on Sociology of Sport: Ten Questions, Ten Scholars, Ten Perspectives
Research in the Sociology of Sport, Volume 10, 153−169
Copyright © 2018 by Emerald Publishing Limited
All rights of reproduction in any form reserved
ISSN: 1476-2854/doi:10.1108/S1476-285420170000010010

Females: Critical Issues in the History and Sociology of Women's Sports"
(Hargreaves, 2003).

ABOUT THE AUTHOR

Mentors and Influential Figures

My academic career began in Bochum, Germany (1976–1981) and Horst
Überhorst, the supervisor of my PhD project and one of the most influential
scholars in the emerging academic field of sport history, was an excellent mentor in this important period of my career. Überhorst did pioneering research in
various areas of sport history, ranging from the workers' sport movements to
German *Turnen* in the United States. He encouraged me to explore physical
education and sport from a gender perspective, and I published my first articles
in his "World History of Physical Education and Sport" (Pfister & Langenfeld
1980, 1982). Another important member of the scientific community of sport
historians is Hans Langenfeld, whom I met at my first sport history conference.
He co-authored my first articles and became a reviewer and advisor of many of
my further publications. The third scholar who has had a decisive influence on
my career is Dieter Voigt, a sport sociologist who left the German Democratic
Republic – with great difficulty – and started a new career in Bochum. He
invited me to cooperate on many of his projects – for instance on a project
about male and female students' attitudes to and practises in PE.

However, I was also influenced, and supported, by a number of colleagues
of the same age or younger, such as Sabine Kröner, Kari Fasting, Sheila
Scraton, Susanna Hedenborg, Tansin Benn, Susan Bandy, and Annette
Hofmann. We all share an interest in women's sports and physical cultures
from a feminist perspective, have conducted research projects together and co-
authored publications on the results. One of the first of the joint projects with
Kari Fasting involved travel to Ankara and an exploration of the "opportunities and barriers for women in sport in Turkey." Kari also was a coauthor of
an article on the beginning of women's football in European countries
(Scraton, Pfister, Fasting, & Bunuel, 1999). With Tansin Benn I worked on several projects, in particular on Muslim women and their opportunities and challenges in sport. We both participated in a meeting in Oman in 2000 where
especially women from Muslim countries discussed several issues concerning
women and sport and adopted the declaration "Accept and Respect" of
Muslim athletes' decisions about their sporting practises. A further result of
our cooperation was an edited book on "Muslim Women and Sport" (Benn,
Pfister, & Jawad, 2010) and the compilation of articles about women and sport
in Latin America (López de D'Amico, Benn, & Pfister, 2016). I also cooperated
on several small-scale projects about Turkish women and sport with Ilknur

Hacısoftaoğlu, and we published several articles, for example, on Turkish female migrants in Denmark (Hacısoftaoğlu & Pfister, 2012).

A number of other scholars were, and still are, important role models and/ or sources of inspiration and, as such, supporters of my academic career: Roberta Park, Patricia Vertinsky, Ann Hall, Jennifer Hargreaves, Annelies Knoppers, Margaret Talbot, and many more. Currently, I am sharing a number of projects and publications with Gerald Gems. For instance, we edited a book about American football which aims to explain various aspects of the game for readers who are not familiar with it (Gems & Pfister, 2017). I was, and still am, inspired by my 20 PhD students. With Marie-Luise Klein I published a book about the gendered representation of female athletes in the mass media in 1985 (Pfister & Klein, 1985). Klein is currently Professor of Sport Sociology at the Ruhr-University Bochum. Perhaps the most famous of my PhD students is Reinhard Sprenger, who embarked on a successful career as consultant and presents himself today, not only as a manager but also as a philosopher and musician. Verena Lenneis is one of my last PhD students. She conducted, among other projects, a physical activity intervention with female cleaners (with a migrant background). She contributed to several articles, not only with empirical data but also with her expertise in various theoretical approaches, for example to gender and minorities (e.g., Lenneis & Pfister, 2016).

However, not only my mentors, colleagues and students, but numerous "extraordinary women" are in the focus of my research and have become "influential figures" in my life: I explored, for example, the biographies of female boxers in the 19th century. Many of them were Americans, but some e.g., Violette Morris, lived in Europe. Morris, a French athlete who was (maybe wrongly) suspected of spying for Nazi Germany and killed by the French Resistance. But it may have been her preference for men's clothes which made her an enemy of a bourgeois society. One of my recent publications focused on Halet Cambel, a famous Turkish archaeologist, who was one of the first two women from a Muslim country to participate in the Olympic Games (1936) in fencing (Pfister & Hacısoftaoğlu, 2017).

Research Trajectory

My interest in adventures was not "inherited." My father taught mathematics and physics at high school; my mother was a kindergarten teacher. I studied physical education/sport sciences and Latin in Munich because I loved to play various sports and to teach them, skiing in particular, and I trained for years to emulate the famous skiers of the time. However, I did not become an athlete, but a professional ski instructor.

After my studies in Munich I wanted to get more deeply involved in "sport sciences" before embarking on a career in teaching. Therefore, I pursued a PhD in Regensburg under the supervision of Professor Adolf Lippold, a renowned scholar in Ancient History. My PhD focused on the "iuventus" − an organiza-tion of young noblemen in the Roman Empire who underwent military training which included "sports" and exercises. After finishing my thesis in 1976, I got a position as a research assistant of the sport historian Horst Überhorst at the University of Bochum (although my research had not focused on modern sport). One of my first tasks was to write a chapter about women in his "World History of Sport," and I was glad about this task because I identified myself as a feminist. Later, in the 1990s, I became a member of a network of women who explored the situation of females in sport and physical education, published their results, and conducted seminars and workshops with a focus on feminist sport studies and their application to various fields of practise. Working on projects dealing with the opportunities and challenges of girls and women in sport became one of my favorite occupations.

New opportunities and challenges emerged when the sociology professor at the sport department, Dieter Voigt, asked me to participate in one of his pro-jects − an enquiry in male and female students' opinions, attitudes, and prac-tises with regard to PE. As preparation for my work on this project, I took relevant courses at the sociology department. The findings of this project are published in several articles which I used for obtaining a PhD in sociology in 1980.

In 1981 I was appointed professor at the Freie Universität Berlin and became a very active member of the international "scientific community." This was one of the reasons why I was offered a position at the University of Copenhagen in 2000. There I had the opportunity to conduct several exciting research projects − for example, about women in leadership positions of sport organizations, about attitudes of female athletes toward doping, and about female football fans in Europe, a project which was funded by the European Union. I also participated in several projects supported by the Center for Team Sport and Health at Copenhagen University − for example, the evaluation of a physical activity intervention with female cleaners. Other studies focused on women with PCOS (polycystic ovary syndrome) or on overweight individuals.

ABOUT SPORT

Why Does Sport Matter?

The answers to this question depend largely on the definition of the term "sport" and on the definitions, practises, and perspectives of those who do sport and/or talk or write about it (e.g., Maguire, 2006). As the term *sport* has various meanings which differ in different cultures and time periods, it is not easy to identify the importance of "sport" as its aims and practises differ depending on the context – the time period and the place. In Europe, the term "sport" includes various physical activities which do not – in contrast to work – aim at delivering a product. However, the same movements (e.g., throwing or running) can be work, a religious ceremony, fitness exercise, or sport, depending, among other things, on the intentions of the participants.

In the early 19th century, three different "movement cultures" emerged in Europe: *Turnen* in Germany, sport in England, and specific concepts of gymnastics in several countries such as Sweden and France (Pfister, 2003). These "movement cultures" "matter" in different ways. They had and still have a decisive influence on current sport systems and activities. *Turnen* (German gymnastics) is a physical education system developed at the beginning of the 19th century. The *Turners'* aims were, among others, the liberation of Prussia from French occupation, and the establishment of a German national state. They not only performed exercises on and with various equipments but also participated in "athletics" such as running or jumping. However, in contrast to "modern sport," performances were not "abstract" but measured in relation to the body of the *Turner*. High jumping, for example, was evaluated according to the height of the athlete, and runners were expected to arrive at the finishing line "in good health" (Pfister, 2003).

At the same time, a specific gymnastic system was developed by Per Henrik Ling in Sweden. Swedish gymnastics had a focus on health and fitness and consisted mostly of calisthenics and free-standing exercises. This system soon spread to other countries such as the United States, where it was used particularly in girls' schools (Pfister, 2003). A third contemporary movement culture, "modern sport," emerged in England, where rowing competitions and horse races became increasingly popular (Holt, 1995). Sport in the form of codified, organized, and competitive physical activities spread worldwide in the context of the globalization processes of the 19th and 20th centuries. Allen Guttmann identified the characteristics of "modern sport" as the quantification of performance, its assessment through competitions, as well as the comparison of performances independent of time and place, for example by setting and breaking records (Guttmann, 2012; see also Maguire, 2006). This definition indicates that in principle all physical activities can be "sportified" if the participants agree on the organization and the common rules of competitions.

The global sport system enforces compliance with this "logic," independent of the traditions and cultures, aims and intentions of the people involved. In the course of "sportification processes", the principles of sport transformed "movement cultures" worldwide (Pfister, 2003, 2007). Relatively recent examples of "sportification" are dragon-boat racing, originally a Chinese folk ritual, and skateboarding, a leisure activity of young men which became one of the central sports at the X Games (see e.g., Thorpe & Wheaton, 2011).

However, the "character" and the meaning of sport has changed with the emergence and popularity of the "sport-for-all" movement, which has spread across Western countries since the 1950s and 1960s, when many inhabitants began to integrate sport into their everyday lives, not least because sport activities seemed to hold out the promise of health and well-being, fun and enjoyment, social interaction, and social integration (e.g., European Commission, 2014, 2016, p. 47; see also Jütting, Schulze, Müller, & Pfister, 2009; Palm, 2003).

The various "movement cultures" matter in different ways depending on the aims and the activities as well as on the expectations of the individuals and groups involved as participants, spectators, providers, or consumers. From my perspective, sport matters most for those individuals and groups who are actively involved because they are able to take pleasure in the well-researched benefits such as fitness or enjoyment. Despite these benefits, compliance with physical activity recommendations seems to be a problem in many societies, and this also applies to Europe, where on average less than half the population engages in sport and exercise in their leisure (e.g., European Commission, 2014, 2016, p. 11). These and other differences can − at least partly − be attributed not only to the different traditions, but also to the different organization of sport in the different countries.

In particular in northern and central European countries, large groups of the population (in Germany, e.g., around 35% of the inhabitants) are members of sport organizations. The umbrella organization, the German Olympic Sport Confederation (DOSB), reports 27 million memberships (DOSB, 2016). Sport clubs are voluntary associations which organize competitive sports and provide opportunities for sport for all. Sport federations represent their members and their sports in the society at large.

Since the 1950s, in Germany (as well as in numerous other countries) new forms of physical activities or unorganized forms of "sport for all" have emerged such as "trim and fitness" exercises with or without apparatus, aerobics, jogging, and hiking, as well as "street sports" like roller skating or skateboarding, street soccer, or street basketball. Whereas fitness exercises attract the "mainstream population," risk and street sports are the domains of young men. In contrast, girls and women are overrepresented in various forms of gymnastics and in horse riding, which have become female preserves. The concept of "sport for all" has been taken up by many sport organizations, and also by city administrations in industrialized countries. In many urban areas people enjoy illuminated jogging trails, fitness equipment, climbing walls, or skateboard parks, as well as numerous other sport facilities which transform cities into "sporting grounds for all." However, we should not forget that there is only a small group of municipalities which have the financial means, the spaces, and the people with inspiration who can and want to engage in "sport in the city" (e.g., Pfister, 2017).

The Eurobarometer surveys − reports about opinions and habits (including physical activities) of Europeans provided by the European Commission − show a considerable increase in sporting activities in recent decades, particularly in countries in northern and central Europe. These surveys also reveal that a considerable number of the inhabitants — between 15% and 27% — are members of sport clubs. This is the case for instance in Germany, Belgium, and France, as well as in the Scandinavian countries, where gymnastic and sport clubs have a long tradition (e.g., European Commission, 2014, p. 4).

It goes without saying that sport — and in particular elite sport — is not only important for participants but also for the numerous fans of athletes and teams who identify with them and "bask in reflected glory." Although success in sport takes many forms, successful athletes and teams are — incorrectly — considered by many to be an indicator of the "quality" of a group or a society and used (also by modern states) to represent the country in the international community of nation states.

To conclude: the information provided in this section shows that sport and, in particular, "sport for all," matter. Its representatives emphasize the crucial importance of sport and exercise for fitness, as a means to counteract the health risks of a sedentary lifestyle and to provide various social and psychological benefits. However, joy, fun, relaxation, social relations and interactions, or pride in one's performance are further important assets of sporting activity. In particular in modern industrial societies, where the building density in cities prohibits spontaneous play and games, provisions for sport for all are indispensable.

The question of whether sport matters also addresses sport consumption. It cannot be denied that watching sport provides entertainment for large percentages of populations worldwide. Following athletes and teams may trigger identification, enjoyment, and distraction from troubles and problems in everyday life, which, however, will not allow disappear. In addition, "sport matters" for the sport industry, that is, media conglomerates, producers of sport goods, organizers of events and professional athletes, as well as for other individuals and groups, such as for journalists, coaches, or architects, who may profit in one or the other way from sport. For them sport, in particular elite sport, is a business which matters.

Elite sport in particular is supported in many, if not in all countries (which can afford this), and used for the presentation of a society in the international community. Although victories in international events may contribute to the prestige of a country, a closer look at successful "sport nations" such as the German Democratic Republic or the Soviet Union in the 1970s and 1980s reveals that sport can be used not to solve but to cover over numerous problems — for instance with regard to economy or human rights issues.

How Should Sport be Studied?

As shown above, sport has different meanings. Whereas this term can be used in some European languages (e.g., in German) as an overarching term for recreational and for competitive physical activities — including physical education – the term refers in English to competitive sports. In a similar way, "sport studies" may have different aims and contents which will attract different groups of students.

In European countries academic sport studies are provided by colleges and universities. They mostly include a variety of scientific disciplines ranging from sport history to sociology, and also to biomechanics and to physiology. Sport students who wish to become PE teachers also have to become familiar with didactics, and may have to learn how to teach skills in various sports to different target groups, including students of both genders and of different ages. However, sport studies differ decisively in different contexts and different countries, not least because they prepare students for a number of professions besides that of a PE teacher. They may want to become administrators in sport clubs or federations, trainers in rehabilitation centers or sport journalists. Therefore, the question of how sport should be studied depends, among other things, on the demands of the students future profession. Whatever the case, the course of study should contain a broad overview of a variety of subjects and should also allow a measure of flexibility – for example, with regard to the disciplines studied and the issues on which the students should concentrate, depending on the demands of the students future profession. Sport studies at some colleges or universities may have a focus on the natural sciences (e.g., on physiology and biomechanics); at other academic institutions students will concentrate more on the social sciences and humanities but also have to take basic courses in natural sciences. These are necessary to understand central principles of exercising and training, but in-depth insights into these disciplines are not important for students who want to become teachers, sport journalists, or sport managers. The curriculum for these students has to have a strong focus on the human and social sciences and offer a range of subjects, topics, theories, and methods, thus providing qualifications which allow students to set priorities, depending on both their interests and career plans, as well as being flexible with regard to the situation on the "job market." Students should also be familiar with the different "movement cultures" and their aims and potentials; with the organization of "sport for all"; and with the habits and tastes of different groups such as young men who may love risk sports and girls who love horses.

Sport studies should take a critical approach – for example, with regard to the expectations people have of sport, to the promises of sport leaders, as well as to the large variety of theoretical and epistomenological approaches ranging from critical theory to post-positivism. The study programs should be accompanied by small-scale projects which draw on pedagogical, psychological, or sociological theories, use relevant quantitative and/or qualitative methods, provide sound interpretations, and indicate potential application to various fields of practise. Social constructivism, feminism, as well as gender and socialization theories might provide guidelines for interpretation and for an in-depth understanding of results and their consequences for different groups. Particularly since the 1960s, there has been a debate in Europe on whether – and, if so, to what degree − sport students must be able to play sports in order to be good teachers of their subject. During the periods of student protest and the new women's movements it seemed more important to adopt a critical political position rather than to train in one's particular sport discipline. I do not doubt that (bodily) experiences gained in sport provide an understanding of exercising, training, and playing, which is important for dealing with various target groups. Sport studies should be provided by universities which can make use of students' integrative powers to create links between sport sciences and the "mother disciplines" on which they draw, such as history, sociology, or psychology. Cooperation with scholars working in these fields will contribute toward raising the academic standards of "sport studies" and increasing the job opportunities of alumni.

Is Sport a Panacea for Social Problems?

For the large majority of participants sport is a leisure time activity, and even those who participate in competitions do this mostly in their leisure. In addition, it must be kept in mind that sport may be played only during short periods of the participants' lives, that is, during childhood and youth. This is especially true in the United States, where many students at colleges and universities are athletes. Although leisure sports may attract all age groups, membership statistics of sport organizations as well as surveys such as the Special Eurobarometer on Sport and Physical Activity (2014) show a decline of participation in sport with increasing age. Thus, participation in sport cannot be a "panacea" in many situations and periods of people's lives. However, there is also the question of whether − and, if so, how − sport can at all have a positive influence on various social groups in different societies. Physiologists and psychologists provide convincing evidence that sport can have a positive impact on health (e.g., body weight or blood pressure), and also on well-being and personal satisfaction. However, when evaluating the benefits of sport participation, one must also consider that participation in strenuous physical activities or in risk sports may also cause frustration and health problems through overexertion or injuries.

When discussing the potential benefits of sport, we should not forget that sport and its organizations and adherents neither aim nor are able to solve major problems of current societies such as poverty, social inequality, gender stereotyping, racism, or wars, etc. However, I do not deny that sport has some potential to counteract social problems. In Chicago, churches have created a midnight basketball league to keep gang members off the streets and limit violence. Other examples are a number of women and sport projects, which have been implemented in developing countries: an excellent example of such initiatives is the initiative Women Win, which not only supports sport programs for girls and women but includes also the education of women and their prepara-tion for leadership roles. A further initiative with a focus on education is the "global sport development initiative" of Seoul National University, South Korea. Funded by the Korean Ministry of Culture, Sports and Tourism (MCST) and the Korea Sports Promotion Foundation (KSPO), the university's Dream Together Master's program is a graduate program to educate future global leaders in various areas of sport. Around 20 students from developing countries – men and women with different but sport-related backgrounds – are invited to live and study for two years in Seoul. When the students return to their countries, they are expected "to become active leaders who promote international sport development. We dream for the day when all the countries throughout the world enjoy and appreciate the benefits of sport" (see the web-page of SNU). This statement reflects a widespread belief and the hope that sport can be used to solve at least minor social problems, yet this claim may be too general and too vague: What kind of problems should be solved, and in which ways may sport – as either an activity or its organizations – provide benefits for social groups or societies as the whole? It might also be asked why sport – its organizations or participants – should feel responsible for solving problems of individuals, groups, or societies in need?

I do not doubt that sport and exercise may be beneficial. However, their effects depend on, among other things: the duration, intensity, type, and setting of the activity; the gender, age, and health of the participants; and, finally, their skills as well as their intentions. This also means, though, that sport is not – and cannot be – a general panacea, and that the opportunities and challenges connected with playing sports also depend to a large degree on the aims and contexts. Competitive sport creates winners and losers, which may lead to pro-blems for both groups. It may, moreover, be doubted that success in sporting competitions has positive effects for the population of the athletes' home coun-tries. We should not forget that only decades ago the countries with the highest success rates in the international sport arena, that is, the Soviet Union and the German Democratic Republic, ranked very low with regard to the performance of their economies or the level of their citizens' rights – and finally collapsed and disintegrated. Neither is sport for all a general panacea, especially when clear aims and strategies are lacking. When sport is used as an intervention aiming at, for example, the social integration of migrants or at breaking the iso-lation of seniors, it will only be successful if this intervention is a planned pro-cess and the members of the target groups, too, take on responsibilities for these projects.

In sum, playing sport has many potentials but whether or not these have the desired effect depends on how, why, and by whom sport opportunities and pro-grams are provided, which target groups are aimed at and which are actually reached, and if and how these groups react to participating in sport and exercise.

ABOUT PRACTISING SOCIOLOGY OF SPORT

Is Teaching Sociology of Sport Easy?

The answer to this question is not "easy" as it depends on the aims, target groups, and the circumstances of teaching. Sport sociology is an academic course of study and a "science" which can be applied and used in many contexts since sociological approaches and insights contribute to an understanding of reasons and backgrounds concerning a large number of situations and developments. However, teaching is "easy" only when the topics and the methods used to study them, that is, the aims and the processes of teaching and learning, meet the needs and expectations of both the teachers and the students. As sport is popular and not only of interest to those who study it but also to people who participate in sporting activities and/or follow sport and games as spectators or via the mass media, there are numerous topics which can be used as a peg for motivating students to reflect about sport and for initiating discussions.

Aims of sport sociology classes should also be to provide the students with sociological methods and theories, as well as with their application. This might be done by asking students to conduct "mini projects" in which they have to use both a specific method and a theoretical approach. "Student projects," which were part of my "standard repertoire" were, for instance, analyses of the gendered sport coverage in newspaper editions on a Monday morning. First, the students were asked to guess the percentage of coverage devoted to women's sport and then measure the actual space given to both genders. In many cases, the numerous sports pages focused entirely on men, in particular on men's football, without a single article on women's sport. Although the students guessed that most coverage would focus on male athletes and players, none had expected that women would not be mentioned at all. As the mass media are important "socialization agents," we used socialization theories and discussed the potential effects of gendered media coverage from a socialization perspective (e.g., Grundmann, 2006; Heinemann, 2007). As quite a lot of the students in my courses worked in sport-related fields (for instance, with interventions for migrants or as coaches in children's sports), they could contribute information and ideas to issues of sport participation — among working-class women or migrant girls, for example. They were able to provide insights into their own (lack of) opportunities to play sports, and we discussed their experiences drawing on gender theories (e.g., Connell, 2008; Lorber, 2012).

A further relevant topic which is easy to teach because of the numerous examples in the students' environments is "sport for all" with a focus on large cities. I worked with students, for example, on the city in which they lived: Copenhagen. This city provides numerous examples of "sport-for-all facilities" ranging from skateboard parks to fitness equipment and from climbing walls to fenced-in basketball courts in several parts of the city center. The transformation of

Copenhagen into a "sport city" (which has taken place in the last decade) offers numerous examples of small-scale research studies, such as conducting interviews with (or observations of) people engaged in sporting activities; the "findings" might then be analyzed and from a gender perspective and/or with a focus on the social backgrounds of the informants or in the context of their sporting biographies. The students can use their findings not only for discussion in the classroom (and writing papers) but also for designing interventions and approaching sport architects or city administrators with new ideas and concepts. As sport sociology offers students theoretical approaches and tools to explore relevant themes and as there are numerous topics which are extremely relevant not only for the students but also for society in general, attracting the interest of students and teaching sociology of sport can be easy.

Do Sociologists of Sport Like Sport?

I know very little about the "sport tastes" of other sociologists. Moreover, I do not quite know what this question is aiming at; nor do I know what "like" refers to: like playing sport or like watching sport? And what is meant by the term "sport"? On reading this question, I asked myself whether I liked sport; and there is no doubt: yes. I even love sport! However, my relationship to sport is not quite so clear-cut as it may appear. I have always liked to play sport, for example tennis − although I was never a very good player. I loved, and still love, skiing, biking, or running. However, I very seldom watch sport. If I do, then perhaps women's football championships or track-and-field events. As I am not aware of any survey or any study about the attitudes and practises of sport sociologists with regard to their own sport participation and/or consumption, I know very little about their preferences and can only provide more or less qualified guesses.

First of all, I assume that many sport sociologists have studied sport as an academic subject − however, this may differ according to the country of study − and it seems likely that they have a positive attitude toward sport; otherwise they would not have chosen sport as their course of study and later as a focus of their research and publications. As a sport sociologist, I am familiar with the research, approaches, and studies of many colleagues. However, given the large number of scholars working in this field, my insights into the scientific community of sport sociology, in particular into the personal lives of its members, remain restricted. Nor do I have access to work which is not published in German, English, or one of the Scandinavian languages. And most of the work of my colleagues in sport sociology provides no information about their personal lives, their feelings toward sport, or their participation in competitive sport or recreational physical activities. I am also aware that there have been a fair number of sociological studies with a critical approach to sport in general or to certain sports in particular, especially those in which large amounts of money are at stake. Doping, match fixing, and violence are issues which seem to be intrinsically interwoven with elite sport, and the lack of an effective response from governing bodies may give rise to doubts whether elite sport can be "liked" at all. Although women have achieved "gender equality" at the Olympics, at least with regard to access to sports, there is still a considerable measure of sexism. The list of "issues" which may prevent sociologists from "liking sport" is long; but initiatives such as the "Accept and Respect" declaration, which aims at the acceptance of Muslim women in sport competitions, and Michelle Obama's program "Let's move," addressing children in the United States, are examples of sport policies which may be positively evaluated not only by myself but also by other sport sociologists.

Is the Sociologist of Sport a 'Public Intellectual?

As my own experience and the exchange of information with colleagues show, we are indeed sometimes considered experts who can provide information and formulate messages to the general public. I am often approached by journalists with questions about women's sport participation, female athletes in "men's sports," the gender of coaches, body and beauty ideals of women in Western countries, or about migrant women and their attitudes to and participation in recreational physical activities. For over a decade, I was one of the nine members of the president's committee of the German Turner Federation, the second largest sport federation in the country with around five million members. As vice-president of this organization (and a professor of sport science), I was approached with numerous issues and demands for my expertise – ranging from questions about adequate exercise for migrant girls to questions on sources for the compilation of a booklet about the history of a sport club. I have also been involved in several groups which support girls and women in sport. As one of the authors of the declaration "Accept and Respect" (drafted in Oman in 2000), I spoke with numerous sport leaders and journalists in order to spread this message and to gain support.

Generally, however, I do not strive actively to propagate messages to the general public; I publish my research findings in books and articles addressed to the scientific community. Having said that, I am glad if my knowledge can be used in a nonacademic context. I am often addressed by various people with various questions and concerns, and I attempt to provide information and support. Very seldom, though, do I have the time (and perhaps also the right topics) to actively approach the media and act as a "public intellectual."

There are a number of influential commentators in the area of sport. James Dorsey, for example, has impressive knowledge about the use of sport, in particular football, for political purposes, and this knowledge he shares with his readers. Although I admire this way of imparting knowledge and having an impact, I do not believe that I have the type of information or insights which can be used for political messages and publications. However, I do plan to work more intensively in the overlapping field of sport and politics, for example with regard to gender issues, in the future.

ABOUT THE SOCIOLOGY OF SPORT IN THE ACADEMY

Does Sociology of Sport Face Institutional/Industry Barriers?

Sport sciences, including sport sociology, are established academic disciplines devoted to research and teaching in many, if not all, universities in Europe. However, this was not always the case. In many countries, including Denmark, sport was a subject which consisted in mostly of sport practise, that is, learning sport skills and how to teach them in order to become a physical education teacher. At the turn of the 20th century, teachers at these institutions (or other educational theorists) developed specific methods and didactics for teaching PE. Since the end of the century, sport studies re provided at universities with the consequence that the teachers have to have academic qualifications, e.g., a Phd, have to conduct research and publish their findings in "acceptable" journals or books. At the turn of the 21st century, for example, Copenhagen's Physical Education College was integrated into the University of Copenhagen, with the result that renowned work physiologists were integrated in the institute. The teachers, coming from the college, were given the opportunity to obtain a PhD degree; some succeeded, others did not want and became "outsiders". In the last decade, the pressure on staff members to obtain research grants and to publish in journals with a high impact factor has become an increasing burden, in particular for those who regard themselves as teachers rather than scientists. However, as I came from a university with a focus on research and had experiences with grant applications, I was not negatively affected by these new policies; on the contrary, I took the opportunity for developing and conducting several research studies. Currently, it is difficult but still possible to obtain grants for sport sociological research, such as from the Danish Ministry of Science, and also the Department of Nutrition, Sport and Exercises of the University of Copenhagen. My latest projects have included studies on the evaluation of physical activity programs for female cleaners, along with an exploration of their everyday lives; research on the "sport socialization" of obese people; and the project "Football Research in an Enlarged Europe" (together with colleges from eight countries, funded by the 7th Framework Programme for Research of the European Union).

In 2000, physiologists of the Department of Nutrition, Sport and Exercises founded the "Center for Team Sport and Health," which conducted interventions with, and research on, participants in small-sided team games such as floorball and football (often with four or five players on each side). As these games demand a high intensity of physical activity and are at the same time experienced as enjoyable, the participants in this project not only increased their fitness level but also attended the training sessions regularly. They were also willing to participate in sociological and psychological studies. Similar projects have been conducted with older people in senior centers, with children in schools, and with members of sport clubs. Since 2000, I have been a member of the executive board of this Center, which still provides funding and other resources for into team activities. Three of my projects were funded by the center (besides the project with the cleaners), among them an intervention with girls in school breaks and an evaluation of a program for seniors. In addition, I have obtained funding from either my university or my faculty to conduct regularly conferences and Summer Schools with a focus on human and social sport sciences.

To sum up, I faced no specific barriers as a sociologist at the two universities or in the organizations and institutions for which I worked as a volunteer. Particularly in Denmark, I was supported in many ways and with relatively large resources. However, not all of my colleagues had similar opportunities.

What is the Future of the Sociology of Sport?

As described above, sport sociology is an important discipline in sport studies, which must be financed by the universities along with research in this field. There are numerous topics and issues in the broad area of sport and exercise which need to be studied from a sociological perspective. These include: the role of sport in populations with rising life expectancy; Muslim women and their opportunities and challenges in various sports; and the influence of the new media on sport participation. Concepts as well as evaluations of programs for refugees, for the increasing numbers of older people, and for many other target groups are also in high demand. In addition, gender and race are still important predictors of sport participation; and more knowledge is needed – for example, about women pioneers also in sports hitherto defined as male domains. A crucial topic which needs much more attention is the choice and use of theory in sport-related sociological research.

Sport sociology is – and always will be – needed; therefore, it should – and hopefully always will – be adequately funded. However, it cannot be denied that there is increasing competition in academia and that especially applied approaches of the natural sciences are becoming dominant "players" in sport studies. (The question arises, though, whether very specific insights into physiological processes, for example during training, or knowledge about details of bio-mechanics are truly important for university students who wish to become sport teachers, administrators or sport journalists, for instance.) However, these disciplines contribute – hopefully – to new knowledge about the benefits of sports, and sociology is needed in particular to provide insights into the role of sports in society and in particular in the opportunities and barriers of various groups of people to make use of sport and exercises.

REFERENCES

Benn, T., Pfister, G., & Jawad, H. A. (Eds.). (2010). *Muslim women and sport*. London: Routledge.

Connell, R. (2008). *Gender*. Cambridge: Polity.

DOSB. (2016). Bestandserhebung (yearly membership statistics German Olympic Sport Confederation. Retrieved from https://www.dosb.de/

European Commission. (2014; 2016). Special Eurobarometer. Sport and Physical Activity. Brussels.

Gems, G., & Pfister, G. (Eds.). (2017). *American football*. Berkshire: Great Barrington.

Grundmann, M. (2006). *Socialization*. Basel: Beltz.

Guttmann, A. (2012). *From ritual to record: The nature of modern sports, Updated Edition*. New York, NY: Columbia University Press.

Hacısoftaoğlu, I., & Pfister, G. (2012). Transitions: Life stories and physical activities of Turkish migrants in Denmark. *Sport in Society*, *15*(3), 385–398.

Hargreaves, J. (2003). *Sporting females: Critical issues in the history and sociology of women's sports*. London: Routledge.

Heinemann, K. (2007). *Einführung in die Soziologie des Sports*. Schorndorf: Hofmann.

Holt, R. (1995). *Sport and the British: A modern history*. Oxford: Clarendon Press.

Jütting, D. H., Schulze, B., Müller, U., & Pfister, G. (2009). *Sport for all – opportunities and challenges in different sport systems*. Münster: Waxmann.

Klein, M.-L., & Pfister, G. (1985). *Goldmädel, Rennmiezen und Turnküken*. Berlin: Bartels & Wernitz.

Lenneis, V., & Pfister, G. (2016). Health, physical activity and the body: An inquiry into the lives of female migrant cleaners in Denmark. *International Journal of Sport Policy and Politics*, *8*, 647–662.

López de D'Amico, R., Benn, T., & Pfister, G. (2016). *Women and Sport in Latin America*. London: Routledge.

Lorber, J. (2012). *Gender inequality: Feminist theories and politics*. New York, NY: Oxford University Press.

Maguire, J. (2006). *Power and global sport: Zones of prestige, emulation and resistance*. London: Routledge.

Maguire, J. (2011). Studying sport through the lens of historical sociology and/or sociological history. *Sport in Society*, *14*, 2011, 872–882.

Malcolm, D. (2005). The emergence, codification and diffusion of sport: Theoretical and conceptual issues. *International Review for the Sociology of Sport*, *40*, 115–118.

Malcolm, D. (2015). Durkheim and sociological method: Historical sociology, sports history, and the role of comparison. *The International Journal of the History of Sport*, *32*, 1808–1812.

Palm, J. (2003). *Global perspectives on sport, community and inclusion: 'Sport for all' in policy and practice*. London: Routledge.

Pfister, G. (1977). *Die Erneuerung der römischen iuventus durch Augustus*. PhD thesis.

Pfister, G. (2003). Cultural confrontations: German Turnen, Swedish gymnastics and English sport – European diversity in physical activities from a historical perspective. *Sport in Society, 6*, 1, 61–91.

Pfister, G. (2007). Sportification, power, and control: Ski-jumping as a case study. *Junctures: The Journal of Thematic Dialogue, 8*, 51–67.

Pfister, G. (2017). Copenhagen – A city becomes a sporting ground. In G. Pfister & G. Gems (Eds). *Sport in cities*. Meyer & Meyer Sport.

Pfister, G., & Hacısoftaoğlu, I. (2017). Women's sport as a symbol of modernity – a case study in Turkey. *International Journal of the History of Sport, 29*(3), 1–13.

Pfister, G., & Langenfeld, H. (1980, 1982). Die Leibesübungen für das weibliche Geschlecht – ein Mittel zur Emanzipation der Frau? In H. Ueberhorst (Ed.), *Geschichte der Leibesübungen, Bd. 3/1; 3/2* (pp. 485–521, 977–1007). Berlin/München/Frankfurt: Bartels & Wernitz.

Scraton, S., Pfister, G., Fasting, K., & Bunuel, B. (1999). Women and football – a contradiction? The beginnings of women's football in four European countries. *International Review for the Sociology of Sport, 34*(2), 99–112.

Thorpe, H., & Wheaton, B. (2011). 'Generation X Games', action sports and the Olympic movement: Understanding the cultural politics of incorporation. *Sociology, 45*, 830–847.

INDEX